# The
# Spirit
# Moving
# the Church
# in
# the
# United States

# The
# Spirit
# Moving
# the Church
# in
# the
# United States

Francis A. Eigo, O.S.A.
Editor

The Villanova University Press

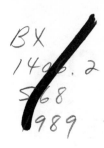
Copyright © 1989 by Francis A. Eigo, O.S.A.
The Villanova University Press
Villanova, Pennsylvania 19085
**Library of Congress Cataloging-in-Publication Data**
The Spirit moving the church in the United States.

   Includes index.
   1. Catholic Church—United States—History—20th
century. 2. Holy Spirit. I. Eigo, Francis A.
BX1406.2.S68 1989      282'.73      88-33883
ISBN 0-87723-052-8

Pour

mon filleul,

Jean

(à l'occasion de sa réception

du sacrement de l'eucharistie):

". . . que vous soyez enraciné(s),

fondé(s) dans l'amour.

Ainsi vous recevrez la force de comprendre . . .

ce qu'est la Largeur, la Longueur,

la Hauteur et la Profondeur,

vous connaîtrez l'amour du Christ

qui surpasse toute connaissance . . ."

(Épître aux Éphésiens 3:17-19).

# Contents

# Contributors

ELIZABETH DREYER, a member of the faculty of the Washington Theological Union, lectures widely, conducts workshops and retreats, and has published extensively in a number of scholarly journals and books as well as authored *Passionate Women: Two Medieval Mystics* and *Manifestations of Grace.*

JOSEPHINE MASSYNGBAERDE FORD, Professor of New Testament Studies at the University of Notre Dame, has most recently published *My Enemy is My Guest, Bonded with the Immortal: a Pastoral Introduction to the New Testament,* and *The Silver Lining,* and she is currently working on a revision of her *Anchor Bible Commentary on the Apocalpyse.*

JOHN C. HAUGHEY, S.J., currently serving as pastor of Saint Peter's Church in Charlotte, North Carolina, and ministering to the Business Community there, is the author of such well known books as *The Conspiracy of God, Should Anyone Say Forever?,* and *The Holy Use of Money* as well as the editor of *The Faith That Does Justice, Theological Investigations of the Charismatic Renewal,* and *Personal Values in Public Policy.*

JOSEPH A. KOMONCHAK, ordained a priest of the Archdiocese of New York and currently on the faculty of the Department of Religion and Religious Education at the Catholic University of America, has published many articles, particularly on contemporary ecclesiological issues, in such scholarly publications as *Theological Studies, The Thomist,* and *Concilium,* and is presently working on the history and theology of the Second Vatican Council.

MARIE AUGUSTA NEAL, S.N.D., Professor at Emmanuel College, holder of a number of lectureships, officer and member of prestigious committees and commissions, recipient of various honors, contributor to scholarly publications and books, counts among the books she has authored *A Socio-Theology of Letting Go, Catholic Sisters in Transition from the 1960s to the 1980s,* and *The Just Demands of the Poor.*

JEROME THEISEN, O.S.B., presently abbot of Saint John's Abbey and a faculty member of Saint John's University, Collegeville, Minnesota, has contributed to a number of scholarly journals and books as well as authored such books as *The Ultimate Church and the Promise of Salvation* and the forthcoming *Community and Disunity: Symbols of Grace and Sin.*

# Introduction

Focusing on the Holy Spirit moving the Church in the United States, this twenty-first volume of the *Proceedings* of the Villanova University Theology Institute begins with Joseph A. Komonchak's introductory essay ("The Church in the United States Today"), considers the biblical understanding of the Spirit (Josephine Massyngbaerde Ford's essay), then examines the questions of power, authority, and charism (Jerome Theisen's essay), the Spirit in the quest for Justice (Marie Augusta Neal's), the many ministries in the one Spirit (Elizabeth Dreyer's) and closes with John Haughey's study on living in the Spirit.

I am indebted to a number of people who have figured in the production of this volume: the members of the Theology Institute Committee (Walter Conn, Edward Hamel, O.S.A., Bernard Lazor, O.S.A., Thomas Ommen, Suzanne Toton), Patricia Fry, and all the essayists.

Francis A. Eigo, O.S.A.
Editor

# The Church in the United States Today

## Joseph A. Komonchak

Anyone would feel intimidated by having to prepare an essay on "The Church in the United States Today." Consider the dimensions: geographically, from Alaska to Florida and Hawaii to Maine; economically, from Wall Street to the grape fields; politically, from Washington power-brokers to the frightened and undocumented alien; culturally, from Hollywood to the Amish; educationally, from the Ph.D.s to the illiterate. How united are these states?

Then, turn to the other subject, "the Church." Restricting our attention to Roman Catholics, we find the restorationists of *The Wanderer* and the revolutionaries of "Womanchurch," and some even to the right and to the left of them! Alongside hierarchs and bureaucrats, there are "the communal Catholics," and between them, one suspects, millions of others. We have a Michael Novak and a Daniel Berrigan, a Phyllis Schlafly and a Rosemary Ruether. Our prisoners of conscience include Joan Andrews and the Plowshare group. Our liturgies range from the formality of Tridentine Latin to the enthusiasms of the charismatic and the psycho-babble of "I'm O.K., you're O.K." Of all this can one use the word "Church" in the singular?

Another problem arises from the place of this essay within a volume devoted to the theme, "The Spirit Moving the Church in the United States." Here, one's hesitations arise from the memory of Jesus' words: "The Spirit blows where he will, and you hear his sound, but you do not know whence he comes or where he goes" (Jn 3:8). The discernment of the Spirit is a special charism, and there is little evidence that it is given with ordination or with a Ph.D. in theology. And, what movement in the Church is there today which does not claim the Spirit's impulse? And, how common is it not for people to invoke him in the absence of other reasons and in order to prevent or deflect criticism?

I can offer only what I have to give. I am by ordination a priest and by interest and training a theologian. Most of my work in recent years has been in the theology of the Church, where I

1

have given special attention to the relationship between ecclesiology and social theory; that is, to the relationship between
what Christian faith says about the Church and what may be
known about this social reality from the perspective of the social
sciences. This has led me into two more specific areas of inquiry.
The first is the theology of the local Church; that is, an understanding of what Vatican II meant when it said that "it is in and
out of the particular Churches that the one and universal
Church exists" (*LG*, 23). The second is an attempt to understand the impact of the Second Vatican Council on the Catholic
Church, for the more concrete one's ecclesiology becomes, the
more one needs to try to understand the process of the Church's
self-constitution; and few ages have seen more dramatic changes
than ours in the self-realization of the Church.

These are, then, the background and the perspectives from
which I write. What I have to offer is perspectives and sets of
categories in which we might together undertake a study both of
the topic assigned to me and of the larger theme of this volume. I
offer, in other words, not an empirical study, but a heuristic
framework which we might find helpful in a common task.

I will begin with proposals for a general methodology with
which to consider the Church, move on to discuss the self-
constitution or genesis of the Church, show the way it requires
that ecclesiology be focused on the local Church, and only then
offer some reflections on the present state of the Church in the
United States in the light of the impact of Vatican II.

## METHOD IN ECCLESIOLOGY

Perhaps I can best clarify my methodological starting-point
by saying that one of the principal tasks of ecclesiology is to avoid
two forms of reductionism. The first is often cited: *sociological*
reductionism, which would consider the Church as simply
another form of a social body organized for religious purposes.
What is distinctive about the Church would not enter into consideration except to the degree that it needs to be taken into
account as this social body's own self-designation. But, its claim
to be a unique, transcendent, and indeed divine reality would
not be accepted. The danger of this type of reductionism is
regularly invoked by Church officials and theologians, many of
whom seem to be unable to use the word "sociological" without
putting the adjective "merely" in front of it.[1]

But, there is another kind of reductionism which is far less
often remarked: *theological* reductionism.[2] This consists in the
assumption, tacit or explicit, that the only appropriate language
with which to speak about the Church is biblical, spiritual, or

liturgical. Here, the unique, transcendent, and divine dimensions of the Church are so stressed that it is easy to forget that they are true of a very human social body. It is not rare for the human and social dimensions of the Church to appear only when they are needed to explain the deficiencies, failures, or sins of the Church. And, systematic ecclesiology is considered largely or even exclusively a matter of reflecting on, reconciling, and understanding the various biblical and traditional affirmations about the Church.

Sociological reductionism is rather rare among serious theologians, although it is hard to deny that it can be found among many non-theologians. But, there are, I believe, many instances of theological reductionism. An example was offered at the 1985 Synod of Bishops, whose "Final Report" warned that "we cannot replace a false, one-sided, merely hierarchical view of the Church with a new and also one-sided sociological concept of the Church."[3] The first false view is what Congar called "hierarchology," the reduction of ecclesiology to a study of the distribution of authority within the Church. Two things seem to be intended by the second one-sided view: (a) a new, but this time, very critical discussion of authority, and (b) some efforts to equate such notions as "People of God" with various types of political reality, whether the "popular Church" of Latin America or various efforts at "democracy in the Church" in Europe and the United States. At the Synod, the German language-group had warned of "the widespread ideology of general and technical feasibility [*Machbarkeit*], which practically denies the created character of man and the world and the attitudes that correspond to it," and they found an example of it in the Church in "the tendency to want to make the Church *ourselves* instead of receiving it as a gift. The correct statement, 'we *are* the Church,' often becomes the mistaken view that 'we *make* the Church.' "[4]

Against this danger, the Synod called for a renewed emphasis on the Church as "mystery" and as "communion." In its deepest reality, the Church is a common participation in the mystery of Christ, a work of God, brought about by the Word of God and the sacraments, a *koinonia* that cannot be reduced to organizational questions or to questions about power.[5]

Now, the Synod is surely correct in insisting that communion in Christ's mystery is at the heart of the Council's ecclesiology and perhaps even in remarking that this dimension has been neglected in some post-conciliar ecclesiologies. But, the issue is poorly posed if it requires a choice between an ecclesiology of communion and an ecclesiology which takes seriously the institutional and sociological dimensions of the Church, including the distribution of authority in the Church. Perhaps this is clear-est when the phrase, "we *make* the Church," is considered an instance of an all-pervasive ideology of *Machbarkeit,* counter-posed to an attitude of receptivity. This framing of the issue is typical of the theological vision of Joseph Ratzinger (who was a member of the German group at the Synod).[6] The human dimension of the Church, the sort of thing that underlies St. Paul's regular references to our "building up" the Church, is quite missing. The impression is given that all we members of the Church do is to "receive" the Church. This is so incomplete as to at least border on theological reductionism.

Vatican II offered a more balanced view in *Lumen gentium*:

> The one mediator, Christ, here on earth established and unfail-ingly supports his Church, the community of faith, hope, and love, as a visible structure through which he pours truth and grace out upon all. The society equipped with hierarchical organs and the mystical Body of Christ, the visible assembly and the spiritual community, the earthly Church and the Church endowed with heavenly gifts, are not to be viewed as two reali-ties, but constitute a single reality, which consists in a human and a divine element (*LG*, 8).

This is a description precisely of what it means to call the Church a mystery. This term "does not simply indicate something unknown or abstruse; . . . it designates rather a divine, tran-scendent, and saving reality which is revealed and manifested in some visible way."[7] Take away either element, the transcendent or the visible, and the mystery disappears. The Church con-tinues, as the conciliar text went on to say, the law of incarna-tion: the presence and power of God's saving grace and truth in human history and society.

It can be argued that a primary task of ecclesiology is to understand and to show the way this can be the case: that there are not two Churches, but only one, at once divine and human, spiritual and sociological, transcendent and empirical. It is easy enough to distinguish them, as, for example, when people speak of the *Ecclesia ut mysterium* and of the *Ecclesia ut societas,* but the distinction becomes a separation unless a serious effort is made to unite them in a synthetic theological vision.[8]

I am myself convinced that this will not be possible unless theologians overcome their fear and suspicion of social theory and learn to use it to help develop the categories needed to speak of the social phenomenon which is itself the created sign and instrument of God's redemptive purpose in the world. As Claude Welch argued, the created character of the Church as a community constituted in response to the divine initiative

belongs to the very ontology of the Church.[9] And, this legiti-
mates a theological approach which moves from the common to
the unique,[10] from what the Church has in common with other
human communities in order to discover precisely in and
through, and not in spite of, those common elements where and
how the Church is a distinct and transcendent reality. For, it is
only if the unique and transcendent are realized in the common
that the Church participates in the mystery of Christ, the Word
made flesh.

For that reason, theologians can usefully begin by considering
what it is that makes a group of human beings a community; that
is, the way communities come to be and then continually, daily,
reproduce themselves. For this, I have found it useful to follow
Bernard Lonergan's heuristics of community, which I find strik-
ingly confirmed by at least certain social theories. Lonergan
speaks of community as constituted by common meaning and
value. A group of people have the potentiality to become a
community when they share a common field of experience,
something they can think and talk about together. This potentiality is given form when their conversation leads to common or
at least complementary understandings and judgments about
this experience: when they can say, "Yes, this is what it means,"
or "No, that is not what it means." And, this becomes an actual,
effective community when, on the basis of their common interpretation of their common experience, they commit themselves
to common goals, common commitments, and common decisions. Such common meaning and value are what distin-
guishes a genuine community from a mere assemblage of people
in the same place and at the same time. They are distinct from
other human communities if different meanings and values constitute their common reality. And, they remain across time the
same community to the degree that the same meanings and
values draw them out of their individuality into one concrete
social body.[11]

This constitution of community is as precarious an achievement as the self-constitution of an individual through the understandings and commitments which define his existence. As our
existential identity requires that we each every day realize ourselves by our acknowledged meanings and chosen values, so a
community continues to exist to the degree that its distinctive
meanings and values continue to be accepted and lived out by its
members. As Anthony Giddens has persuasively argued, social
bodies are recreated and reproduced by the free acts of their
members: "*The production of society* is a skilled performance, sustained and 'made to happen' by human beings."[12]

Such heuristic descriptions of the constitution and re-
constitution of social bodies provide a helpful way to approach
the concrete self-constitution or self-realization of the Church.
They suggest certain questions to ask precisely about this unique
and transcendent reality. What common experiences ground the
potentiality for the human community we call "the Church"?
What common interpretations and judgments give it form?
What values, goals, commitments, and decisions make it effectively real in human history? Notice that these questions do not
separate the transcendent and the empirical. On the basis of a
formal heuristic of human community, shared with other social
bodies, they ask about the empirical realization of the unique
and the transcendent. Putting it in other terms, they ask what
are the common meanings and values that constitute and distinguish this group of human beings as the People of God, the Body
of Christ, and the Temple of the Spirit? To approach an answer
to them, we may move to a second step in our reflections and
speak about the genesis of the Church.

## THE GENESIS OF THE CHURCH

I borrow the metaphor of genesis from the words of St. Bede:
"Everyday the Church gives birth to the Church."[13] We will
have to return to the at least paradoxical idea that the Church
can give birth to the Church, but for the moment I wish to
emphasize the underlying metaphor of genesis or birth.[14]

The paradigmatic historical event, of course, is the emergence
of the Christian Church. The Church had its origins when a
group of Palestinian Jews of the first century began to stumble
after one Jesus of Nazareth. Drawn by his preaching and his
call, they tried to understand who he was and what he was about,
relating his unique message to their religious tradition, looking
for the categories in which to make sense of him, finally coming
to hope "that he was the one who would liberate Israel" (Lk
24:21). His arrest and execution appear to have shattered that
hope, and they were at the point of abandoning their common
life in order to return to their individual destinies, when they
became convinced that he had been raised from the dead and
constituted Lord and Messiah. Experiencing a new power,
which they called "the Holy Spirit," they began to tell others
what they had themselves experienced and witnessed and drew
them now into what they considered the fulfilment of the ancient
promises of a restored Israel, the assembly of the last days. Their
new and distinctive community, centered on the memory of
Jesus of Nazareth and the confession that he is Lord, was the concrete effect in human society and history of his redemptive ministry.

All the other language with which the early Christians spoke of the Church was an effort to make sense to themselves and to others of this fundamental and abiding common reality. What was born in them from their encounter with Jesus and from their Easter and Pentecost experiences continued to be born and reborn whenever they told of him, and others came to believe, to hope, and to love as they had been given to do. And ever since, the genesis of the Church has been accomplished through that same process, summed up in the words of the First Epistle of John: "What we have seen and heard we proclaim to you, so that you may have fellowship with us, and our fellowship is with the Father and with his Son, Jesus Christ" (1 Jn 1:3). If this event does not take place again and again, day after day, the Church does not exist; and where it does take place, again and again, day after day, the Church continues to be born.

To take the argument further, let us distinguish two moments in this process by which daily the Church gives birth to the Church. The first of these moments is the communication by one generation of believers of "what they have seen and heard." "Faith comes from hearing," St. Paul said (Rom 10:17). The message comes from without; it stands over and against a new generation as promise, call, and demand. A world is held out to them, a fellowship which they are invited to enter, a fellowship with God and the Son whom he has sent. By our time, today, this objective element in the genesis of the Church is represented in the various carriers of Christian meaning and value which over the centuries have been built up as the historical and communal realizations of that fellowship. Catholics find these in the scriptures and the monuments of the Tradition, in the sacraments, in the apostolic ministry, in the institutions and roles, customs and habits, images and language, stories and legends, exemplary individual and communal histories, in all of which earlier generations of Christians embodied the interpretation and evaluation of human life which they drew from and centered upon Jesus Christ. This is the Church as already constituted and realized, as a given to be received or rejected. It is the Church, to use the ancient metaphor, as the matrix of faith and Mother of believers.

But, the Church is not reborn again today unless this offer is subjectively received and appropriated in the faith, hope, and love of a new generation of believers. This reception and appropriation are the second, subjective moment in the genesis of the Church. The Church is the *congregatio fidelium,* the assembly of believers, and the fellowship with the Father and with his Son continues only if what was seen and heard by the first generation of witnesses continues to be accepted and appropriated in the

individual and communal lives of a present generation. The
Church is possible only because of the offer of the word and
grace of Christ, but it is not real unless that word and grace are
received in faith and love. And, when a new generation comes to
believe and love what another generation has seen and heard,
the Church is born from the Church, the *Ecclesia congregans* giving birth to the *Ecclesia congregata.*

This perspective helps us appreciate the reason the Eucharistic assembly has always been taken as the central realization of
the Church. Let me refer to a dramatic example. I know a pastor
who once had to prepare a homily for the funeral of a white teen-
ager who had been murdered by a black teen-ager. This was the
second such tragedy in a parish in which racial tensions were
already high, and many of the white parishioners were threaten-
ing revenge. Put yourself in the pastor's place. You will be
addressing a congregation which will enter the Church, not only
sunk in grief over a senseless death, but with some of them
tempted to hatred and violent revenge. You will be the one
responsible for bringing this tragedy and the grief and anger it
has caused before what once was seen and heard by the disciples
of Jesus of Nazareth. Once again, you will tell what they saw and
heard, what promise and comfort it can offer, what attitudes and
decisions it demands. And, that is all you can do. You can be the
instrument of the offer, of the possibility for there being once
again, here and now, in *this* assembly, a Church.

But, will the Church be born again, here and now, in this
assembly? That will depend on whether, by the power of the
Spirit, those who came in grieving can find comfort in their faith
in him who also died a senseless death, and whether those who
came in with hatred and revenge in their hearts can at least begin
to try to forgive. Will the offer be received? Will the comfort be
appropriated? Will the forgiveness of God generate the forgiveness of man? Out of the tense division between whites and blacks
will the Body of Christ be built up once again, when all, blacks
and whites, though many, share in the bread which is the Body
broken on the cross and in the blood poured out for forgiveness?

The example is dramatic, but what was at stake in that actual
funeral assembly is what is at stake each day in less dramatic
ways when the Word of Christ is again communicated and a
generation invited to believe in it. The Church gives birth to the
Church when the "objective" element, the offer, is received and
appropriated through the free subjectivity of those to whom it is
proclaimed.

The example also illustrates how concrete an event is the

genesis of the Church. When the subjective moment is understood to be central to and constitutive of the self-realization of
the Church, it becomes immediately clear that ecclesiology cannot remain content with a simple description of the objective
moment. The Word and grace are constitutive of the Church, of
course, as are the various ways in which they are carried from
generation to generation; but, that mediation is always a concrete process, in which the Word is preached to specific interpretative contexts and the grace is offered as comfort and healing
and confirmation to specific groups of men and women. Just as
there is no Eucharist in general, but only specific worshipping
communities, so also there is no Church except in assemblies of
faith, here and there, yesterday and today. The genesis of the
Church is thus a hermeneutical achievement, an event of proclamation and interpretation, reception and appropriation. And,
because this hermeneutical event is an existential event, the
genesis of the Church is itself an event constitutive of history. [15]

Two implications of this recognition must be noted. The first
is the impossibility of separating the nature and mission of the
Church. [16] It is possible, of course, to distinguish these insofar as
one can locate the "nature" of the Church in its distinctive
generative principles common to all communities of faith,
whereas the reception and appropriation constitute its mission,
which varies from place to place. But, since this nature is never
generative of the Church except as received and appropriated as
local and historical mission, the distinction should never become
a separation. The Church's nature is realized as its mission. As
the incarnation represents God's insertion into human history,
into the process of man's self-constitution, so the Church is the
sign and instrument through which that redemptive intervention in word and grace continues to be socially and historically
effective. That is the reason ecclesiology is the place where soteriology, the theology of redemption, becomes a theology of
history, a theory of the divine response to the great drama of
human self-realization. [17] The genesis of the Church is an event
within and with regard to the genesis of the world of human
history.

Perhaps a comparison with the concrete process of an individual's conversion can be helpful here. It is possible to construct a
theology of grace in somewhat general terms, focusing on the
reality of sin, the processes of repentance, the experience of
justification, et cetera. But, in any single person, what is
described there is realized in specific ways. This man is engaged
in a task of self-realization through his own personal exercise of
his freedom. By the time he is an adult, that freedom is already
existentially oriented through a complex of factors, some of

them of his own choosing, some of them not, some of them
genuinely human, some of them not. The call to conversion is a
call for him to face himself, in all his concreteness, and to decide
for himself what he will make of himself in the light of the Gospel
of Christ. The decision he will have to make is not a decision in
general, but a decision about a very concrete and existential
history: will his past history determine also his future history? or
will a new freedom create a new self and the new self create a new
history? For example, will he continue to be addicted to his past
habits, to his habitual relationships to others, or will there
appear, in his private life and in his relationships, a different
habit of living, displayed in quite specific ways of thinking,
choosing, speaking, et cetera?

Something similar happens with the genesis of the concrete
Church. A concrete group of men and women, in a specific
historical moment, with specific habits of inter-relating and of
relating as a group to the larger world, is faced with the choice of
its own historic future. It is a collective subject of history-making
decisions: shall there appear, here and now, in the face of these
opportunities, a group of men and women who come to believe
and who make choices because of, in the name of, and for the
sake of Jesus Christ? The very emergence or genesis of the
Church, when viewed concretely, means the assumption of
responsibility for a collective future. Human history in general
and in this specific instance will be one thing if a Church is born
and reborn and something else if it is not. One set of historic
possibilities will be either realized or not. Christ's word and
grace will continue to affect human history or they will not. An
ecclesiology of the concrete genesis of the Church is a theology of
history.

This leads to our second implication: the need to focus on the
local communities in which this genesis occurs; i.e., on parishes
and other small communities. Here, we need to note a certain
difficulty with regard to the notion of the local Church. We
included in our description of the constitutive generative principles of the Church the apostolic ministry. That phrase was meant
to point to the Catholic belief that a structure of ministry, gathered around a bishop in the particular Churches and around the
ministry of universal unity in the person of the Bishop of Rome,
belongs to the essence of the Church. In this sense, the local
Church is described in terms of the diocesan Church. This
particular way of seeing the issue is itself the result of an historical development, nicely summarized by Jean-Marie Tillard:

> It is thus every local community assembled by the Eucharist
> which is the Church. Originally, it seems, each city having only

one Eucharist, the Churches were reckoned and distinguished after the places where the eucharistic assembly took place. The local eucharistic community was the local Church. But with the expansion of the Church outside the cities, the eucharistic communities multiplied, this occurring at the same time as the Church felt the need to organize and structure itself. Around the city, but in connection with the leaders of the Church—with a "president" authorized for them, as Ignatius of Antioch would say—communities would celebrate for themselves the Memorial of the Lord. Often the link with the eucharist of the city, presided over by the one now called a bishop, was symbolized by the rite of the *fermentum*. The local Church thus becomes the totality of eucharistic communities in communion with this bishop and gravitating around his see. It is thus itself a *communion* of local communities. In today's language, it is the diocese (entrusted to a bishop), itself composed of parishes, each of these being a eucharistic community.[18]

The role of the local eucharistic assemblies as constitutive of the Church was acknowledged in an important passage of *Lumen gentium*:

This Church of Christ is truly present in all legitimate local congregations of the faithful which, adhering to their pastors, are themselves called "Churches" in the New Testament. For in their locales, these are the new People of God called by God in the Holy Spirit and in full conviction (see I Th 1:5). In them believers are gathered by the preaching of Christ's Gospel and the mystery of the Lord's Supper is celebrated. . . . In every altar community, under the bishop's sacred ministry, is manifested the symbol of that love and 'unity of the Mystical Body, without which there can be no salvation.' In these communities, although often small and poor or living.in the diaspora, Christ is present, by whose power the one, holy, catholic and apostolic Church is gathered together (*LG*, 26).

We are brought by this text to consider the Church not only in terms of the diocesan Church, but in terms also of the individual communities of which the diocese, in its fundamental reality, is the living communion.

These communities are, of course, the parishes, but they also include non-territorial communities of faith and smaller communities within the parishes. Here is the place to bring in the powerful movement since the Council towards grassroots Christian communities.[19] These have emerged not only as ways of overcoming some of the anonymity of large parishes, but also as ways to promote the genesis of the Church, as we might put it, from below up. Official Church documents have occasionally referred to them as "cells" of the Body of Christ, which may be a useful metaphor. A body is alive and healthy only if all its cells are alive and healthy, and in turn the cells are alive and healthy only with the life of the whole body. Similarly, the Church is alive and healthy only if all its communities are alive and healthy, and they are alive and healthy with the life of the whole Church. It is not necessary, in fact it is fatal, to distinguish these.

The issue this raises is, of course, the one frequently posed in terms of the relationship between the universal Church and the local Churches. In the next section, however, I would prefer to address it in terms of the genesis of the one Church in and out of the many local Churches.

## THE ONE CHURCH IN THE MANY CHURCHES

One of the characteristic developments in ecclesiology since the Council has been the renewed emphasis given to the local Church.[20] This theme was not well developed at all before Vatican II, when ecclesiology was largely developed from a universalist perspective. At the Council itself, this perspective was dominant, but there are conciliar texts which helped to inspire what has been called "a Copernican revolution in ecclesiology."[21]

We may take as our starting-point a sentence in the third chapter of *Lumen gentium*: "The individual bishops are the visible principle and foundation of unity in their own particular Churches, formed in the image of the universal Church, and in and out of which the one and single catholic Church exists" (*LG*, 23). I am interested in the description here of the relationship between the one universal Church and the many particular Churches. The latter are said to be "formed in the image of the universal Church," while this one catholic Church is in turn said to exist "in and out of" the particular Churches.

The way these two affirmations are to be understood and related to one another constitutes one of the most warmly debated issues in contemporary ecclesiology. It is sometimes, perhaps unfortunately, expressed as the question whether "priority" is to be given to the universal or to the local Church.[22] Must not this priority be assigned to the universal Church, since the local Churches are formed in its image? On the other hand, must not the priority be assigned to the local Churches, since it is only in and out of them that the universal Church has any existence?[23]

I suspect that we have here a false dilemma. The Council makes *both* affirmations, and, if they are not to be considered to be contradictory, there must be some sense in which they can be reconciled. Let me offer an interpretation on the basis of our description of the genesis of the Church.

We argued towards the end of the previous section that the Church is always generated locally; that is, in particular communities of believers. We also spoke of generative objective principles which constitute the divine offer of the Word and grace of Christ which constitute the Church as a distinct community. From several conciliar texts, particularly *Lumen gentium* 26 and *Christus Dominus* 11, we may derive the following list of the spiritual principles that constitute the Church: the call of God, the grace of the Holy Spirit, the preaching of the Gospel of Christ, the apostolic ministry, and the celebration of the Eucharist. These are the most important of the means through which by Christ's word and grace the Church is generated. No other human community arises because of and around these generative principles, and so they are the carriers of the uniqueness and transcendence of the Church.

As such, these are also the principles of the unity and catholicity of the Church across generations and across cultures. It is due to the fact that the same principles which gave rise to the Church in its first generation give rise to it today that the present generation is in communion with the first generation of believers. It is due to the fact that everywhere, in America and Africa, Asia and Europe, the same principles gather men and women as assemblies of believers that these communities of faith are the one and universal Church. And, any community which does not arise from the reception and appropriation of these objective representations of the word and grace of Christ is by that fact a different community from the one and universal Church of Christ.

That is the meaning of the statement that every local Church is "formed in the image of the universal Church." The objective principle of the genesis of the Church is thus the principle of the Church's catholicity. To make it concrete, consider the day when there are Churches fully inculturated, say, in Africa, Asia, and the United States. On that day, these Churches will either be in communion with one another as one catholic Church or there will not be one Church, but many Churches not in communion with one another. If they are *one* catholic Church, it will be due to the fact that in their several cultural circumstances one call, one grace, one Word, one Eucharist celebrated under one apostolic ministry have generated each of the inculturated Churches. In other words, the objective generative principles are what one would point to in order to be able to assert that the Church in Africa, the Church in Asia, and the Church in the United States are, for all their differences, *one* Church.

But, what is this one and catholic Church? Where is it to be found? How is it generated? It exists at all only because in each place, the objective principles have been subjectively received and appropriated in concrete communities of faith. The one catholic Church has no existence except because Africans, Asians, and Americans receive in faith the Word of Christ and in love the grace of his Spirit. It does not exist in some super-local, super-cultural, super-historical sphere, but only in the places, cultures, and historical circumstances where groups of men and women have been brought to enter into communion with those who transmitted to them what the first disciples saw and heard.

One can conclude, therefore, only that the question of "priority" is a mistake in principle. There is no local *Church* that is not the one and catholic Church, and there is no one and *catholic* Church except in and out of the local Churches. One is not prior to the other. The great biblical image of this, of course, is the Church born at Pentecost:

> There were living in Jerusalem devout Jews from every nation under heaven; and at this sound the crowd gathered, all bewildered because each one heard his own language spoken. They were amazed and in their astonishment exclaimed, "Why, they are all Galileans, are they not, these men who are speaking? How is it then that we hear them, each of us in his own native language? . . . we hear them telling in our own tongues the great things God has done" (Acts 2:5-6,11).

The Galilean disciples of Jesus were speaking in the city of Jerusalem, but their one message about the marvelous deeds of God was heard and accepted in all the languages of the world. Simultaneously, the Church was born both local and universal. The Church that was born in Jerusalem was the Church that would be born in all the cultures of the world. An ancient liturgical preface caught this beautifully:

> We know no gift of yours more sublime than the one granted at the beginning of the Church, when the mouths of believers proclaimed your Gospel in all languages, so that the sentence justly passed because of the construction of the prideful tower might be absolved and the variety of languages would not hinder the building up of the Church but would rather foster its unity.[24]

If this is the case, then why did the false question arise? It appears because of certain misunderstandings of the relationship between universal and local Churches. Some people understand the universal Church almost as a multi-national religious corporation which from a central office in Rome establishes identical branch offices in the major cities of the world, with these in turn establishing retail outlets in their own regions. This view sees the local Churches as "parts" of a pre-existing whole, the universal Church. Hence the idea of a "priority" of the universal Church. This view is often associated with a view of the papal primacy which detaches it from the role of the pope as the Bishop of the local Church of Rome.[25]

On the other hand, some people who speak of the priority of the local Church imagine that the universal Church arises only in a secondary moment, as the result of a sort of free confederation of local Churches. This view neglects the fact that catholicity or universal communion is of the essence of the Church, founded in the catholic intentionality and effectiveness of the call of God, the Gospel of Christ, and the grace of the Spirit. The local Church is born catholic, or it is not the Church. It is the local realization of the one Church.

With all this as a prelude, necessary to avoid misunderstanding, one must say something further about the concrete meaning of the catholicity of the one Church. The Council gave a splendid description of this attribute of the Church in *Lumen gentium,* 13:

> The character of universality which adorns the People of God is the gift of the Lord himself, by which the catholic Church effectively and constantly seeks to recapitulate the whole of humanity with all its goods under the Headship of Christ, in the unity of his Spirit. In virtue of this catholicity, the several parts bring their own gifts to one another and to the whole Church, so that the whole and its several parts grow by the mutual sharing of all and by a common effort towards the fullness of unity.

Catholicity is thus not mere geographical universality nor is it achieved or realized in spite of, or over and above, the diversities of human societies and cultures, but precisely in and through them. Once Catholics used to boast that they could go anywhere in the world and find the Eucharist celebrated in the same language and the same rite. It is a perfect illustration of the vision of catholicity which the Council sought to overcome: everywhere the central mystery of the Church is celebrated in a language and in forms which have no relationship to the local living cultures. The Council's decision to permit the Eucharist to be celebrated in local languages was the momentous decision to allow the *one* central mystery to be realized in, and not in spite of, the various living cultures. The Eucharist is no less one and universal today than it was thirty years ago; but, the vision of what concrete universality means has changed.

The Council's *Decree on the Church's Missionary Activity* can be read as a description of the concrete catholicizing of the Church. Through the process which has since come to be known as inculturation, the Church is to enter into a creative dialogue with the cultures of the world, acknowledging and assuming their riches, illuminating and redeeming them by the Gospel, and so enriching the catholic unity.

For this reason, the socio-cultural factors are part of the theological definition of the local Church.[26] Attempts to distinguish the "theological" principles of the local Church from "socio-cultural" factors reflect a failure to consider the concrete genesis of the Church, which does not occur solely on the basis of the distinctive principles of the Church, what we have called the "objective, generative principles," but only through their reception and appropriation by groups of men and women living in quite specific social and cultural circumstances.[27] If the Church's catholicity means concrete universality, then the variety of receptions and realizations of the constitutive principles is as much a part of the Church's basic reality as the unity of those principles. As the Council put it in a fine phrase: "This unity-intending variety of local Churches shows all the more resplendently the catholicity of the undivided Church."[28]

The Council's attempt to recover the whole reality of the concretely catholic Church has led, then, to the flourishing of the theology of the local Church. Its practical implementation has led, in turn, on what might be called the cultural level, to the vast effort at genuine inculturations of the Gospel. On the structural level, it has included calls to give a greater decision-making authority to local and regional institutions. Two recently debated aspects of this structural question may be briefly described.

It first appears in the question whether the principle of subsidiarity applies within the Church.[29] In general terms, this principle maintains that where an individual or smaller social unit is able to meet its responsibilities, their freedom of self-realization should not be restricted by removing these possibilities and assigning them to a larger social group. Put in terms of the Church, this would mean that a Christian, a parish, a diocese, or group of dioceses should be given the freedom to exercise their own rights and responsibilities, so that none of the larger ecclesial units arrogates to itself or makes impossible that exercise of freedom.

Objections to applying subsidiarity in the Church are expressed, first, in the general principle that a notion elaborated for civil society should not be considered applicable within the unique social reality which is the Church. This is a principle difficult to reconcile with the millennial practice of the Church in making use of social philosophies and structures found in successive ages. It also borders on the "theological reductionism" to which I referred earlier.

More particularly, the argument is also made that the relationship between the local and universal Church cannot be assimilated to that between a central governmental structure, such as our federal government, and more local administrative structures, such as our state governments. This is, as we have seen, a legitimate comment, but it does not seem relevant here. The Church is catholic and local, inseparably. The local Church is the local realization of the one catholic Church; but, this can *ground* an analogous application of the principle of subsidiarity, because this principle is one way of articulating the genuinely and fully ecclesial character of the local Church.[30]

A second area in which the structural question arises is with regard to the nature and authority of episcopal conferences. This institution developed in the last century and was strongly endorsed at Vatican II. Today, there are more than one hundred of them, and, since the Council, they have developed into a very important, even indispensable, means for the exercise of episcopal authority in the local Churches. Recently, however, particularly because of post-conciliar developments and especially the frequency with which some conferences have issued doctrinal statements, the objection has been made that they are in danger of restricting the authority of the two constitutive bearers of ecclesiastical authority, the diocesan bishop and the pope. A Roman document has recently been sent out in draft-form which argues that the episcopal conferences are not collegial in the strict sense and that they do not, in themselves, have any doctrinal authority.[31]

The issues here also are complex. There are some practical problems connected with at least some of the conferences, such as the danger of bureaucratization which can in fact inhibit the freedom of the individual bishop (which would, of course, itself be a violation of the principle of subsidiarity). Whether there is a real danger today of a revival of nationalism in the Church is a matter of dispute, one with which we are familiar enough in the United States.

But, the practical questions are not necessarily theological in nature, and here is what I think is one of the major mistakes in the Roman document. It tries to answer practical questions by a theological response. Again, at the heart of the issue, as the text itself implies, is the relationship between the local and the universal Church. In an important paragraph, this document maintains that the universal Church has an ontological and historical priority over the local Churches. It has astonishingly little of a powerful theological nature to say about the reality of the local diocesan Church as a realization of the one Church nor about the role of the bishop as a representative of his local Church to the whole Church.

It is most significant that the text quite ignores the context in which the Council introduced the episcopal conferences: that precisely of those "organically linked groupings of Churches" which arose in the early Church, particularly in the form of patriarchates. This sort of cooperative instinct led the Churches as early as the second century to gather in local and regional councils, which are the first historical evidence we have for what today we call collegiality. This instinct has a contemporary reflection in the emergence and development of the episcopal conferences.

In both of these practical questions is visible what is perhaps the most basic and significant tension in the post-conciliar Church, the tension between the demands of unity and the demands of concrete catholicity. This has been dramatically illustrated in almost all of the meetings of the Synod of Bishops, which has become an expression at once of the issues at stake and of the Church's present difficulty in addressing them, either theoretically or practically.

The tensions are built into the notion of a Church which wishes to be both one and concretely catholic. If unity is identified with uniformity or catholicity with simple pluriformity, the tension does not arise. The problem arises because the Church is supposed to be one by being concretely catholic. This is an important point. Catholicity and unity are not opposites: the one Church is catholic; the catholic Church is one.

But, to the built-in tension must be added the further fact that this recovered sense of unity as concrete catholicity has emerged after and in many respects in reaction to a millennium of centralization and increased uniformity. These were bought at the price of a decline in the importance recognized to belong to local diocesan Churches and to various types of regional associations of Churches. These practical developments were assisted and legitimated by an ecclesiology of the universal Church, which at times ran the danger of regarding the local Churches as simple administrative units of the world-wide organization. This became something simply taken-for-granted in the minds of many churchmen and theologians. The questioning of this pre-supposition can lead us to the last section of my remarks, on the impact of the Second Vatican Council.

## THE IMPACT OF VATICAN II

In the United States, as almost everywhere else, the question of the present state of the Church must be posed concretely in terms of the extraordinary changes which have taken place in the Catholic Church since the Second Vatican Council. It is perhaps unnecessary here to try to demonstrate that the Church changed more in the twenty years after the Council than it had for centuries before. If something like consensus on that remark is fairly easy to find, it is another question when one asks for the causes of this remarkable transformation and for an evaluation of it. Disagreement on these matters greatly charges the contemporary effort to interpret the Council itself.[32]

Roughly speaking, three interpretations of the conciliar event are now vying for acceptance. The first may be called the "progressive" interpretation, which assumes an extremely negative evaluation of pre-conciliar Catholicism and counterposes to it the Spirit-filled and liberating event of the Council. The second, "traditionalist" interpretation, reverses the value-judgments, assigning modern Roman Catholicism an eternal validity and seeing in the Council and its impact a capitulation to the principles and movements which produced the modern world and which the Church had consistently opposed until the days of Pope John XXIII. Attempting to occupy a middle-ground between these two interpretations, a "reformist" view argues that the Council intended a needed "reform" but not a "revolution," and that if the latter has, unfortunately, happened, it is the fault of those progressives who distorted the Council's "letter" in favor of their own interpretation of its "spirit."[33]

The black-and-white, almost apocalyptic, antitheses of the first two views render them, in my view, unhelpful. They suffer equally from a lack of historical and sociological perspective. I will, therefore, concentrate on the "reformist" attempt to exonerate the Council from responsibility for the post-conciliar transformation.

It seems to me, first, to be unfaithful to the dynamics and the experience of the Council itself. Anyone who took part in the Council or even witnessed it can remember the dramatic character of its sessions, particularly the first one. For good or ill, it was experienced as a moment of "*krisis*," of critical decision, when a series of movements largely suspect suddenly gained respectability and when a whole set of attitudes and strategies officially sanctioned before were called into question. This sense of dramatic change was a characteristic mark of the conciliar experience.[34]

Secondly, the question of responsibility cannot be addressed solely in terms of the intentions of the popes and bishops of the Council. One can probably argue that they did not anticipate or even desire the dramatic changes the Council would provoke, and in that sense one might agree that they intended only "reform." But, according to a well-known law of history and sociology, people can be the causes of effects which they did not foresee. And on this basis, I would argue that the Council is responsible for the dramatic transformation of modern Catholicism in that it made three decisions which called radically into question basic elements of the social form of the pre-conciliar Church.

The first of these is visible in the two chief aims which Pope John set out for the Council: renewal and up-dating. The Council was to go back to the sources of the Church's life, and by that criterion to examine its concrete activities in terms of its fidelity to Christ's will. *Aggiornamento,* on the other hand, required the Church to examine its activity in terms of its appropriateness to the world of the late twentieth century. The inevitable tension between these two movements and their criteria should not make us overlook the fact that they had in common an intention to subject the everyday life of the Church, in almost every one of its aspects, to a critical re-examination for the sake of whatever reforms might be required.

This, I submit, was already a jolt to the social system that was the modern Church. All of the processes by which it reproduced itself day by day came under examination. What operated most successfully by being taken for granted was no longer to be taken for granted. And, particularly because in its official claims the Catholic Church had prided itself on not needing change, this came as a psychological and sociological shock to many Catholics. If the genie of reform suddenly appeared to have revolutionary size and strength, that does not excuse those who rubbed the bottle and called him forth.

Secondly, already implicit in the slogan of *aggiornamento* was a far more nuanced attitude towards the modern world than had characterized the Roman Catholicism that had been constructed in the previous century and a half.[35] That at least suspicious and not infrequently hostile attitude had inspired the Church to construct itself as a sub-society, marked by clear lines of demarcation from all other groups and by powerful structures of centralized authority. Pope John XXIII, in his opening address, challenged this view at its root, and he was echoed by Paul VI when he devoted his first encyclical to the theme of dialogue. The Council followed the two popes in its documents on ecumenism, religious freedom, and the Church in the modern world.

This was not, as Archbishop Lefebvre would have it, a capitulation to modernity, but it was something more than a minor "reform." Much of the sociological consistency and identity of pre-conciliar Catholicism derived from the suspicious attitude and its corresponding strategies. Suddenly, the lines of demarcation from others were blurred, and Catholics were asked to look for another identity than anti-modernity. A second way in which what might have been meant as a mere reform had revolutionary potential.

The third decision of the Council challenged the structuring of authority familiar in pre-conciliar Catholicism: the call for genuinely local Churches, which we have reviewed above. Modern Roman Catholicism was highly centralized and increasingly uniform. The underlying image was that of a single, world-wide Church engaged in a battle with world-wide forces of evil, and nothing is more crucial in a war than clear instructions from the single commander-in-chief and immediate obedience. But, now the Council, because it had changed the goal, was also changing the strategy. The role of the Church could still be stated as being that of a sacrament, sign, and instrument of the unity of the human race (*LG*, 1), but this unity would be achieved as concrete catholicity, involving a genuine dialogue between Gospel and local cultures, and this required that the task be taken up in and by the local Churches, as the subjects of the self-realization of the one Church in their own areas. This is, of course, part of what Karl Rahner has made familiar as the shift from a Eurocentric to a genuinely "world-Church," a shift he compared in epochal importance to the shift from Jewish to Hellenized Christianity.[36]

What this change has meant has varied, of course, in the various Churches.[37] The specificity of the new charge itself makes generalizations impossible. In our own North American circumstances, however, I do not think it inaccurate to speak of the rapid collapse of the pre-conciliar form of Roman Catholicism, in evidence of which I need only suggest a reading of works written at the time or evoking it later.[38]

I am not suggesting here that the Council is solely responsible for what happened or indeed that it is responsible for all that happened. The Council began in 1962 and ended in 1965. Its beginning coincided with a period of remarkable optimism and its end with the beginning of an extraordinary challenge to the taken for granted habits of mind and action of Western societies. It is as tempting as it is futile to wonder what would have happened to the Church had the Council not occurred. The point is that it did occur and that it occurred when it did, and that its own commitment to a greater engagement with contemporary historical movements was quickly given a form and a momentum which its protagonists almost certainly never envisaged. In any case, we have no other choice but to engage our own task of ecclesial self-realization in the conditions created by and after that remarkable event.

I have introduced these points because I think they are pertinent to a discussion of "the Church in the United States today." The Church today is a product of the Council in fact, if not always in the intention of the Council members themselves. The Church, while in many respects the same Church, is in many other respects a different Church today. This startles those by whom the concrete genesis of the Church over successive historical generations has never been given serious theological consideration. There are others who believe that the Council's own decisions need not have had the iconoclastic consequences which in fact often followed it. One can agree with that regret, even while maintaining that the answer is not a return to or restoration of the *status quo ante* nor in an appeal to a theological reductionism which in effect denies the Council's central insistence on the historic responsibility of Christians to be and therefore to make the Church what it should be in and for each historical moment and situation.

In his later writings Bernard Lonergan often referred to the existential moment when a person recognizes that it is up to himself to decide for himself what he will make of himself. It can be argued that the Council represented such a moment in the development of the Church; that is, when its existential self-responsibility became conscious. As it is impossible for the individual to go back from that discovery—so that to choose not to choose his own future becomes an impossibility, so also the Church now understands itself to be inescapably the subject of its own self-realization, no matter how much it may try to pretend something else. No more than in the case of the individual does this mean that this self-realization ought to be undertaken in some mad, global repudiation of the Church's past, as if self-realization must mean the refusal to receive anything from others, from our parents in the faith or, indeed, from Christ himself. But, it does mean that the Church is born from the interaction of two freedoms: the freedom of the God of salvation, creating and liberating the genuine freedom of those who are saved. No one else can be the Church for us; it is our historical moment, and it is we who will decide whether and what kind of Church there will be in the United States today.

To say that does not mean, of course, that we undertake this task by ourselves, without communion with others undertaking this task in their situations or with the one who exercises the ministry of universal unity. What we wish to see continually born here is the same Church which was born in generations past and which is being born elsewhere today. And, this living communion with the other Churches which today are realizing the one Church of Christ is not only a necessary element of the very being of the Church, but an important challenge, stimulus, and criterion for the fulfilment of our task. What we want to see born is "the Church in the United States today," and all the elements in that phrase must be given equal attention. It is to be "in the United States today," and it is to be "the Church" here today.

## HEURISTIC OBSERVATIONS ON THE CHURCH IN THE UNITED STATES

I have offered heuristic foundations for a theology of the local Church, what Catalino Arevalo, S.J., has called "a field-theory in ecclesiology." It is not itself a theology of the local Church. This can be constructed only on the basis of reflection on the process by which a local Church is generated when the constitutive principles that make the Church the Church are received and appropriated in the hermeneutical and historical process that makes it a *local* Church, the Church in *this* time, place, and culture. I take it that the rest of this volume's reflections can be considered a contribution to such a local ecclesiology in this country.

It is only right, however, to acknowledge that there is a good deal of resistance today to the post-conciliar emphasis on the local church. It is visible at one level in the criticism of the phrase, "the American Church," at another in Cardinal Ratzinger's insistence that "the national level is not an ecclesial dimension,"[39] and at yet another in a series of recent efforts on the part of Rome to restrict the autonomy of the local Churches. Let me say a few things about each of them.

The dispute about the term to be used, "American Church" or "the Church in the United States," is relatively trivial. Similar objections do not seem to be raised, even in Rome, when people speak of the "French Church" or the "Italian Church." The real issue here is not the term itself, but differing judgments about the degree of variety compatible with Catholic unity and about the relationship between local and Roman authority. Here is where the issue should be joined.

As for Cardinal Ratzinger's comment, one can agree that the Church's inner and distinctive reality has nothing to do with nationhood, at least as this is understood in the modern world.

The Church in a particular cultural or geographical area can
remain quite the same, however the political constitution of the
people there may change. Moreover, history has enough examples of nationalism becoming a principle of schisms for us not to
overlook the possibility of it today. On the other hand, in organizing itself, the Church has long respected political realities, as
does Church law today when, for example, it adopts them as
guides for episcopal conferences. Furthermore, even modern
nationalism can be seen as an expression of a people's effort to
defend its right to cultural identity and self-direction, an effort
which Pope John Paul II has recently endorsed as part of the
Church's concern for human rights. In his recent Encyclical,
*Sollicitudo rei socialis,* the Pope makes this concern an integral part
of the Church's evangelizing and redemptive effort, and it
seems it can quite appropriately be considered one of the elements involved in the reception and appropriation of the generative principles of the Church's self-realization.[40] Pope John
Paul's powerful endorsement of the American political experiment during his last visit here can also be seen in this light.

The third level is by far the most important one. We see
working itself out a tension which ought to be expected in any
age between unity and diversity in the Church, made more
acute, of course, by the fact that the post-conciliar drama is
defined in good part as a reaction to the period in which Roman
centralization and uniformity reached their highest degree in
history. This sociological form of the Church was defended by a
universalist ecclesiology which attained the status of something
simply taken for granted. Attempts to loosen the tight bonds of
dependency upon Rome are, therefore, often resisted as threats
to the unity of the Church. Particularly when they are exercised
in a heavy-handed way, the Roman reactions are sometimes
regarded as external interference and denials of local rights. As
often happens, the extremes feed on one another.

I think we need to cool the rhetoric and accept the fact that we
will be engaged in this tension for a very long time. In principle,
of course, there is nothing wrong with such tension; it can even
be a sign of life: that we are taking our local responsibilities as
Churches seriously and that Rome is taking seriously its task as a
ministry of catholic unity. We might also note that in the United
States both appreciation for and opposition to Roman interven-
tions often are rather selective. Those delighted with Roman
reminders of Catholic teaching on sexuality often are far less
impressed by its comments on our geopolitics, while those
delighting in the Pope's recent encyclical on social questions
often are eloquently silent on his teachings on marriage and

sexuality. The Petrine ministry of unity exists precisely in order to prevent the efforts at inculturation from collapsing into cultural capitulation, that ethnocentrism which we have no reason to think does not tempt us. The only positions which are not useful are those which deny either the demands of catholic unity or those of concrete catholicity.

There are two other aspects of the question of "the Church in the United States today" which need to be raised. Both concern the use of the singular in this phrase, but address it from apparently opposite directions. There is a certain legitimacy in speaking of a single Church in the United States, since so much of the Catholic Church's organization follows political lines. But, as I suggested in my first paragraphs, the political reality of the United States covers greatly different economic, social, and cultural realities. Following an idea first expressed by a reporter in *The Washington Post, USA Weekend* recently started to try to attract advertisers by speaking of "The Nine Nations of USA Weekend."[41] As the reporter put it, "We saw patterns in the news—and even got good at predicting events—by observing that North America was working as if it were nine separate civilizations. They ranged from MexAmerica in the Southwest to New England in the Northeast—each with its own economy, politics, boundaries and value structure." If this is the case and one wishes to speak of the concrete genesis of the Church, then I wonder whether we do not need to speak of the *Churches* in the United States, in the plural. Two considerations support this suggestion.

First, the Church does not come to be on the national level, or at least it is a reality at that level only because it comes to be at levels far more local and particular. More specifically, the Church arises in and out of local communities of faith, whether parishes or other small communities, which are linked with one another through the spiritual and institutional bonds of communion into diocesan Churches, which have certain spiritual and institutional bonds on a national level, with this national level itself being bound spiritually and institutionally into the one great catholic communion of all Churches. To speak of a single Church in the United States runs the risk of neglecting this fundamental genetic process by which the Church comes to be in the many Churches.[42]

Second, when we use the singular, we are tempted to take a single economic, social, or cultural element in our country as the norm. I have not studied this in detail, but I have a hunch that most people who use such phrases as "the American experience" or "experiment" mean it in terms of the dominant economic, social, and cultural phenomena, which, of course, are white, middle-class, Anglo-Saxon, and male. Now, one does not have to engage in another round of WASP-bashing to note that this is not the whole, or even the best part, of "the American experience." It is culturally dominant, of course, and may, particularly through the influence of the media, one day become simply the common social reality. Whether that will be a good thing, I leave to another day's discussion. My point here is simply to point out that the phenomena of daily American life are too diverse for only the singular to be used of the Church, at least if the genesis of this Church is understood in its full concreteness. If there is one Church in the United States, it exists in and out of the many Churches which are born within dioceses in the many local communities of faith, facing the variety of local challenges.

I suppose it can be asked whether this social and cultural diversity will remain very long in our country, so powerful is the hegemony of culture presupposed by our economic system and communicated massively through the media. It does not take many hours of watching television to recognize that there are meanings and values being communicated, sometimes explicitly, sometimes simply by being taken for granted, which run quite counter to Christianity. They are present, and one is almost tempted to say inextricably linked with other meanings and values which are not only compatible with Christianity but can make a genuine contribution to universal catholic life. One of the redemptive roles of the local communities of faith should be precisely to be a place for people to see held out to them, not just in the form of creed and moral code, but as lived out, a different way of viewing and evaluating human life, its mysteries and its challenges.

Having questioned the use of the singular of the Church in the United States, let me now defend it in the light of another consideration. If there is only one Church here, it exists only in the many Churches; but, the many Churches are genuinely Churches only if they are also consciously one Church. On a universal level, the more the Church becomes genuinely local Churches, the more challenging will be the task of communion. Communication and mutual comprehension will become more difficult, requiring a dialogue not needed when unity was uniformity and a charity one might have believed was less necessary when obedience was all.

This same dialogue and charity are needed if communion among the many local Churches is to be real. I sometimes feel that the sense of this communion as one Church in the many

Churches has been lost in our country. A good number of Catholics seem to find it easier to converse with courtesy and charity with non-Catholics than they do with those Catholics who differ from them with regard to a whole host of issues: abortion, catechesis, feminism, liturgy, nuclear war, et cetera. I cite in evidence typical contributions to *The National Catholic Reporter* and to *The Wanderer*. It is particularly distressing to see the issues painted in apocalyptic terms, as a part of warfare between the children of light and the children of darkness, particularly when political and social options are legitimated by religious conviction. This represents a real danger of sectarianism, and sects classically are a repudiation of the Catholic principles of reconciled diversity and of the Church's mixed character as a community at once holy and in need of constant purification (*LG*, 8). We will not be able to claim that we are one Church if we cannot even talk to one another civilly and with charity.

I may have disappointed hopes that I would attempt a global theological analysis of the title of my talk. Instead, I have tried to indicate what it can mean to ask the questions which will lead, first, to a description of the concrete Churches in which the one Church is realized in our country today; second, to a theological justification of the effort to construct genuinely local Churches in the United States; third, to the actual genesis of such Churches here, and, finally, to an understanding of the reasons for some of the tensions being experienced today as we undertake this challenge in communion with the other Churches and particularly with the Bishop of the Church in Rome. I have given you what I can. I hope it will be useful for our further discussion.

## NOTES

[1] For examples, see André Rousseau, "Emploi du terme 'sociologie' dans les textes du magistère central de l'Eglise," *Social Compass* 17 (1970): 309-20, which studies allocutions of Pope Paul VI. A similar study of major contemporary theologians would be illuminating.

[2] I borrow the term from James Gustafson, *Treasure in Earthen Vessels: The Church as a Human Community* (New York: Harper & Row, 1961), p. 101; see also p. 105: "A doctrinal reductionism refuses to take seriously the human elements in the Church's life, or if it acknowledges them it does not explore or explicate them except in doctrinal language. The definition of the Church may focus on what is considered to be the essence of the Church; this may be defined in such a way as to exclude the social functions and structures that the Church shares with all societies. . . the reader occasionally has difficulty in knowing whether some theologians are referring to anything historical and social in character in their treatises on the Church."

[3] "Final Report," II, A,3. See H. Pottmeyer, "The Church as

Mysterium and as Institution," in *Synod 1985—An Evaluation,* ed. G. Alberigo and J. Provost (*Concilium,* 188; Edinburgh: T. and T. Clark, 1986), pp. 99-109; J.A. Komonchak, "The Theological Debate," Ibid., pp. 53-63; and "The Synod of 1985 and the Notion of the Church," *Chicago Studies* 26 (1987): 330-45.

[4]See *Synode Extraordinaire: Célébration de Vatican II* (Paris: du Cerf, 1986), p. 481.

[5]See "Final Report," II, A,3, and II, C,1.

[6]For the clearest example among many, see his *Introduction to Christianity* (New York: Herder and Herder, 1970), pp. 25-47. For an application to post-conciliar ecclesiology, see *The Ratzinger Report* (San Francisco: Ignatius Press, 1985), pp. 45-49.

[7]From the official *Relatio* of the Doctrinal Commission in presenting chapter I of *Lumen gentium*; see *Constitutionis Dogmaticae Lumen Gentium Synopsis Historica,* ed. G. Alberigo and F. Magistretti (Bologna: Istituto per le Scienze Religiose, 1975), p. 436.

[8]It is not an answer to separate these two dimensions and on that basis to defend distinct "models" of the Church. I would argue that any model of the Church must bring these two dimensions into intelligible unity; see Giuseppe Colombo, "Il 'Popolo di Dio' e il 'mistero' della Chiesa nell'ecclesiologia post-conciliare," *Teologia* 10 (1985): 97-169.

[9]"The Church may be fully dependent on God's act, but it is not simply God acting. It is a people believing, worshipping, obeying, witnessing. Thus we can and must make fast at the outset our understanding of the church as a body or community of human beings, albeit existing in response to the activity of God. In this sense, the ontology of the church means in the first instance the humanly subjective pole of the relationship" (Claude Welch, *The Reality of the Church* [New York: Scribner's, 1958], p. 48).

[10]This is the method employed to great effect by Gustafson in *Treasure in Earthen Vessels.*

[11]Bernard Lonergan, *Method in Theology* (New York: Herder and Herder, 1972), p. 79.

[12]Anthony Giddens, *New Rules of Sociological Method: A Positive Critique of Interpretative Sociologies* (London: Hutchinson, 1976), pp. 15-16.

[13]"Nam et Ecclesia cotidie gignit Ecclesiam" (*PL,* 93, 166d), quoted by Henri de Lubac, *The Splendour of the Church* (New York: Paulist Press, 1963), p. 65 and p. 269, n. 102.

[14]For other uses of the idea of "ecclesio-genesis," see Leonardo Boff, *Ecclesiogenesis: The Base Communities Reinvent the Church* (Maryknoll: Orbis, 1986), and Severino Dianich, "Soggettività e Chiesa," in *Teologia e progetto-uomo* (Assisi: Cittadella, 1980), pp. 105-28, and "Ecclesiologia ed ecclesiogenesi," *Rassegna di Teologia* 21 (1980): 415-18. My position is closer to Dianich's and attempts to fill out his theological insight with sociologically informed notions.

[15]For very good observations on this aspect of the genesis of the Church, see Marcello de C. Azevedo, *"Basic Ecclesial Communities in Brazil: The Challenge of a New Way of Being Church"* (Washington: Georgetown University Press, 1987), pp. 178-94.

[16]The best treatment of this issue is Severino Dianich, *Chiesa in missione: Per una ecclesiologia dinamica* (Milano: Ed. Paoline, 1985).

[17]This point was made by Bernard Lonergan in the "Epilogue" to *Insight: A Study of Human Understanding* (New York: Longmans, Green and Co., 1957), pp. 742-43.

[18]J.-M. R. Tillard, *Eglise d'Eglises: L'ecclésiologie de communion* (Paris: du Cerf, 1987), p. 47.

[19]A fine introduction with a large bibliography can be found in Azevedo's book, *Basic Ecclesial Communities.*

[20]See Herve Legrand, "La réalisation de L'Eglise en un lieu," in *Initiation à la pratique de la théologie,* ed. B. Lauret and F. Refoule, tome III: dogmatique 2 (Paris: du Cerf, 1983), pp. 143-345; J. A. Komonchak, "Towards a Theology of the Local Church," *FABC Papers,* No. 42.

[21]See E. Lanne, "L'Eglise locale et l'Eglise universelle: Actualité et portée du thème," *Irénikon* 43 (1970): 481-511, at p. 490.

[22]The conciliar documents are not consistent in their use of "particular" and "local" as modifiers of the Church. "Particular" has since been adopted by the Code of Canon Law as the term to refer to a Church presided over by a bishop; but the argument has been made that this canonical language should not be considered to settle the issue. I will use by preference the term "local Church," clarifying, where the context does not make it clear, whether I am referring to a parish, a diocese, or some other groupings of Churches.

[23]This argument is made by Bruno Forte, *La Chiesa icona della Trinità: Breve ecclesiologia* (Brescia: Queriniana, 1984), and, more briefly, in *Laicato e laicità* (Genova: Marietta, 1987), pp. 67-89.

[24]From the Leonine Sacramentary, cited by J.-M. R. Tillard, *Eglise d'Eglises,* p. 105. For Pentecost as the reversal of Babel, see *Ad gentes,* 4, and Herve Legrand, "Inverser Babel, mission de l'Eglise: La vocation des églises particulières au sein de la mission universelle," *Spiritus* 11 (1970): 323-46.

[25]While using the language of communion, the recent Roman text on episcopal conferences argues for "the ontological and historical priority of the universal Church" and maintains that "the Petrine primacy itself, understood as '*plenitudo potestatis,*' has no meaning and theological consistency except within the primacy of the one and universal Church over particular and local Churches" (see "Draft Statement on Episcopal Conferences," *Origins* 17 [1988], 735). For a different and more traditional view of the papal role, see Joseph Ratzinger's comment: "The pope is not, then, bishop of a particular community only secondarily, in some awkward sense and in addition to his universal task; rather it is only *because* he is bishop of *one* Church that he can be *episcopus episcoporum* in such a way that all the Churches must orient themselves to the one Church of Rome" ("Die bischofliche Kollegialitat nach der Lehre des Zweiten Vatikanischen Konzils," in *Das neue Volk Gottes: Entwürfe zur Ekklesiologie* [Düsseldorf: Patmos-Verlag, 1970], pp. 171-200, at p. 185).

[26]For the other position, see the distinction between "the theological basis" of the particular Church (i.e., the diocese) and the "primarily

contingent and occasional, even if providential factors, such as those associated with a socio-cultural territory,'' which is assumed by Gian-domenico Mucci, ''Concili particolari e conferenze episcopali,'' ''*Civiltà Cattolica* 138/2 (1987), 341. Mucci follows de Lubac on this point; see *The Motherhood of the Church* (San Francisco: Ignatius Press, 1982), pp. 189-90.

[27]''. . . the local—with what it entails of the cultural, the 'contextual,' the geographical, the religious, the historical—belongs to the material in which the *Ekklesia tou theou* is incarnated in its truth. Inculturation or 'contextualization' should not constitute an *a posteriori* undertaking. It belongs to the very emergence (*surgissement*) of the Church of God. It is woven in catholicity'' (Tillard, *Eglise d'Eglises*, p. 30).

[28]*LG*, 23; see also *OE*, 2. Pope Paul VI echoed this conciliar view when he said that ''the Church welcomes such pluralism as an articulation of its very unity,'' and then went on: ''And precisely in the Oriental Churches is found an historical anticipation and exhaustive denomination of the validity of the project of pluralism, so that modern efforts at realizing the relationships between the Gospel proclamation and human civilizations, between faith and culture, have in the history of these venerable Churches significant anticipations of conceptual developments and of concrete forms with regard to this twofold unity and diversity'' (quoted by Ary Roest Crollius, ''Inculturation: Newness and Ongoing Process,'' in *Inculturation: Its Meaning and Urgency* [Kampala: St. Paul Publications-Africa, 1986], p. 37).

[29]For the present state of the discussion and bibliography, see Joseph A. Komonchak, ''Subsidiarity in the Church: The State of the Question,'' *The Jurist* 48 (1988): 298-349.

[30]See Tillard, *Eglise d'Eglises*, pp. 343-46.

[31]See ''Draft Statement on Episcopal Conferences,'' *Origins* 17 (1988), 731-37. For four preliminary reactions to this text, see *America*, March 19, 1988. See also the papers delivered at the January 1988 Salamanca colloquium on the conferences, published as *The Nature and Future of Episcopal Conferences*, ed. H. Legrand et al. (Washington: The Catholic University of America Press, 1988).

[32]See *The Reception of Vatican II*, ed. G. Alberigo, J.-P. Jossua, and J.A. Komonchak (Washington: The Catholic University of America Press, 1987).

[33]The third of these positions, of course, is that of Cardinal Ratzinger; see *The Ratzinger Report*, pp. 27-44.

[34]See, for example, Joseph Ratzinger, *Theological Highlights of Vatican II* (New York: Paulist Press, 1966).

[35]See Joseph A. Komonchak, ''The Enlightenment and the Construction of Roman Catholicism,'' *Annual of the Catholic Commission on Intellectual and Cultural Affairs* (1985), pp. 31-59.

[36]See Karl Rahner, ''Basic Theological Interpretation of the Second Vatican Council,'' in *Concern for the Church: Theological Investigations XX* (New York: Crossroad, 1981), pp. 77-89.

[37]See Joseph A. Komonchak, ''The Local Realization of the Church,'' in *The Reception of Vatican II*, pp. 77-90.

[38]I have found the first two chapters of Garry Wills, *Bare Ruined Choirs: Doubt, Prophecy, and Radical Religion* (Garden City: Doubleday, 1972), very useful for the increasing number of my students who have no memory of the pre-conciliar Church.

[39]*The Ratzinger Report*, p. 60; for the larger perspective of this comment in Ratzinger's earlier theological writings, see Aidan Nicholls, *The Theology of Joseph Ratzinger: An Introductory Study* (Edinburgh: T. & T. Clark, 1988), pp. 136-49.

[40]In the Encyclical, the Pope's chief interest appears to be the emerging nations (see #15, 21-22, 26, 32-33, 39), but he has also been greatly concerned to maintain the close link between the Church and the efforts of his native Poland to recover its national rights.

[41]See Joel Garreau, "My $7-Million Gift to Al's USA," *The Washington Post*, 8 May 1988, Outlook section, p. B5.

[42]This is where the objections to episcopal conferences' becoming a sort of bureaucratic super-government have a certain validity, but this problem is not properly addressed by denying the legitimacy and necessity of regional associations of bishops in favor of a universalist ecclesiology.

# The Biblical Understanding of the Spirit

## Josephine Massyngbaerde Ford

> As you enter the city, you will meet a band of prophets, in a prophetic state, coming down from the high place, preceded by lyres, tambourines, flutes and harps. The spirit of the Lord will rush upon you, and you will join them in their prophetic state and will be changed into another man (2 Sam 10:5b-6).

> But you are a chosen race, a royal priesthood, a holy nation, God's own people, that you may declare the wonderful deeds of him who called you out of darkness into his marvelous light. Once you were no people but now you are God's people; once you had not received mercy but now you have received mercy (1 Pet 2:9-10).

I have chosen to quote these two texts to demonstrate two spectra of pneumatology, the theology of the Holy Spirit. I plan to trace briefly the evolution of the Spirit in the Hebrew Scriptures and then to turn to the New Testament,[1] with special emphasis on the baptized Christian and the gifts of the Spirit bequeathed to him or her through the sacrament of baptism. I shall make some references to the biblical background of the early Syriac baptismal liturgy as representative of the Semitic theology of baptism within the early Church.

### The Spirit in the Yahwist[2]

a) The Spirit as wind and as might in battle: *Ruah* in the J source of the Hexateuch denotes a powerful and invisible force under the control of God. It is the storm wind, the zephyr which rends mountains, drenches the earth with rain, sways trees, and drives chaff into the air. More importantly, the same divine force cleft apart the waters of the Reed Sea to that the Israelites could cross over dryshod and swept them back to engulf their Egyptian pursuers. The triumph of Yahweh is celebrated in the Song of the Reed Sea which commemorates the *magnalia dei* (Exodus 15:1-21). This is the victory of the Divine Warrior over his rival, Pharoah.

b) The same violent and mighty force fell[3] upon the first charismatic leaders of the tribal confederacy who led the defensive wars against the enemies of Israel in the land of Canaan. They shared the Spirit of the Divine Warrior. The prime example is Samson. In the power of the Spirit, he tore in pieces the lion (Judg 14:6); the cords with which he was bound became soft, and Samson killed a thousand Philistines:

> . . . the spirit of the Lord came upon him: the ropes around his arms became as flax that is consumed by fire and his bonds melted away from his hands. Near him was the fresh jawbone of an ass; he reached out, grasped it, and with it killed a thousand men. Then Samson said,
> "With the jawbone of an ass
> I have piled them in a heap;
> With the jawbone of an ass
> I have slain a thousand men" (Judg 15:14).

In a similar, but not so dramatic, way, the Spirit gave power to Gideon (Judg 6-8). Deborah and Barak appear to be inspired by the same Spirit, but the actual phrase, "Spirit of God," is not found in the text (Judg 4-5). The spirit fell on other charismatic leaders to endow them with strength: Othniel (Judg 3:10) and Jephthah (Judg 11:29). Through these human agents the Spirit of the Lord conquered military forces which were vastly superior to those of the Chosen people.[4] The Spirit was seen as the source of anger (e.g., in Saul, 1 Sam 11:6), strength, and courage.

c) Closely akin to the charismatic war figures are the Spirit filled prophets who were often also associated with war.[5] As we saw from the opening quotation, the pre-classical prophets often functioned in large groups of prophets. For example, when Queen Jezebel murdered the prophets of the Lord, Obadiah hid a hundred fifty in two separate caves (1 Kgs 18:4), and at the contest on Mount Carmel there were four hundred and fifty prophets of Baal and four hundred of Asherah who ate from Jezebel's table (1 Kgs 18:19, 22). These prophets were filled with the ecstatic spirit. At times their possession was psychologically induced by music, dancing, clashing themselves and, perhaps, the use of drugs. They prophesied in a body and through mass hypnosis drew Saul into a similar prophetic state (1 Sam 10:1-12). Often when they were in ecstasy, they were not in control of their words and actions. Pre-classical Israelite prophecy was not unlike the prophecy, sometimes frenzied, that affected the prophets and prophetesses in surrounding cultures.[6]

Such prophetical figures were credited with the powers of telephany, clairvoyance, perhaps glossolalia and other "gifts" of a similar and demonstrative nature.

In the case of these prophets and prophetesses also, the recipients received the Spirit, but did not always retain self-control. They were under the compulsion (literally speaking) of the Spirit who at times caused violent agitation. We may compare the modern day "holy rollers" and the phenomenon of slaying in the Spirit common among some evangelic healers. The association of the Spirit with violent agitation will become important to us later in this essay.

d) From this rather dubious background, the great figures of Elijah and Elisha stand out. Despite their moral stance and the role which they played in encouraging the people to keep the covenant, they still possessed some of the characteristics of the pre-classical prophets. For example, the Spirit caused them to perform remarkable physical feats, such as Elijah running forty miles beside the chariot of Ahab (1 Kgs 18:46). When the double portion of the Spirit of Elijah fell on Elisha, he struck the waters with Elijah's mantle, and the waters were cleft asunder (2 Kgs 2:13-14). Both Elijah and Elisha performed signs and wonders; for example, providing "miraculous" nourishment for widows: Elijah (1 Kgs 17:7-16), Elisha (2 Kgs 4:1-7), and curing their sick children: Elijah (1 Kgs 17:17-24), Elisha (2 Kgs 4:18-37). More miracles are attributed to Elisha than to Elijah: the healing of the water (2 Kgs 2:19-22); the destructive curse on the boys who mocked Elijah for his bald head (2 Kgs 2:23); cf. Elijah calling down fire on the Samaritans (2 Kgs 1:9-12); providing a remedy for poisoned stew (2 Kgs 4:38-41); multiplication of loaves (2 Kgs 4:42-44), and the cure of Naaman the Syrian leper (2 Kgs 5:1-27).

## The Spirit in the Deuteronomic Literature up to the Exile

It is interesting to note that until "this factor of ecstasy could be eliminated, or reduced to a minimum, the message of the prophet would be discredited. This elimination of ecstasy occurred in the Deuteronomic period, which we will date in the seventh century."[7]

But, even before this in the eighth century, the prophets Amos, Hosea, and Micah (a composite work) showed their disparagement of ecstasy and the Spirit. Amos distanced himself from the group prophets (Amos 7:14) and insisted on his individual call:

To Amos, Amaziah said: "Off with you visionary, flee to the land of Judah! There earn your bread by prophesying, but never again prophesy in Bethel; for it is the king's sanctuary and a royal temple." Amos answered Amaziah, "I was no prophet, nor have I belonged to a company of prophets; I was a shepherd and a dresser of sycamores. The Lord took me from following the flock, and said to me, "Go, prophesy to my people Israel" (Amos 7:12-15).

Hosea called the prophet a "fool" (Hos 9:7,8; cf. 2 Kgs 9:11 and Jer 29:26); Micah stated that prophets lied and staggered like drunken persons (Mic 2:11). None of the classical prophets of this period (Amos, Hosea, first Isaiah and Micah) claimed to prophesy by the Spirit of God. On the contrary, they empha-sized the Word (*dabar*) of God which has no ecstatic behaviour (or "pecuniary" benefit) associated with it.

Jeremiah continued in the tone of the eighth century prophets. He said that the prophets would become like *wind* because the *Word* was not in them (Jer 5:13). The phrase, "the Spirit of God," does not appear in the main corpus of literature in this period. Shoemaker avers:

> It is not found in D of the Hexateuch (only once in the Book of Deuteronomy and that in a late text), nor in the Deuteronomic portions of the books of Kings, nor even in the prophecies of Jeremiah, Zephaniah, Nahum, and Habakuk. This abandon-ment of the term spirit of God was probably due to the disrepute into which the ecstatic prophets had fallen. The period had at its heart the religio-ethical revival of Josiah, and ethics and ecstasy have little in common.[8]

Yet, there are a few references to the Spirit which must be considered. There are two passages where the Spirit falls on persons and enables them to prophesy. In Num 11:17-20, the seventy elders are endowed with Moses' spirit, and in Num 11:29 Moses exclaims, "Would God that all the Lord's people were prophets, that the Lord would put his spirit upon them." In this case, we have "his spirit" rather than the "Spirit of God." Each elder shared in one spirit shared with Moses. Another case where the simple phrase "spirit" occurs is the instance of Micaiah (1 Kgs 22:10-24). Also in this period the "spirit" is occasionally used to denote strength or courage. But, these cases need not detain us. The important point is that in the literature of this period "Spirit" is still not used in an ethical sense.

### The Use of Ruah in the Sixth to the Fifth Centuries BCE

In this period we find a considerable development in the meaning of "Spirit."

a) The "Spirit of God" is no longer a term of reproach but has religious and ethical connotations.

b) It is used in the sense of "breath," which is a synonym for "life." The most dramatic example is the valley of dry bones when the *ruah* is blown into the bones and they become alive like an army (Ezek 37:1-10). Breath is put into a human person by God (Ezek 37:5,6; Num 16:22; 27:16; Mal 2:15), and he protects it (Ps 31:5 (6); cf. 143:7). Although breath is not identified with a person's soul, yet it is one of the most precious possessions (Lam 4:20). *Ruah* is now a synonym for *neshamah*, the older word for breath which is used in Gen 7:21.

c) The meaning of "spirit" in a human being is extended to include a certain aspect of conduct and character.

d) The phrase, "the Spirit of God," occurs very frequently in the prophetic writings of this period, but less often in the priestly source. In Ezekiel, the Spirit is also transporting power of God (Ezek 2;3:12,14,24;8:3;11:1; 43:5;11:24). The Spirit is also the directing power of the theophany (Ezek 1:12,20,21;10:17). It impels the living creatures and the wheels of the chariot-throne to go where God wishes. It co-ordinates the whole complex phenomenon.

But, one must reiterate that the most striking feature of this period is the absence of the ecstatic from association with the Spirit of God. "Spirit" is the "energizing, directing, guiding, and enlightening power of God."

e) The Spirit is the enlightening and directing power of God in persons who are called by him to perform some great task. In this sense it is found in three passages in P (the Priestly strand). The Spirit gives technical skill and knowledge, e.g., those who make the priestly garments (Exod 28:3); to Bezalel to make the tabernacle (Exod 31:3). Compare also Exod 35:31. Joshua is filled with the spirit of wisdom (Num 27:18 P; Deut 34:9).

f) The Spirit not only guides the individual but the nation. The ideal king is charactered by the sixfold[9] spirit of wisdom, understanding, counsel, strength, knowledge, and fear of the Lord. The Spirit helps those who judge (Isa 28:6); she will bring forth judgment for the Gentiles (Isa 42:11). The Spirit of the Lord inspires his servant to preach good tidings to the meek and proclaim liberty to the captives (Isa 61:1; cf. Lk 4:16ff). The Spirit accompanies the Servant in his work (Isa 48:16). Zerubbabel is assisted in rebuilding the temple by the Spirit of the Lord (Zech 4:6; cf. Ps 143:10).

g) The Spirit represents the presence of God directing and protecting his people, not as individuals, but as a nation. In recalling the Exodus experience, the writers of this period see

God's Spirit "hovering over, guiding and prospering them."[10]
The Spirit is the spirit of holiness[11] and comes to the wayward
and sinful (Ps 51:11 (13); Isa 63:10,11). She is the spirit of
correction and instruction (Neh 9:20; cf. 9:30; Ps 139:
51:11,13). But, above all, the Spirit is associated with the Covenant: "This is the pact that I made with you when you came out
of Egypt, and my spirit continues in your midst; do not fear"
(Hagg 2:5). We may compare Jer 31:31-34 where this idea is
implicit, but the text does not actually mention "Spirit":

> "The days are coming," says the Lord, "when I will make a new
> covenant with the house of Israel and the house of Judah. It will
> not be like the covenant I made with their fathers the day I took
> them by the hand to lead them forth from the land of Egypt; for
> they broke my covenant and I had to show myself their master,"
> says the Lord. "But this is the covenant which I will make with
> the house of Israel after those days," says the Lord. "I will place
> my law within them, and write it upon their hearts; I will be their
> God, and they shall be my people. No longer will they have need
> to teach their friends and kinsmen how to know the Lord. All
> from the least to greatest, shall know me," says the Lord, "for I
> will forgive their evildoing and remember their sin no more."

Thus, the Spirit is the way in which God becomes immanent
and omnipresent, not only over all of humankind, but also
creation (Gen 1:2 P; cf. Isa 40:13). However, the Spirit is still
not an individual "person" in the godhead. She is an aspect of
God.

h) *Ruah* is used of the human spirit as in a former period
(Ezek 3:14) and is the seat of the emotions (e.g., Ezek 21:7).[12]
Furthermore, the human spirit is the energizing and directing
power or faculty in the human person, guiding his/her conduct
towards God. To stray from God in one's spirit is considered one
of the greatest follies (Ps 32:2; cf. Hos 7:16). The spirit of the
broken and contrite heart (Ps 34:18; Isa 57:15; 66:2) is pleasing
to God, and the divine presence is near to those who possess this.

### The Use of Ruah in the Later Persian and the Greek Periods, Dating from about 400 BCE to Maccabean Times

*Ruah* still has the sense of "wind."[13] It is still used in the sense
of "vanity" or "nothingness."[14] This is especially so in the
Wisdom literature. However, the actual phrase, "Spirit of
God," is not used in Job, Proverbs, Canticles or Ecclesiastes.
The priest relied upon the Torah, and the wise person upon his/
her human wisdom.

More pertinent to our enquiry is the prophetic function of the

Spirit of God. The text of most interest to us is Joel 3:1-2 (2:28-29):

> Then afterward I will pour out
> my spirit upon all mankind (the text reads "all flesh").
> Your sons and daughters shall prophesy,
> your old men shall dream dreams,
> your young men shall see visions;
> Even upon the servants and the handmaids,
> in those days, I will pour out my spirit.

Here, the important aspect is the universality of the gift of the Spirit. She is the personal possession not only of every true Israelite but of all flesh.[15] The Lord stirs up the spirit of Cyrus, who was a Gentile (2 Chron 36:22 = Ezra 1:1) and of those whom he wishes to build the temple (Ezra 1:5). But, the universal extension of the Spirit is not expected to occur before the Messianic age. The Spirit brings messages from God (2 Sam 23:2; 1 Chron 28:12; 12:18; 2 Chron 15:1; 20:14; 24:20). In Daniel, the Spirit helps to interpret dreams (Dan 4:8 (5); 5:11,12,14; 6:3 (4). The Spirit is the helpful presence of God with his people. Zech 12:10 predicts that God will pour on Israel the spirit of grace and supplication, and Isa 32:13 speaks of the pouring out of the Spirit so that the wilderness becomes a land of gardens.

In the interest of time, I omit discussion of the use of pneuma in the Classical Writings, the Septuagint,[16] Qumran,[17] the Pseudepigrapha, Philo,[18] Josephus,[19] and pass immediately (if reluctantly) to the New Testament.

## The Use of Pneuma in the New Testament[20]

To some extent, the meaning of *Pneuma* in the New Testament follows that of the Greek Old Testament and the *Pseudepigrapha*, but it rapidly becomes exclusively religious and psychological.[21] The most significant aspect is the use of the phrase, the "Holy Sprit" (often, literally, the Spirit of Holiness). Here, we find a revival of the prophetic concepts, which are frequently predicated of the non-professional-sacerdotal members of the people of God. This modifies or complements the priestly ideals in applying them to all the faithful rather than one privileged class.

The New Testament is pre-eminently the age of the Spirit. Indeed, Acts of Apostles has often been called the Acts of the Holy Spirit. Yet, curiously enough, the Holy Spirit is not an "entity" distinct from Father and Son. Rather, She is the Spirit of Jesus (Christ) and of God (cf. 2 Cor 3:17). A binitarian, rather than trinitarian, theology still obtains. There is only one clear reference to the Spirit as a distinct person; namely, in Matt 28:19: this may be a redactional or additional pericope in that Gospel.

Further, when we turn to the Synoptic Gospels, it is surprising how rarely Jesus speaks of the Holy Spirit and, indeed, how comparatively seldom the Spirit is mentioned at all in the Gospel. Perhaps it was not until the Christian community could experience the Spirit that She became a reality to them. In all three Synoptic Gospels, the Spirit descends upon Jesus at his baptism. It is the Spirit who urges him into the desert where he is tempted with regard to his concept of his messianic mission. Matthew identifies Jesus as the Servant of the Lord (from Isaiah) because God has endowed him with the Spirit. Through the same Spirit he casts out demons (Matt 12:28) and performs miracles of healing (Matt 12:18).

When we turn to consider the followers of Jesus and their relationship to the Spirit, we find that the only occasion when Jesus definitely promises the gift of the Spirit to believers is the promise that the Spirit will speak on their behalf when they are apprehended and put on trial:

> When they deliver you up, do not be anxious how you are to speak or what you are to say; for what you are to say will be given to you in that hour; for it is not you who speak, but the Spirit of your Father speaking through you (Matt 10:19-20; cf. Mk 13:11 and Lk 12:12, both of whom say "Holy Spirit").

Even Luke, the author of Acts of Apostles (Acts of the Holy Spirit), does not emphasize the Spirit in his Gospel. The only references additional to those in Matthew are: in the infancy narratives where Gabriel announces to Mary that the Holy Spirit will come upon her (Lk 1:35) and where Simeon is led by the Spirit into the Temple to identify Mary's Son as He Who Cometh (Lk 2:27); Jesus' return in the power of the Spirit from the temptation in the desert (Lk 4:14; cf. 4:1), and his assertion at the commencement of his mission (Lk 4:18) that he is the prophet upon whom rests the Spirit of God; Jesus' rejoicing in the Spirit when he utters his song of jubilation (Lk 10:21; cf. Matt 11:25), and his assurance to his disciples that God will give the Holy Spirit to those who ask for Her (Lk 11:13).

Finally, in all three Gospels we have the curious statement of Jesus that the unforgivable sin is blasphemy against the Spirit of God (Matt 12:31-32):

> Therefore I tell you that every sin and blasphemy will be forgiven men, but the blasphemy against the Spirit will be not forgiven. And whoever says a word against the Son of Man will be forgiven; but whoever speaks against the Holy Spirit will not be

forgiven, either in this age or in the age to come (cf. Lk 12:10, and Mark 3:21-29).

In the context (common to all three Gospels), the unforgivable sin appears to be attributing the charismata of Jesus to the power of the devil (Beelzebub).

It seems, therefore, that the specific missionary activities of the disciples of Jesus before his exaltation are evangelization, healing and exorcism, but after Pentecost the Christian community is endowed with the Spirit of Christ and relives his ministry, passion, death and resurrection to the full.

### Acts of Apostles

Indeed, this is what we find in Acts of Apostles. There is a distinct change in the disciples. Luke has carefully modelled his second volume, Acts, on his Gospel. He shows the way the Christian communities, as the Body of Christ, relive the life of Christ in their ministry, suffering, death and resurrection. Goulder[22] has prepared a chart to illustrate this.

Acts opens with the Risen Christ's promise that the Spirit would descend upon his disciples and they would be his witnesses to the end of the earth (Acts 1:6-8). It is not fortuitous that Luke presents the descent of the Spirit upon those in the Upper Room as taking place on the Jewish Feast of Pentecost. This feast does not have a separate tractate assigned to it in the *Mishna*; but, according to Josephus (*War* 3:1; *Ant* 17:10,2; cf. *Pes* 68b), it was a very popular feast to which many of the Jews from the Diaspora travelled. Paul expressed the wish to be in Jerusalem for the feast of Pentecost (Acts 20:16; cf. 1 Cor 16:8). We now have evidence for the feast from the Temple Scroll found at Qumran.[23] Interestingly enough, it is the feast of New Wine which is celebrated fifty days after Passover (cf. Acts 2:13: " . . . they are filled with new wine," and the symbolism of the miracle at Cana).

### The Jewish Feast of Pentecost

The Jewish feast of Pentecost celebrates the giving of the Covenant on Mount Sinai.[24] Some scholars suggest that it was on the Feast of Pentecost that the members of the Qumran community met to initiate new members into the community and to renew their own allegiance. The ceremony includes a recitation by the priests of the benefits which God had bestowed upon the Israelites, a recitation by the Levites of the disobedient deeds of Israel, formal admission into the community through a solemn promise to keep the Covenant and purificatory baths

(See especially 1 QS 1:16-4:14). Some fragments[25] from the scrolls appear to belong to this Pentecost liturgy. Bardtke[26] finds three elements which were important for the Qumran candidates who entered into the community: they acquired knowledge of God's truth and insight into His mysteries; they cleansed themselves from sin and made a consecration to God; they were united in a covenant community of the children of truth. These privileges were possible through the Spirit of Yahweh. The Qumran member could say: "I know that with thy good pleasure I have a part in Thy Holy Spirit" (1 QH 14:13). He could speak of the Holy Spirit falling upon him (1QH 7:6-20). Among the gifts of the Spirit (many of which were comparable to the six in Isa 11) was the certainty that the recipient would receive the Holy Spirit and come to understand God (1 QH 14:12f) and have a right understanding of the prophetic word and its application to the final age (1 Qp Hab 2:9f; 7:4-5).[27] This Jewish background is important for our understanding of the Christian Pentecost. There is some evidence for an expectation of the outpouring of the Spirit upon all persons during the messianic and/or eschatological age. This belief was based on Joel 2:28-32 (3:1; cf. Acts 2:17-21).

### The Christian Pentecost

In writing Acts of Apostles, Luke portrays the Christian Pentecost as the fulfillment of the Covenant on Sinai.[28] His description of the Jerusalem Pentecost (Acts 2) vividly recalls both Sinai and has some affinity with the pneumatology of the pre-classical prophets. The Spirit descends with panache, like the storm wind with tongues of fire, and causes the whole building to vibrate (cf. also Acts 4:31). These phenomena are followed by glossolalia, Peter's preaching with boldness, and subsequently the baptism of three thousand converts (Acts 2:41). A similar phenomenon appears to occur when the Samaritans accept the Gospel as preached by Philip and receive imposition of hands from Peter and John (Acts 8:14-17), although glossolalia is not explicitly mentioned. The text is a difficult one to understand because one would expect the Spirit to come through baptism, but I think that Bruner may have arrived at the most reasonable interpretation:

> It was evidently not the divine plan, according to Luke's understanding, that the first church outside Jerusalem, should arise entirely without apostolic contract. For this to have occurred could have indicated the indifference of the apostolic tradition — viz., of the history of Jesus Christ — and of the unity of the church. Both the tradition and the union were preserved through the apostolic visitation. The Samaritans were not left to become an isolated sect with no bonds of union with the apostolic church in Jerusalem. If a Samaritan church and a Jewish church had

arisen independently, side by side, without the dramatic removal of the ancient and bitter barriers of prejudice between the two, particularly at the level of ultimate authority, the young church of God would have been in schism from the inception of its mission.[29]

The phenomenon of glossolalia (and prophecy) occurred also on the occasion of the Gentile Pentecost (Acts 10-11:18), when Peter baptized the first Gentiles (or proselytes). The Spirit fell upon the assembly prior to baptism. Acts 19:1-7, the Ephesian Pentecost, also describes the disciples of John the Baptist receiving glossolalia and prophecy when they were baptized in the name of Jesus.

In these four incidents we have characteristics similar to those of pre-classical prophecy, although speaking in tongues is not associated with ecstasy[30] or loss of control. Consonant with such religious experience, Acts also records miraculous bursting asunder of bonds and escape from prison (Acts 12 and 16); the "magical" transportation of Philip after the conversion of the eunuch (Acts 8:39-40). We also have destructive miracles, e.g., the death of Ananias and Sapphira (Acts 5:1-11) and the blinding of Elymas (Acts 13:4-12). Again, these happenings resemble the feats of the pre-classical prophets, especially Elijah and Elisha. Perhaps they, too, became socially unacceptable.

On a less dramatic level, we find the guidance of the Holy Spirit in the missionary work of the Church. Through the praying community, She elects Barnabas and Paul for missionary work. She forbids them to speak in Asia (Acts 16:6,7). She enables them to speak with boldness (see especially Acts 6 and 7 for the martyrdom of Stephen) and to accept suffering with fortitude and joy. Through the prophetic spirit, She warns of affliction which is to befall Paul (Acts 20:22-33; 21:11).

However, such occurrences fade in significance in the face of the belief that it was on the Day of Pentecost that God did in reality fulfil Joel 2:28-32 and pour out the Spirit upon all flesh.[31] This is clearly explicit in Peter's first speech in Acts and his extended quotation of the relevant text of Joel (Acts 2:17-21). The Spirit will come upon all, men and women, and, perhaps, in the phrase "all flesh," creation as well. The universality of the Spirit is also symbolized in the list of peoples[32] in Acts 2:5-11 and in Luke's concept of the reversal of the myth of Babel through the Pentecost experience.[33]

Nevertheless, the climax of the fulfillment of Joel 2:28-32 comes in the conversion of the Gentiles. Luke foreshadowed this in Acts 1:8 through the words of Jesus which predicted that the Gospel would be preached in Jerusalem, Judea, Samaria, and to the end of the world. First, the Gospel is preached in Jerusalem (Acts 2), then Samaria (Acts 8), and then to the end of the world, beginning with the conversion of Cornelius and his household (Acts 10:11-18) and ending with Paul's preaching in Rome (Acts 28:30-31). Christianity became a world religion. Sinai Transformed brings a New Status to the People of God.

## Pneumatology in John

However, pneumatology is more richly and delicately developed in the Gospel of John. For John, the Spirit brings new birth (Jn 3:5-8); She gives life (6:63; cf. 7: 37-39); She is not given by measure (Jn 3:34). She enables one to enter into true worship (Jn 4:23,24; cf. 16:13). The words of Jesus are Spirit and life (Jn 6:63). The Spirit is the bearer of truth (Jn 14:17, 26; 15: 26; 16:13). On Easter Day, Jesus breathes the Spirit into the disciples and gives them the spirit of discernment for good and evil and the divine prerogative to forgive or retain sin. The Spirit is the helper and director of the believer, especially in the work of establishing the Kingdom of God on earth.

In a word, in the Gospel of John there is a wholly new order of functions predicated of the Spirit, all of which are found first attributed to Jesus and through him transmitted to "his own." These functions are exemplified in the use of two special titles of the Spirit; namely, the Spirit of Truth and the Paraclete. The final redaction of the Gospel of John must have taken place when the Christian communities had frequently experienced the Spirit.

## The Spirit in the Farewell Discourses of John

In John 14:16-17, 26, Jesus says that he has asked the Father for "another paraclete" who will be with the disciples permanently (in distinction from his own temporary sojourn with them). Jesus identified this Paraclete with the Spirit of Truth. She will lead the disciples into all truth and will cause them to remember all that Jesus has taught (Jn 14:26). This complements the concept of the Spirit as cleansing and regenerating water in Jn 1:33 and as breath or vitality in Jn 20:22. Here, the function of the Spirit is to teach, guide, and defend. This Paraclete will witness concerning Jesus (Jn 15:26f), lead the disciples into all truth (Jn 16:12-15), and convince the secular world that they have misconceptions about sin, righteousness, and judgment (Jn 16:8-9): concerning sin, because the world puts its trust in earthly and secular power, not Jesus' power; concerning righteousness, because it sees righteousness as the observance of legal requirements rather than love; and concerning judgment, because it condemns Jesus and his followers rather than the "ruler of this world."[34]

Johnston states:

> . . . He (the Paraclete) is a prophetic teacher who verifies and completes Jesus' revelation. Only in the difficult passage 16:8-11 is any suggestion of a lawsuit found. But there the Paraclete is not the advocate for the disciples. He is a prosecuting counsel, listing the charges against the cosmos at the judgement seat of God and securing a conviction.[35]

For Johnston, the Spirit-Paraclete in the Church is Inspired Teacher, Preacher, Prophet, Advocate within the Christian community. In other words, it is the Spirit or Paraclete who enables the baptized Christian to perform his or her function as prophet and teacher (*vide infra*).

### The Spirit and the Concept of Baptism in the Early Church

#### The Spirit and Sacred Time

a) Scholars of religion divide time into ordinary, historical time and sacred time. The sacred time is not concerned with sequence of events. As Brock says:

> . . . Rather the concern of sacred time lies in the salvific content and meaning of an event or events that take place either in primordial time, "in the beginning," or . . . at a point or points in historical time. These salvific events continue to be effective throughout history, and can be "recaptured" at any point in historical time, since they are eternally present in sacred time . . . The feast and the salvific event it celebrates likewise run together in sacred time, even though far separated in historical time.[36]

It is the Spirit who brings us into sacred time and, as it were, removes the "generation gap" among that of the Hebrew Scriptures, the time of the historical Jesus and of the exalted Christ, and our own ordinary time. The liturgical celebration "recaptures" the events of Jesus' life and enables us to experience them with him through a genuine ontological union. Thus, in Romans 6:5-6, Paul can speak about our dying, being buried, and rising with Christ. It is baptism that effects this, and baptism is the vehicle of the Holy Spirit. In more developed liturgical practice, the outward signs are water, oil, and the imposition of hands.

b) As the Spirit moves us into sacred time, She also effects for us a new and supernatural (divine) relationship. She brings us the status of sonship and daughterhood with God. Paul states: "The Spirit whom you received is a Spirit that makes us sons (supply daughters), enabling us to cry, 'Abba, Daddy' (supply 'Mummie') . . ." (Rom 8:15).

This filial gift gives the newly baptised the privilege of reciting the Lord's prayer. One notes with interest the variant in the Lukan form of the Our Father: " . . . let your Holy Spirit come upon us and cleanse us . . . " (Lk 11:2).

One might ask whether this variant came about because of the baptismal liturgy.

The Syriac Church makes a close association between the baptism of Jesus and our own. Jesus was proclaimed "Son" at his baptism, and, consequent upon this, the Spirit descended upon him in the form of a dove.[37] Similarly, when men and women are baptized, as they emerge from the water, through the power of the Spirit they become new creatures in a new creation. A felicitous image occurs in a hymn of Ephrem who speaks of the neophytes as divers who go through the baptismal waters to secure the Pearl of Great price: "In symbol and in truth Leviathan is trodden down by mortals: the baptized, like divers, strip and put on oil, as a symbol of Christ they snatched you (the Pearl) and came up: stripped, they seized the soul from his embittered mouth."[38]

Brock notes the play on the Syriac word "diver" (*amoda*) and "baptised" (*amida*) and also the appropiate symbol of the pearl for Christ because the pearl is pierced and suffers before it is raised in a place of honour to adorn the wearer (cf. the idea of "putting on" Christ).[39]

Just as Christ is proclaimed Son at his baptism, so the neophyte is proclaimed "son" or "daughter" at his/her baptism.

c) Together with sonship and daughterhood, the Spirit makes us co-heirs with Christ. Our inheritance is the Kingdom of God (heaven); Christ having died bequeathed this to us. Within this Kingdom, as we shall see below, we live as prophets, priests, and sovereigns (kings and queens). Nevertheless, baptism gives us a "pledge of the Spirit" rather than a "full measure." We still await with eagerness the full revelation and realization of the Kingdom and our new and full potentials. As the Biblical version *Good News for the Modern Man* (*sic*) translates the Greek, all creation waits on "tiptoe" with us for the fulness of the Spirit (Rom 8:21-22). This expectation is no individual affair, for through the indwelling of the Spirit we are all brothers and sisters both of and in Christ. We, too, wait on tiptoe as a community, whether we are baptized by water or by desire, for the fulness of our humanity, our adulthood in the Spirit.

d) This possession of the Kingdom "recaptures" and implements the promise made by God on the occasion of the covenant of all covenants, the Sinai Covenant (Exod 19-24). On this occasion, the Israelites accepted the sovereignty of God instead of Pharaoh, and they became to him a "precious" people. The baptized lives through this experience again, but in a richer way. This is expressed lucidly and emphatically in 1 Peter 2:9-10:[40]

> But you are a chosen race, a royal priesthood, a holy nation, God's own people, that you may declare the wonderful deeds of him who called you out of darkness into his marvelous light. Once you were no people but now you are God's people; once you had not received mercy but now you have received mercy (Cf. Rev 1:5-6; cf. also 2 Cor 4-5).[41]

I should like to enquire more closely in this essay into this status of prophet, priest, and sovereign for all Christian believers. It is not merely a special class who possesses this status. It is the essence of Christianity to have no special class of priests, prophets, and sovereigns, but to see the whole community as such, a community which is theo-democratic. But, before I address this particular issue, I wish to make a few preliminary remarks. I shall also be making some references to the early Syriac liturgy of baptism as presentative — to some degree — of early (Semitic) Jewish-Christianity.[42]

### A Chosen Race, a Royal Priesthood

Returning to the text from 1 Peter 2:9-10, I should now like to enquire whether the gift of the Spirit brings to each Christian the status of prophet, priest, and sovereign. The text under consideration is, of course, based on Exod 19:5-6a: "Therefore, if you hearken to my voice and keep my covenant, you shall be my special possession, dearer to me than all other people, though all the earth is mine. You shall be to me a kingdom of priests, a holy nation."

Through the Christian Pentecost, which is the fulfillment of the Covenant on Mount Sinai, the believer accepts the regality of Yahweh and together with his Christ shares in sacerdotal regality; that is, becomes prophet, priest, and sovereign. In the early Christian communities, although not explicitly in the New Testament, the outward symbol of this sacerdotal regality is the anointing(s) (cf. the meaning of Messiah, the Anointed One) in the rite of baptism. This regality is an important aspect of the supernatural sonship and daughterhood of the believer. If we might quote the Syriac theologian, Severus, who comments on

1 Peter 2:9: "We who believe in Christ receive the same things that he did; since he was of royal stock and high priest by birth, we have received the same dignities by his grace."[43]

We may compare Paul's words in Rom 12:1 and Rom 15:15-16. The gift of the indwelling of the Spirit makes us temples of the Spirit and priests who minister in this temple, which is the Body of Christ. We may compare Jn 2:21-22 where Jesus, or a redactor, identifies the new temple with his Body after he had risen. Paul says that the body is the temple of the Holy Spirit (1 Cor 6:19) and, therefore, we should have no relationship to Satan (cf. 2 Cor 6:14-7:1). In Rom 12:1, he speaks about this priestly service: "I appeal to you therefore, brethren, by the mercies of God to present your bodies as a living sacrifice, holy and acceptable to God, which is your spiritual worship." And later, in the same epistle, he describes his work for the Gentiles in sacerdotal terms: " . . . the grace given me by God to be minister of Christ Jesus to the Gentiles in the priestly service (*leitourgon . . . hierourgounta*) of the Gospel of God, so that the offering of the Gentiles may be acceptable, sanctified by the Holy Spirit" (Rom 15:14-16). This is Paul's ministry of reconciliation (the Gentiles to the Jewish Christians) as the ambassador of Christ (cf. 2 Cor 5:18-21).

## The Priestly and Kingly Investiture

We also "put on" the Spirit (Rom 13:14; Gal 3:27). This is sometimes interpreted as putting on the robe of light or glory. There is a Jewish tradition that the garments of skin provided for Adam and Eve[44] replaced the "garments of honour" which were the original robes of Adam and Eve. The robe of glory is also the robe of priesthood and the robe of royalty. The Peshitta[45] of 1 Pet 2:9 reads: "a chosen race, which serves as priests for the kingdom." In Sir 50:11, the robe of the high priest is the robe of glory: "Vested in his magnificent robes, and wearing his garments of splendour, as he ascended the glorious altar and lent majesty to the court of the sanctuary."

The "robe of glory" is put on at baptism. It sums up the effects of the various gifts of the Spirit in terms of re-entry into Paradise, a restoration to the pre-Fall state of Adam and Eve who reflected the image, as yet uncorrupted, of Christ, the Second Adam.[46]

I quote another Syriac prayer which succinctly expresses this Christian character of priesthood and regality:

> . . . grant through this imprint the union of your living and holy Spirit, and the honour of priesthood and the heavenly kingdom to those who are sanctified; and grant, in the coming of your

> Christ, glorious honour and priestly produce, since to you all things are simple and easy; and may they be made worthy to offer up, together and in company and companionship with us, praise for your mercies towards us, Father, Son and Holy Spirit, now and always and for eternal ages, Amen.[47]

So, the sacrament of baptism, with its symbolic use of oil and the white garment, endows every Christian with priesthood and sovereignty.

### Prophethood and Baptism

In the Old Testament, not only kings and priests were anointed, but also prophets. Thus, Aphrahat refers to "the illumination of the mind and the fruit-bearing of the light-giving olive, with which the *rushma* (mark) of the mystery of salvation takes place, and by which Christians are perfected as priests, kings and prophets."[48]

The Pentecost speech of Peter shows clearly the universality of the gift of prophecy. It gives us a bird's eye view of the development of early Christianity; but, if we wish to look at the roles of individual early Christians, we should look into the epistles, especially those of Paul and 1 Peter.

### The Prophetic Gifts and Kindred Ministries according to 1 Corinthians

1 Corinthians is one of the earlier letters of Paul. It reveals a charismatic Christian community that practises some of the more dramatic gifts of the Spirit. Again, these are not without some affinity to pre-classsical prophecy. 1 Corinthians 12 lists nine such gifts. I should like to address myself to two of these: glossolalia and prophecy.

### Glossolalia:[49]

This much discussed gift appears to have been present in ecstatic prophecy,[50] both in the Hebrew Scriptures and contemporary cultures. However, in the New Testament there is no evidence that the gift of glossolalia was associated with ecstatic behaviour. Gundry[51] argues cogently against this. Nevertheless, studies during the last decades would indicate that glossolalia is not a true language in a linguist's sense of the word.[52] Rather, it is "play language."[53] If this is true, then it differs from the gifts of the utterance of wisdom and knowledge because it is not intelligible (1 Cor 14:2). Furthermore, pseudo-glossolalia can be psychologically induced with serious consequences: retrogression of the ego, undue submission to the authority figure, histrionic behaviour, and such schismatic differences as we find at Corinth (1 Cor 1:10-17).[54]

Further, it is important to realize that the gift of tongues in Acts of Apostles is clearly a different phenomenon from that which we find in 1 Corinthians (cf. also the longer ending of Mark 16:17). In Acts of Apostles glossolalia is: a group experience; an extraordinary experience; a temporary phenomenon; it occurs at strategic points in the missionary work of the church; there are only two explicit references to it (Acts 10:46 and 19:6).[55] In Corinthians glossolalia is a gift to the individual; it is a prayer gift, appears to be a permanent one and one which is quite common (1 Cor 14:5).

Glossolalia in Acts of Apostles and 1 Corinthians is a phenomenon of the primitive Church before she grows into the more mature gifts and graces of the Spirit. Like ecstatic prophecy in the Hebrew Scriptures, glossolalia can become socially unacceptable to the more sophisticated Christians and, perhaps, unnecessary as the liturgy developped.

### Prophecy

On the other hand, the gift of prophecy can be found as a phenomenon concomitant with glossolalia, but it can also be distinct and, indeed, separate from it. It is the work of the Word of God, like the *dabar* of the classical prophets. There have been a number of significant works on prophecy in the early Church during the last few decades. Most important are Aune,[56] Boring,[57] Hill.[58]

As Aune avers, prophecy and revelations played an integral role within the early Christian Communities.[59] He adds: "Thereafter the inevitable forces of institutionalization banished prophets from their roles as leaders and marginalized the revelatory significance of their proclamations."[60] We may add that the institutionalization gave rise to a hierarchy of priests and bishops, and with the marginalization of prophecy came the marginalization of women and, perhaps, the less educated or unlettered persons.

Judaism expected the outpouring of the Spirit and the gift of prophecy for both men and women in the eschatological age. Luke sees this to be fulfilled on the Day of Pentecost. The Christian prophet and prophetess usually, but not always, functioned within a community. They were spokespersons for God and may have constituted a "school."[61] A good example is found in the *Shepherd of Hermas:*

> Therefore, when the man (*sic*) who has the Divine Spirit comes into a meeting of righteous men who have the faith of the Divine Spirit, and intercession is made to God from the assembly of

those men, the angel of the prophetic spirit rests on him and fills the man, and the man, being filled with the Holy Spirit, speaks to the congregation as the Lord wills (*Hermas,* Mand 11:9).

Aune calls such a prophet a specialist in mediating divine revelation. According to some scholars,[62] all Christians were potential prophets because all possessed the Spirit of God. Aune thinks that the Christian as a potential prophet is a theological conception, but the concept of individuals having this gift is an empirical one.[63]

The prophet was a type of Christian leader, perhaps second only to the apostles of the early Church. The apostle was sent forth to proclaim the Gospel and may have been sent forth to a number of communities or to found such, but the prophet and teacher usually functioned within the local community. The prophet gave spontaneous revelation, but the teacher preserved and interpreted the Christian tradition.[64] The Christian prophet may have had a function similar to the classical prophet in the Hebrew Scriptures; but, unlike them, there is no evidence that such Christian prophets received an individual call or inaugural vision.[65] Exceptions are found among the Gnostic and Montanist prophets (-esses). In general, the basic content of prophetic speech included announcements of judgment (confronting) or salvation, encouragement, exhortation with regard to ethical issues, legitimization oracles and eschatological oracles. This is not an exhaustive list, but it is sufficient to show the role of prophecy within the Christian communities of the first century CE.

We can take a brief look at the other ministries listed in 1 Cor 12.

## The Utterance of Wisdom and the Utterance of Knowledge

The Christian, like his/her Christ, possesses the spirit of wisdom and knowledge. It is perhaps difficult to distinguish between these two. Both would be *charismata* of the ministry which eventually would be predicated of the teacher and similar ministries within the community. But, in this passage Paul seems to be speaking of a more spontaneous, non-professional ministry. Some see "knowledge" as relating to prophecy and "wisdom" in relationship to the didactic.[66] I think, however, the now dated but still useful commentary of Plummer and Robertson is relevant:

> In each of these it is the *logos* (word) which is divinely imparted, the power of communicating to others: . . . The *logos sophias* (word of wisdom) is discourse which expounds the mysteries of

God's counsels and makes known the means of salvation . . .
Commentators differ as to the exact differences between *sophia*
and *gnosis*; but *sophia* is the more comprehensive term. By it we
know the true value of things through seeing what they really are
. . . By *gnosis* we have an intelligent grasp of the principles of the
Gospel; by *sophia* a comprehensive survey of their relations to one
another and to other things . . . In itself, *gnosis* may be the result
of instruction guided by reason, and it requires no special
illumination; but the use of this knowledge, in accordance with
the Spirit, for the edification of others, is a special gift.[67]

Plummer and Robertson observe that our lack of acquaintance
with the situation of Corinth makes it impossible to distinguish
clearly between the two terms; the difference would be obvious
to the Corinthians as they experienced these gifts, as, indeed, it
should to us in the twentieth century.

## Faith

Some commentators[68] relate this charism to the performance
of miracles. I believe, however, that a better interpretation is to
view it in the light of faith as seen from the magnificent eulogy of
faith in the Epistle to the Hebrews: "Faith is the realization of
what is hoped for and evidence of things not seen" (Heb 11:1).

Here, the writer gives a long list of Jewish persons who lived
the life of faith (or practised *chesed*) in the face of much uncer-
tainty and intense suffering.[69] These are the confessors and
martyrs. They include Abel, Enoch, Noah, Abraham and
Sarah, Isaac, Jacob, Joseph, Moses, Rahab, Gideon, Barak,
Samson, Jephthah, David, Samuel and the prophets. The list
comes to a climax with the reference to Jesus: " . . . Jesus, the
leader and perfecter of faith. For the sake of the joy that lay
before him he endured the cross, despising its shame, and has
taken his seat at the right of the throne of God" (Heb 12:2).

## The Charism of Healing

Although this ministry naturally refers to miraculous healing,
such as we find in the Gospels and Acts of Apostles, I feel for
contemporary pastoral ministry the gift of healing can also be
meaningful if it is related to professional help from doctors,
psychologists, et cetera. We might also recall that Scripture
speaks of the healing of the broken heart, of the penitent, and
also of the waters (2 Kgs 2:21) and land (2 Chron 7:14); we
might say "ecological healing."

## The Working of Powers

This gift seems to be a more comprehensive one than that of healing. Within the world view of the early Christian, it could include exorcisms, "cursing miracles"; for example, the blinding of Elymas (Acts 13:4-12), and nature miracles, such as the multiplication of the loaves (Mark 6:34-44; 8:1-9).

These are the main Corinthian *charismata*. It is interesting to note that, if we compare and contrast the three major lists of ministries in the new Testament, 1 Cor 12; Rom 12 and Eph 4, the prophet and teacher is the constant feature. The ministries which disappear are the miracle worker, the speaker and interpreter of tongues et cetera, that is, the more dramatic and superhuman ministries.[70] The more flamboyant ministries of the Spirit which are listed in 1 Cor 12-14 may be the "milk" to which Paul refers, and the more socially orientated, the "meat" (1 Cor 3:2; 9:7; cf. also 1 Peter 2:2, and Heb 5:12,13). But, perhaps more important is the development of service orientated ministries, especially seen in Rom 12. These include administrator, teacher, one who exhorts, one who gives, and one who shows mercy. All are seen as ministries of the Spirit.

### The Ministries in Romans 12:6-8

These ministries include prophecy; service (*diakonia*) — compare the men chosen to serve the widows in Acts 6: 1-7 and the widows in 1 Tim 5:9-16; teaching; exhortation; contributing or distributing (*metadidous*); presiding (*proistamenos*), and one who performs an act of mercy (*eleon*).

a) *Metadidous* (distributing or sharing) can refer to one who distributes his or her own goods or distributes common goods. In Herodotus 4:145, it is used of assigning allotments of land.[71] Paul may refer, therefore, to one charged with the distribution of the community goods or even of public goods. We may cite the apostles in Acts 4:32-35 and Peter's confrontation with Ananias and Sapphira in Acts 5:1-11 (although *metadidomi* is not the verb used here). Nevertheless, it may be used of Christian stewardship with regard to one's own wealth, and this meaning would seem to be implied if the prepositional phrase *en haploteti* is taken in the sense of "with liberality." If, however, it is translated "with uprightness" or "with sincerity," Paul may be exhorting his readers to adminster the community goods with honesty, faithfulness and without respect of persons. Similar qualifications were required of the charity officers in Jewish communities in the first century. *Metadidomi* can, of course, be used of sharing spiritual gifts.

b) *Proistamenos*: Some scholars have taken this to refer to official offices within the Church in the sense of ruler over the life of the congregation. They have linked it with elders (elderesses) and bishops (cf. also 1 Thess 5:12, and 1 Tim 5:17, but also 1 Tim 3:4,5,12, of ruling over one's household). But, this seems unlikely. I should agree with C.K. Barrett[72] that it refers to a function performed by several persons either together or in rotation. There is no clear indication that it points to presiding over the Eucharist; but, rather, as *proistamenos* stands between *metadidous* and *eleon*, it may point to the administration of alms et cetera or to a person who was a patron or protector in virtue of his social status of those in need of advocacy in various forms (e.g., slaves, resident aliens, widows, and orphans). The feminine form of the cognate noun is used of Phoebe who is said to have been the patron of Paul and others (Rom 16:2). *En spoude*, diligently, attentively or devotedly, is appropriate for a patron.

c) *Eleon*: This appears to refer to those who perform acts of mercy or loving kindness (cf. Matt 25:31-46) for the sick, the poor, the aged, the disabled, and the stranger, perhaps in need of hospitality. The adverbial phrase, *en hilaroteti* — with cheerfulness, with graciousness, is appropriate. Cranfield says:

> A particularly cheerful and agreeable disposition may well be evidence of the special charisma that marks a person out for this particular service; but an inward *hilarotes* in ministering will in any case come naturally to one who knows the secret that in those needy and suffering people whom he (she) is called to tend the Lord is Himself present . . .[73]

These ministries in Romans are more service orientated and have a theological depth which is not apparent in the Corinthian community. Riesner,[74] in a short monogram, addresses the theological aspect. He states that Christian ethic must be consequent on the proclamation of salvation; that this ethic presupposes conversion; that it is related to the whole of humankind; it nourishes its environment, but it also provides a real option to and transformation of secular society. Christian ethic must be approached with all seriousness and have a width of horizon. Its character is distinctive when seen against the scope of salvation history. It is essentially orientated toward community life and lives in expectation of the spiritual gifts. Christian ethic offers positive goals. In summary, Christian ethic in Rom 12 means God, the community, and the world.

This aspect of the ministries of the Spirit in Romans contrasts with the rather parochial, ephemeral and, perhaps, histrionic approach to the ministries in 1 Cor 12-14.

## The Ephesian Ministries

In Eph 4:11-16, we have the fivefold ministries which are directed towards the building up and maturation of the Body of Christ which is the Church, especially in the face of heterodoxical teaching. They are five aspects of the messianic gift given in baptism and promoting the unity of the Church. These ministries include apostles, prophets, evangelists, pastors and teachers. They all appear to be ministers of the Word except, perhaps, the pastors. Here I should like to comment briefly upon them.

a) *Apostle*

This office is not confined to the "twelve," but rather is used of those who are sent forth by the community under the guidance of the Spirit as authorized preachers.

b) *Prophet*

The prophet appears to function within the community, although some may have been itinerant (*vide supra*).

c) *Evangelist*

This is the only reference in the primo-Pauline corpus to this office, although in 2 Tim 4:5 the bishop is to do the work of an evangelist and fulfill his ministry. In all likelihood, at this date it does not refer to the composer of any of the Gospels (canonical or uncanonical); rather, it would seem to convey the idea of the missionary who brought the Gospel to new areas (cf. Philip in Acts 21:8 who is so designated and similarly Timothy in 2 Tim 4:5).

d) *Pastor*

The absence of the article before the next minister (teacher) persuades Barth[75] to see this as a hendiadys and to translate "teaching shepherds" and to relate the ministry to that of a bishop. He states:

> Our translation "teaching shepherds" seeks to do justice to the stress laid upon the teaching capacity of a bishop, but it leaves open the possibility that at Paul's time some bishops considered other tasks their first responsibility, e.g. administrative functions mentioned in 1 Cor 12 and Rom 12.[76]

It should be noted, however, that the hellenistic sense of *poimen* refers more generally to those who lead the Church and in non-Christian Greek literature to leaders of religious guilds.[77]

The complexity and wealth of the ministries of the Spirit are indicated above, and it is important to add that patristic literature gives us an even greater variety of ministries.

All the ministries of the Spirit lie within the context of the fruits of the Spirit. 1 Cor 12 and 1 Cor 14 stand either side of Paul's great hymn to love.[78] Rom 12:6-8 is also placed within the context of faithfulness, hope, and love (Rom 12:9-13) and reaches its climax in Paul's teaching on love for one's enemies. The listing of the ministries in Eph 4:11-12 follows the author's great prayer for familial love and divine love within the community and his plea for meekness, patience, and love (Eph 3:14-4:3) which will foster the sevenfold unity within the Church (Eph 4:4-6). All three discussions of the ministries of the Spirit include reflections on the Church as the Body of Christ (1 Cor 12: 12-31; Rom 12:3-5, and Eph 4:4,15-16).

It would seem appropriate to include these "service" ministries under the regal character of Christians. It was (is) the function of the sovereign to administrate or preside (Rom 12:8 *proistamenos*), to be liberal in distributing the "wealth" of the community (Rom 12:8 *metadidous*), to exhort (Rom 12:8 *parakalon*), to implement acts of mercy (Rom 12:8 *eleon*) and, perhaps, the capacity to judge and make decisions. However, nowhere in the New Testament is there evidence to suggest that these ministries were permanent. It could be possible that they rotated in the community or that a person might have one gift, relinquish that, and develop another.

### The Transforming Power of the Spirit

But, over and above all these ministries, for Paul the Spirit is the transforming power in the believer; she brings a filial relationship (Gal 4:6; cf. Rom 8:15). It is Spirit who generates life (Gal 4:20; 5:25; Rom 8:2,6,11; 2 Cor 3:3,6,8). This life sanctifies (Rom 15:16; 1 Cor 6:11; 3:16; 1 Thess 4:8; 2 Thess 2:13; Titus 3:5; 1 Pet 1:2). The Spirit gradually transforms the earthly body into one fitted for God's eternal abode (Rom 8:11, 23; 2 Cor 5:1-5[79]). She helps one to pray (Rom 8:26-27; cf. Eph 6:18). The term which epitomizes the prophethood, priesthood, and sovereignty of all Christians is "ministers of reconciliation":

> All this is from God, who through Christ reconciled us to himself and gave us the ministry of reconciliation; that is, in Christ God was reconciling the world to himself, not counting their trespasses against them, and entrusting to us the message of reconciliation. So we are ambassadors for Christ, God making his appeal through us. We beseech you on behalf of Christ, be reconciled to God (2 Cor 5:18-20).

Our ministry of reconciliation is effected through the fruits of the Spirit, "love, joy, peace, patience, kindness, goodness, faithfulness, gentleness, self-control" (Gal 5:22-23). The ministries may be a revelation of supernatural activity; they are not necessary for salvation; they can be counterfeit, and they are dispensable. But, the fruits are a revelation of the very essence of godhood and humanhood; they are indispensable and necessary for salvation; they cannot be counterfeit. The fruits of the Spirit are all aspects of Love. In the words of Campbell Morgan:

Joy is Love's Consciousness;
Peace is Love's Confidence;
Patience is Love's Habit;
Kindness is Love's Activity;
Goodness is Love's Quality;
Faith is Love's Quantity;
Gentleness is Love's Tone;
Temperance is Love's Victory.

*Conclusion*

We have looked at the bare outline of the theology of the Spirit of God in the Hebrew Scriptures and seen it develop from a "holy roller" phenomenon into an energizing, enlightening, and moral power in the later prophets to the point where Joel predicts the Spirit as the graced possession of the community as a whole.

Joel's prediction was fulfilled on the Jewish Feast of Pentecost when, by outpouring of the Spirit, the Sinai Covenant was brought to its fullest expression and implementation. The early Jewish Christians became a community which shared efficaciously the messiahship (sovereignty), prophethood, and priesthood of Jesus. Endowed with these characteristics, it transformed itself into a world religion, sharing the Pentecostal experience with Jew and Gentile, men and women, slave and free (Gal 3:28). The individual members of the community were seen as sovereigns, but they ruled by service (cf. Mk 10:45), by sharing of wealth, by the implementation of peace and justice, by the discernment and encouragement of the special *charismata* which their fellow community members possessed. The community was a conventicle of the Spirit, comprising equality of discipleship. They manifested their prophethood by freedom of speech and charitable confrontation within the community; by their interpretation of Scripture and tradition: all members of the community were spokesmen and spokeswomen through the gift of the Paraclete, whom we may call the "constant innovator," which they received in the ordination of baptism. They exercised their priesthood by their ministry of reconciliation (2 Cor 5), being ambassadors for Christ: "So we are ambassadors for Christ (*Huper Christou oun presbeuomen hos tou theou parakalountos di' humon*), God making his appeal through us" (2 Cor 5:20). They were solemnly ordained to forgive or retain sin when Jesus breathed the Spirit upon them, saying: "Receive the Holy Spirit. If you forgive the sins of any, they are forgiven; if you retain the sins of any, they are retained" (Jn 20:22-23). They were continually engaged in the offering of pure and acceptable sacrifices when they offered them as confessors and martyrs in the witness of the faith. With Paul, they could say:

> For I am already on the point of being sacrificed; the time of my departure has come. I have fought the good fight, I have finished the race, I have kept the faith. Henceforth there is laid up for me the crown of righteousness, which the Lord, the righteous judge, will award to me on that Day, and not only to me but also to all who have loved his appearing (2 Tim 4:6-8).

In conclusion, I submit that the ability to realize our baptismal potential to be prophets, priests, and sovereigns lies within each of us. How can we make this a pastoral reality? The decision lies not only with the hierarchy but with you and me under the inspiration of her Majesty, the Holy Spirit.

## NOTES

[1]I am indebted to a dated but very useful article by William R. Shoemaker, "The Use of ruah in the Old Testament and of pneuma in the New Testament," *JBL* 23 (1904): 13-67. Revision is, of course, needed, especially now that the Qumran material must be considered.

[2]For the four sources in the Pentateuch (Hexateuch), J, E, P, and D, see L. Boadt, *Reading the Old Testament, an Introduction* (New York: Paulist Press, 1984), 94-106.

[3]The Hebrew is *slh* ("to rush upon").

[4]Cf. M. Lind, *Yahweh Is a Warrior, The Theology of War in Ancient Israel* (Scottdale: Herald Press, 1980).

[5]As were the Nazirites.

[6]See Joseph Blenkinsopp, *The History of Prophecy in Israel* (Philadelphia: Westminster Press, 1983), 61-68.

[7]Shoemaker, 20.

[8]Ibid.

[9]The *MT* has a sixfold; the *LXX* sevenfold.

[10]Shoemaker, 27.

[11]This phrase is found frequently in the Qumran literature.

[12]Cf. also Isa 61:3; 54:6; 65:14; Ps 77:3 (4); 142:3,4; 143:4.

[13]Jonah 1:4; 4:8; Eccles 8:8; Prov 27:16; 30:4.

[14]Job 6:26; 8:2; 15:2; 16:3 and 20:3; Eccles 1:14,17; 2:11,17,26; 4:4,6,16; Isa 26:18.

[15]"All flesh" is found in Gen 1-11; the translation "all mankind" or "all humankind" is incorrect, for the author, doubtless, wishes to include all creation, as in the covenant with Noah.

[16]See especially *TWNT* 6, 357-443, and David Hill, *Greek Words and Hebrew Meanings*, 202-300, and the literature in J. Fitzmyer, *The Dead Sea Scrolls: Major Publications and Tools for Study: with an addendum* (Missoula, Mont, 1977).

[17]See the brief discussion and the bibliography in George Johnston, *The Spirit-Paraclete in the Gospel of John* (Cambridge: CUP, 1970), 5-9.

[18]Mary Jo Weaver, *Pneuma in Philo of Alexandria*, Ph.D. dissertation, University of Notre Dame, Indiana, 1973.

[19]See Shoemaker, 35-46.

[20]It is not my purpose here to deal with the Apocalypse of John. See my Anchor Bible Commentary on *Revelation* (Garden City, New York: Doubleday, 1975), 19-20, 386-422.

[21]For the meaning of breath, see James 2:26; Rev 11:11; 13:13; Acts 17:23 (here *pneo*), and John 19:30. Cf. also Lk 8:55; 23:46; Acts 7:59. For breath, see 2 Thess 2:8. Heb 4:12 may mean "breath," but it could also mean "mind."

[22]M.D. Goulder, *Type and History in Acts* (London: SPCK, 1964), 74. This chart is also reproduced in the writer's book, *Bonded with the Immortal* (Wilmington: Michael Glazier, 1987), 112-113.

[23]G. Maier, *Die Tempelrolle von Toten Meer* (Munchen, Basel: Reinhardt, 1978; E.T. Sheffield, 1985).

[24]There is some tradition that the Spirit of Yahweh was expected to fall on all the people on the occasion of the Covenant on Mount Sinai; but, because of the sin of the golden calf, She came only to the leaders of the community.

[25]A. Dupont-Sommer, *The Essene Writings from Qumran* (New York: Meridian Press, 1962), 335-36; he cites quite a long fragment.

[26]H. Bardtke, "Considerations sur les Cantiques de Qumran," *RB* 63 (1956): 228ff.

[27]See H. Ringgren, *The Faith of Qumran, Theology of the Dead Sea Scrolls* (Philadelphia: Fortress, 1963), 94-151.

[28]See the author's chapter on Acts in *Bonded with the Immortal, A Pastoral Introduction to the New Testament* (Wilmington: Michael Glazier, 1987).

[29]F.D. Bruner, *A Theology of the Holy Spirit* (Grand Rapids, Michigan: Eerdmans, 1970), 176.

[30]R.H. Gundry, "Ecstatic Utterance," *JTS* 17, part 2 (1966): 299-307.

[31]This phrase, "all flesh," recalls the covenant with Noah and does not confine the Holy Spirit to human persons.

[32]See M.D. Goulder, *Type and History in Acts* (London: SPCK, 1964), 152-58, who argues that Luke is influenced by Gen 10 where the grandchildren of Noah are listed.

[33]See J.D. Davies, "Pentecost and Glossolalia," *JTS* 3 (1952): 228-31.

[34]I have spoken generally about this, but further literature will be given in the classic commentaries of C.H. Barrett, *Commentary on John*, 1979; R.E. Brown, *Anchor Bible Commentary on John*, and Barnabas Lindars, *Commentary on John*.

[35]George Johnston, *The Spirit-Paraclete in the Gospel of John* (Cambridge: CUP, 1970).

[36]Sebastian Brock, *The Holy Spirit in the Syrian Baptismal Tradition, Syrian Churches Series* (Poona: Anita Printers, 1979), p. 8.

[37]I am not conforming to an adoptionist theory here.

[38]Sebastian Brock, *The Harp of the Spirit*, 2nd edition (Fellowship of St. Alban and St. Sergius, 1983), 33.

[39]Ibid., 31.

[40]For discussion of this text, see John H. Elliott, *The Elect and the Holy: An Exegetical Examination of 1 Peter 2:4-10* (Leiden: Brill, 1966) and *Home for the Homeless, A Sociological Exegesis of 1 Peter, Its Situation and Strategy* (Philadelphia: Fortress, 1981).

[41]Elisabeth Schüssler Fiorenza, *Priester für Gott: Studien zum Herrschaft und Priestermotiv in der Apocalypsis* (Munster, 1972).

[42]Brock, *The Holy Spirit*, 1, in his introduction to the Holy Spirit within the baptismal tradition of the Syriac Church, says as follows: "Syriac Christianity is unique in that it represents a genuinely Semitic form of the Gospel which itself was preached originally in Aramaic. Although the New Testament itself reached Syriac by way of Greek, the thought forms, imagery, and religious vocabulary of the earliest Syriac writers — above all Aphrahat, Ephrem and the liturgical poets — are purely Semitic and owe little or nothing to the influence of Greek culture. As such, Syriac Christianity can genuinely claim to be an indigenous Asian representative of Christianity, and not a European export."

[43]Ibid., 59.

[44]Ibid., 48-49.

[45]The Syriac Version of the Bible.

[46]See Brock, *The Holy Spirit*,48-50.

[47]Ibid., 58 (from Syrian Orthodox Timothy and the Melkite Basil). Cf. John Chrysostom, *Hom. on 2 Cor (PG* 61, col. 417): "by baptism you too are made king, priest and prophet."

[48]Brock, *The Holy Spirit*, 58.

[49]For one of the most recent studies of glossolalia, see Watson E. Mills, ed., *Speaking in Tongues, a Guide to Research on Glossolalia* (Grand Rapids: Eerdmans, 1986). This is a collection of essays. The present author's article is printed in pages 263-94. Of particular interest are the five articles on the psychological aspects and the four sociological studies of speaking in tongues. For a good linguistic study, see William J. Samarin, *Tongues of Men and Angels* (New York, 1972).

[50]Blenkinsopp, 66.

[51]I have summarized Gundry's article, "Ecstatic Utterance," *JTS* 17, part 2 (1966): 299-307, in my article in Mills, *Speaking in Tongues*, 263-94.

[52]Samarin, *Tongues of Men and Angels*.

[53]Richard A. Baer, "Quaker Silence, Catholic Liturgy, and Pentecostal Glossolalia: Some Functional Similarities," in Mills, *op. cit.*, 313-28.

[54]See John P. Kildahl, *Psychology of Speaking in Tongues* (Harper and Row, 1972).

[55]See my article, "The Political and Social Aspects of the Miraculous in Acts of Apostles," *Festshrift for Horton*, edited by Elberg, forthcoming.

[56]David E. Aune, *Prophecy in Early Christianity and the Ancient Mediterranean World* (Grand Rapids: Eerdmans, 1983).

[57]Eugene M. Boring, *Sayings of the Risen Christ, Christian Prophecy* (Cambridge: CUP, 1982).

[58]David Hill, *New Testament Prophecy* (Atlanta: John Knox Press, 1979).

[59]Aune, *op. cit.*, 189.

[60]Ibid.

[61]In Rev, the seven angels of the churches are, most probably, prophetic messengers.

[62]H. Kraft, *Anfange*, cited by Aune, 200.

[63]Aune, *op. cit.*, 201.

[64]Ibid., 202.

[65]Ibid., 203.

[66]H. Conzelmann, *1 Corinthians, Hermeneia Commentary*, E.T. (Philadelphia: Fortress Press, 1975), 209.

[67]A. Plummer and A. Robertson, *1 Corinthians, International Critical Commentary*, 2nd edition (Edinburgh: T. and T. Clark, 1971), (latest reprint), 265.

[68]Conzelmann, *op. cit.*, 209.

[69]See the forthcoming *Hermeneia Commentary on Hebrews* by Harry W. Attridge.

[70]See the author's pamphlet, *The Ministries and Fruits of the Spirit* (Notre Dame: Catholic Action Office, 1973).

[71]C.E.B. Cranfield, *International Critical Commentary on the Epistle to the Romans* (Edinburgh: T. & T. Clark, 1979), 624.

[72]C.K. Barrett, *A Commentary on the Epistle to the Romans* (London, 1957), 239.

[73]Cranfield, *op. cit.*, 627.

[74]Rainer Riesner, *Handeln aus dem Geist, 12 Thesen zu Römer 12* (Giessen und Basel: Brunnen, 1977).

[75]Marcus Barth, *Anchor Bible Commentary on Ephesians* (New York: Doubleday, 1974), vol 2, 438.

[76]Ibid., 439.

[77]Arndt and Gingrich under *poimen*.

[78]Although some scholars would argue for a non-Pauline authorship.

[79]For a detailed commentary on 2 Corinthians, see V.P. Furnish, *II Corinthians, Anchor Bible* (Garden City, New York: Doubleday, 1984).

# Power, Authority, and Charism in the Church

Jerome Theisen, O.S.B.

## INTRODUCTION

The Holy Spirit that moves through the Church today does not find an exquisitely tidy and ordered house. It is a house that is still under construction, but which receives residents anyway; the Spirit cannot wait for the perfection of form and order before going about the task of healing and bringing together those who believe in the saving power of Jesus Christ. To speak of the Church as a house that receives residents, of course, is inadequate since the residents of the house are themselves the house and the Church. My point is that the Church is still in the process of being formed and that the house is not in perfect shape. We hope for a perfect order in a world to come.

The Holy Spirit finds much activity in the construction of the house. This has always been true of the Church, and the Church of our day is no exception; in fact, we might suggest that feverish activity is present in the Church since Vatican Council II. The Spirit should know because the Spirit is responsible in no small measure for the creaks and groans of the construction process.

This essay will examine only three dimensions of the construction process as they are evident in the Church today; on occasion, I will also refer to the way they were in the past. The three dimensions under consideration here are power, authority, and charism. These topics are not first in any list of Christian realities; but, they touch every aspect of the Christian faith, and they are particularly important in the decades after Vatican Council II.

More than twenty years ago a prophetic voice spoke up from solitude and marked one of our topics as crucial. A year before he died, Thomas Merton said this about authority:

63

> There can be no question that the great crisis in the church today
> is the crisis of authority brought on by the fact that the Church, as
> institution and organization, has in practice usurped the place of
> the Church as a community of persons united in love and in
> Christ...The Church is preached as a communion, but is run in
> fact as a collectivity, and even as a totalitarian collectivity.[1]

Authority issues were prominent in the recent cases of Archbishop Raymond Hunthausen and Father Charles Curran. Was
the Spirit involved in these cases? And, in which direction did
the Spirit push? What other powers were at play? Will we have
to wait another century before we can assess the cases properly?

The Spirit is guiding the Church through a crisis of authority,
one that is not unrelated to the issues of power and charism. In
popular perception authority is an exercise of power, and charism is a gift of God and/or of nature even as it is an expression of
power. The three topics are related to each other and are equally
under the guidance of the Holy Spirit even as they are affected
by cultural events of today. In this essay I intend to focus on the
question of authority as the central object of my study, but with
introductory and final sections on power and charism respec-
tively.

It is only fair to identify as much as possible the ecclesiology or
ecclesiologies that form the context within which I will approach
and critique the topics of power, authority, and charism. I prefer
to understand the Church as a communion of saints, to use the
phrase of the creeds. This model is closely related to the description of the Church as the people of God, a model extolled by
Vatican Council II. It is also close to an understanding of the
Church as a group of disciples who are gathered in the name and
love of Jesus. It is, finally, close to the perception of the Church
as a gathering of servants and friends of Jesus.

It is no accident that I choose the model of communion as the
preferred perception of the Church today. Vatican Council II
turned our thinking in this direction once again, and we are still
sorting out the implications of this shift of models, one that has
consequences for power, authority, and charism. In the words of
the historian Giuseppe Alberigo: "Vatican II appreciably cor-
rected the hierarchical and authoritarian perspective of modern
Catholicism and formulated a criterion of communion as a measure of the life of the Church in all its aspects."[2]

Vatican Council II, of course, did not create for the first time
this model of the Church; it attached itself to communion movements that go back to the New Testament and the original gathering of believers. Specifically, it related well to the stress that
Cardinal John Newman placed on the sense of the faithful in the

last century. The Cardinal found it important to emphasize the community of believers in a time when hierarchy and power held sway.

To regard the Church as a communion of saints is not to deny the presence of sin in the Church. Sinful power and division run through every member and dimension of the Church. The Church is far from perfect, and it is ever in the process of improvement. In particular, sin affects the exercise of power, authority, and charism in the Church, as we shall see later in the essay.

It should be noted, finally, that I am not confining my reflections to the leadership structure of the Church. Everyone in the Church has a measure of power, authority, and charism. The object of the essay is to discover, wherever possible and surely not exhaustively, the place of power, authority, and charism in the Church and the manner in which the Holy Spirit is leading the Church at the present time in its movements of power, authority, and charism.

## I. POWER IN THE CHURCH

Power is a reality of everyday life. We cannot exist without solar power, water power, or wind power. We are set in the midst of powerful forces that determine the way we must carve out our existence on this planet earth. We are moved by cosmic powers, and we depend on them for life and existence.

Besides the physical forces of power and might, we are confronted with many forms of power that stem from our life in human society: economic power, political power, legal power, military power, moral power, psychological power, religious power, et cetera. I cannot attend to all these forms of power in this essay, even through they have their influence on the power that people experience in the Church.[3]

It should be clear that power is good, the creation of a loving God who makes it possible for anything at all to exist and to have power. Our liturgy and our theology call God all powerful, the very source and sustainer of all that has come to be. The Church today continues to confess God as the power of good and the source of all creative power in the universe.

But, as with any creature, power can be corrupted and become an evil force. It then becomes a power of evil and power of sin. Power, for example, can become coercion when someone is pressured by an outside force which is neither willed nor wanted. Corrupt power can also be expressed in social control when political leaders use their positions to determine the thoughts and activities of cititzens for purposes of personal gain.

Or, again, a teacher can manipulate the minds of his or her students by carefully guarding the power of ideas. In short, power can suffer corruption and become the power of sin.

### A. Good and Salvific Power

I am concerned about the power of sin in the Church, but more directly I must note the power of good. The Church, in fact, exists to bear witness to and to communicate the power of God that leads to health and salvation. In this I follow the lead of Saint Paul who says: "I am not ashamed of the gospel. It is the power of God *(dynamis theou)* leading everyone who believes in it to salvation, the Jew first, then the Greek" (Rm 1:16).

Saint Paul boasts of God's saving power, but he also has to account for the paradox of God's weakness. When one considers God's powerful presence in creation and in the history of Israel, one has a difficult time understanding the reason Jesus, the very Son of God, was abandoned and left to die on the cross. All Paul can answer is that the power and the wisdom of God are made manifest in the cross: "Yes, Jews demand 'signs' and Greeks look for 'wisdom', but we preach Christ crucified—a stumbling block to Jews, and an absurdity to Gentiles; but to those who are called, Jews and Greeks alike, Christ the power of God and the wisdom of God. For God's folly is wiser than men and his weakness more powerful than men" (1 Cor 1:22-25). This passage gives us a clue to the way in which we should understand power in the Church. The Church does not march on with might and force from victory to victory, but it manifests the salvific power of God in weakness and folly. The model of power is the weakness of Jesus of Nazareth.

Though the gospel of Luke sees the Incarnation resulting from the power of God's Spririt coming down upon Mary (Lk 1:35), the hymn in the letter to the Philippians prefers the theme of self-emptying and lowliness. Being the Son of God, Jesus could have come in the flesh with pomp and splendor. But, instead "he emptied himself and took the form of a slave, being born in the likeness of men. He was known to be of human estate, and it was thus that he humbled himself, obediently accepting even death, death on a cross" (Phil 2:7-8)! Jesus did not grasp for power, and he even put aside the power and glory that were his due. He thereby provided a picture of *kenosis* for the Church.

The same message comes through the account of Jesus' temptations after his baptism (see Mt 4:1-11). Jesus is tempted to use the power of God that is within him to become a flamboyant Messiah who would rule and impress the world with spectacular powers. Jesus puts the temptation away and proceeds with a ministry of word and healing that shows a hidden power of the kingdom. At the end of his public ministry, he enters Jerusalem riding a donkey, a beast of burden, and not on a horse, the animal of pride and warfare. Again, a model for the Church: power is for healing and ministry, not self-display and domination.

Jesus manifests his power by word and action (cf. Lk 24:19); he overcomes the power of Satan and bears witness to the kingdom of God. He uses his power to bear witness to the truth and to heal the sick. He lives his life with quiet power. He confronts the power of sin in the midst of human society, and at the same time he redeems power by his death on the cross. He both goes to his death through the weakness of God and is raised from the dead through the power of God (see Mt 11:29; Acts 2:24). The power of the cross and the resurrection becomes manifest in his risen life. Thereby he receives all power to bring about salvation for those who believe: "Full authority has been given to me both in heaven and on earth; go, therefore, and make disciples of all the nations" (Mt 28:18). Jesus receives creative and life-giving power to effect the salvation of the nations.

The risen and exalted Christ now becomes a power to save: "There is no salvation in anyone else, for there is no other name in the whole world given to men by which we are to be saved" (Acts 4:12). Saint Paul confesses the same power: "I wish to know Christ and the power flowing from his resurrection" (Phil 3:10). The apostles go forth in the name and power of Jesus to effect healing and salvation. They and their successors continue this work until Jesus comes again in power. The Church's task, therefore, is to minister with a measure of Jesus' power, a means to bring about the forgiveness of sins and the gift of life.

### B. Problems of Power

The power of Christ's resurrection continues in the Church today; so does his powerful word of life and love. But, this salvific power abides in human vessels marked with limitations and sin. People of the Church communicate the powerful message with different and at times contradictory expressions. The message is thereby blunted. The power of new life is communicated through liturgical rites, but in different and at times shabby modes. The power of love is signaled in different and at times minimal ways (a grudging glass of water, a nod to racial equality, a wink at the weapons of war). The power of the resurrection is indeed present in the Church, but its effectiveness is diminished by human shortcomings and sin.

Discipleship of Jesus demands a basic equality of those who are baptized into his death and resurrection and who are gathered around his banquet of word and sacrament. But, the loving interchange that discipleship implies is marred by the human penchant to be number one, to be first. This already happened in the circle of Jesus; Zebedee's sons, James and John, wanted to sit at Jesus' right and left hand in the kingdom. But, Jesus defused that power move with the word about true greatness: "Anyone among you who aspires to greatness must serve the rest; whoever wants to rank first among you must serve the needs of all" (Mk 10:43-44). There is rank among Jesus' disciples, but the requirements for first place are different from those generally acknowledged in society. The number one person should be outstanding in service.

The desire to be number one was not limited to Jesus' circle of friends. It was found early on in Diotrephes, the leader in a Johannine community: "I did write to the church; but Diotrephes, who enjoys being their leader, ignores us" (3 John 9). Diotrephes uses his position of leadership and power to ignore the elder who writes this letter.

How many Church leaders today enjoy being number one, not because of their ability to serve, but because of their capacity to command? How many act with the purest of motives? How many want to control excessively the power of the resurrection by the way they wish the word to be articulated, by the way they want the sacraments to be celebrated, and by the way they want love to be expressed? The problem is not with the necessary offices of leadership and authority (see the next section of this essay), but with the human figures who occupy these positions. There are still those who want to be first for the wrong reasons, and yes, with an array of right reasons as well.

Humans struggle with their limitations and their self-centeredness. When a person is raised to a position where he or she can exercise power over others, the specter of selfishness and shortcomings inevitably stands in the background. We want to control the power of the resurrection according to our modes of thinking and acting. And, we have the ability to limit the power of the resurrection. Such is the awesomeness of the use and abuse of power in the Church on the part of all believers.

Of course, the abuse of power is not limited to those in positions of leadership. All believers have access to the power of the word, sacraments, and love; and all are marked with limitations and sins in various measures so that the power of the resurrection is hindered in its expression and effectiveness.

Another problem of power is the refusal to share it. It may

JEROME THEISEN, O.S.B.                                    69

take the form of being reluctant to communicate the word, to celebrate the sacraments with others, and to join others in works of justice and love. Those in positions of leadership may refuse to share power and authority with others, holding tight to all the reins of power and wanting to control every aspect of the lives of those who form community with them.

Another problem that exists today is the impression that the power of the resurrection comes only through priests and bishops. They are the overseers of the Christian communities, to be sure, and their leadership allows and fosters great access to the power of God's love. But, the power of the resurrection is not confined to their leadership. It is present widely in the community of disciples, and it is expressed abundantly in many forms of prayer and loving action.[4] In point of fact, the Spirit of the risen Christ is active in richly diversified ways among the community of believers and beyond in the world at large.

A final example of the problem of power is its unexplained and unreasoned use. Those in leadership positions and others as well sometimes exercise control and exert power without an adequate communication of reasons and directives: The use of power is not self-explanatory; thus, people today, perhaps more so than they did in the past, wish to hear the rationale for the use of power.

It should be obvious that power is abundantly present in the community of disciples, that it is good and salvific, but that it is straitened by human limitations and faults. Power in any form can be dangerous and surely carries responsibilities, but the power of the resurrection is especially good, and it is this power that we strive to make maximally present in the Church and the world.

## C. The Spirit of Power

What are the new expressions of the Spirit of power in the Church today? Two come to mind. One is consonant with the communion model of the Church promoted by Vatican Council II; the other stems from the modern focus on the condition of the poor and the powerless.

The communion model of the Church fosters a notion of power that recognizes its presence in the community of the faithful as a whole. The model acknowledges that the power of the resurrection extends to everyone in the Church, not just to those in positions of leadership. The Spirit of the risen savior, the power from on high, is seen as the dynamic power behind every disciple's witness to the word of the gospel, every celebration of the sacrament, and every activity of justice and love. Leaders have a power of authority, but the faithful at large have access to the abundant powers of resurrection life and salvific truth. What the Spirit is telling us today is that the whole community of believers is empowered to articulate the word, to celebrate the sacraments, and to perform works of healing. The Spirit of Jesus really is imparted in baptism and becomes a power for good in the wide-ranging life of the Church in the world, both in its testimony to truth and its service of love.

Secondly, and paradoxically, the Spirit of power is manifesting the power of the resurrection in the powerless of the world. A power of the poor and the weak is affecting the Church of today; it comes, not just from Latin American countries where the preferential option for the poor has become a shout for the world to hear, but also from the poor in the United States. Here, too, the poor, the dispossessed, the excluded, the sick and the elderly make demands on the Church.

The powerless are bearing witness to the power of the cross. They are showing the way their condition throws light on the truth of the gospel, especially in matters of justice. They are manifesting an articulation of the gospel that brings out hidden meanings of the saving word of Jesus. They are demanding that the full gospel of love and service be operative in their lives and in the life of the Church generally. They have the power to demand justice, service, healing, and celebration. Their powerlessness is powerful, and it forces the Church to pay attention to its deepest meaning as a community of disciples and friends of Jesus.

The Spirit of God, the power of the resurrection, is moving through the Church today to enliven all aspects of the Church through the power of the powerless.

It seems that the powerless are teaching the whole Church the value of being vulnerable, of making oneself less protected, and of putting down defenses. There is gospel precedent for this, both in the life of Jesus and in the early disciples. Leaders should not be surprised that they experience a good measure of powerlessness in their work of governing the people of God and in witnessing to the saving life of Jesus. Powerlessness is a central reality of the gospel message. The Spirit is moving the Church, especially through the powerless, to appreciate the powerless dimension of the community of believers.

## II.  AUTHORITY IN THE CHURCH

There is no question about the Church's need for authority. If authority is meant to enrich such a reality as the Church, it must be present in both structures and persons. Official authority is present in the structures that lead to an enhancement of the Church. Personal authority is the leader's talent and grace which give him or her the ability to benefit the life of the Church. Quentin Quesnell's definition of authority applies to both official and personal authority: "Authority is the recognized responsibility and/or ability to direct the group to what it wants and needs as a group."[5]

## A. Sources of Authority

By definition, authority is creative of reality in the Church or any other society, and for this reason it can ultimately be traced back to God. At any rate, this is Saint Paul's method. His exhortation to obedience leads him to cite God as the source of all authority: "Let everyone obey the authorities that are over him, for there is no authority except from God, and all authority that exists is established by God" (Rm 13:1). Paul here puts the authorities in the best of lights and even calls them servants of God. He does not take up the case of the tyrannical authority that demands more than conscience can abide.

We have no difficulty in acknowledging that God is the ultimate source of all authority. God creates, sustains, and enriches the reality of our existence, and other authorities are effective only to the extent that they continue the increase and enhancement of our life in society.

God is the source of all authority, but, for us who belong to the Church, it is Jesus whom we regard as our more immediate authority. John's gospel makes this clear: "Father, the hour has come! Give glory to your Son that your Son may give glory to you, inasmuch as you have given him authority over all humankind that he may bestow eternal life on those you gave him" (Jn 17:1-2). The Son and the Son's Spirit provide the Church with the power and the authority to carry out the ultimate purpose of the Church: to assist people in the acquisition of eternal life. Authority exists to enrich the Church with the means to life.

But, is it enough to speak of God, Christ, and their Spirit as sources of authority in the Church? It would seem not, for we need to attend to the people of the Church for whom authority exists. Disciples of Jesus receive the power of the Spirit in their baptism and Christian life. They have the power of the resurrection, and with that they are able to enhance the reality of the Church; therefore, everyone in the Church has a certain measure of authority and exercises this authority in building up the body and in enriching life in the Church. In the same Spirit, they see the needs for administration and leadership, and they readily acknowledge that believers are called from the midst of the community for the service of leadership. In fact, leaders are promoted and sustained by the community in their call to leadership. While the call comes from God, it is not without the sustaining authority of the people of the Church. The power and the authority that are present in the community as a whole find their focus in the leader who becomes their servant.

The person of authority in the Church is not only the leader but also the man or woman of holiness. The power of the resurrection is more plainly evident in such persons, and others are drawn to them for guidance and instruction. History is replete with Christian saints, confessors, and religious whom we regard as holding a special position of authority in the Church. Others look up to them, seek their counsel, and listen to their teaching. In our day we can think of a Thomas Merton, a Mother Teresa, a Dorothy Day, and a Martin Luther King; these Christians bring an increase to the Church through their lives and works.

Another source of authority is competence, especially in knowledge and truth. The person of historical and practical knowledge becomes an authority for those who look to him or her as a guide in Christian existence. People in the Church vary considerably in their knowledge of the truth, but it is generally easy to recognize the important persons of authoritative knowledge. Karl Rahner was such a person. So also was John Courtney Murray.

We are not claiming, of course, that knowledge or reasoning is the sole source of authority in the Church. We do not accept the Enlightenment principle that reason alone should be the authoritative guide in human affairs. We recognize the authority of the Spirit, but the Spirit does not extinguish the human talents that make a person an authority in the Church.

Not all authorities, to be sure, merit the same measure of recognition. We readily respond to the authority of Jesus and his Spirit with quick obedience, but we do it in faith. The following of other religious authorities requires faith in Jesus and trust in the persons who represent Christ and his Spirit. We find it easier to reverence the person of Jesus (he makes no mistakes), but difficult to revere the human person of authority who dwells in our midst and who is marked with deficiencies and sin.

The acceptance of authority depends on the strength of faith that a person places in religious authority. Obedience to authorities is required, of course, but the obedience will vary according to the strength of Spirit that the person perceives in self as well as the strength of Spirit that one perceives in the person of authority.

Thus, we are constrained to acknowledge that authority is

limited, both by the person of authority (his or her measure of expressing the Spirit and of displaying competence) and by the person who is disposed to obey. We must remember that the person of faith is a free human being with personal worth and autonomy. Placing one's confidence in authorities is a limiting experience (from the standpoint of one's autonomy) but also a broadening experience (from the standpoint of the greater access to knowledge and power). The point I am making is that religious authorities are limited, both by the measure of the Spirit and of competence which the authorities possess and by the measure of obedience which people invest in authorities.

### B.  Tasks of Authority

Those who put their trust in authority find that it promotes their journey to God and their personal fulfillment. Accepting authority outside of oneself opens one up to the realm of truth and power beyond the limits of one's mind and heart. Authority is, in the final analysis, meant to be of service to the Church and to the individual. Those who trust authority find themselves served by people of talent and power.

Authoritative leadership functions as an agent of good in the Church. Its tasks are many. John Futrell, S.J., summarizes them well in one paragraph:

> To form a community a group must have some kind of unifying mechanism, some human instrumentality that can embody the whole community, speak, call and send in the name of the whole community, call forth the unique gifts of each member and integrate them into the corporate strength of the whole community to realize its communion and to carry out what the members as free adults came together to do.[6]

It is the task of religious authority to unify the Church, to give it a center of unity. Religious authority should be able to speak for the whole community; it articulates, not some foreign doctrine, but the truths which lie at the basis of the community. Authoritative leadership recognizes and fosters the gifts of the Spirit that are imparted to every member of the community; it acknowledges these gifts and promotes their use for the benefit of the whole Church.

Another task of religious leadership is the encouragement of change and renewal. "Leaders must create an atmosphere that will encourage people to be creative."[7] Leaders need not have all the new ideas; in fact, they might have very few new ones; but, they should be open to the many ideas that come to light in the community of disciples, all of whom are empowered by the

Spirit to be authorities, that is, to enrich the community with knowledge and service. Leadership fosters and critiques the ideas and actions that rise in the midst of the community; it must judge the new movements because not all are sound or of benefit to the body of the Church.

The bishops of the United States, generally not in the forefront of change, surprised the country with their pastorals on peace and the economy. They thereby became agents of change, urging people to think differently about the arms race and about our attention to the poor and the unemployed. They acted as authoritative leaders, but not before studying the issues themselves and consulting widely with the people of the country.

It should be clear that authoritative leaders are not just administrators of a business office, not just governors of order in the Church, but listeners and healers. They listen to the needs of the people and bring the gospel message to bear on the issues of the day, especially such as those that concern the people of faith at the present time: care for the dying, concern for the global community, and proper stewardship of land. Healers can heal only if they are acquainted with the illness and also know the proper medicines.

## C. Models of Authority

To say that leaders must serve the community of disciples is to use the image of servanthood. Leaders are servants of the community, not demi-gods and objects of worship. Leaders look to the person of Christ who came to serve: "The Son of Man has not come to be served but to serve—to give his life in ransom for the many" (Mk 10:45).

Jesus explicitly rejects the model of earthly kings and princes as one that is unsuitable for his disciples. Jesus said: "Earthly kings lord it over their people. Those who exercise authority over them are called their benefactors. Yet it cannot be that way with you. Let the greater among you be as the junior, the leader as the servant" (Lk 22:25-26). Jesus presents himself as the one who rejects lordly power: his is the model of service, even to the point of death on a cross.

At the last supper he did not insist on having his feet washed. Instead, he took up a towel and a basin and washed the feet of his disciples. Then he instructed them: "But if I washed your feet— I who am Teacher and Lord—then you must wash each other's feet. What I just did was to give you an example: As I have done, so you must do" (Jn 13:14-15). Jesus insists on the repetition of the footwashing just as he insists on the repetition of the supper.

Raymond Brown comments wryly on the command to serve in the same way:

> But the washing shows more clearly than does the eucharist the theme of humble service by the Christian. Because it is so sacred, the eucharist has been very divisive in Christian history with almost every aspect having been fought about. Would Christians have argued with each other so fiercely over the washing of the feet? Many Christians vie for the privilege of presiding at the eucharist. How many would vie for the 'privilege' of washing another person's dirty feet?[8]

Christian leaders still prefer to argue over who should preside at the Eucharist, and only rarely do they concern themselves about the command to wash feet. Fortunately, the rite of footwashing has again become part of our liturgy of Holy Week. It never ceases to provoke thought about the true nature of discipleship, especially among those who lead the Christian community.

Saint Paul understood the servant nature of leadership, even though he was not at the last supper to receive the ritual services of Jesus. On his way to Jerusalem, he spoke to the presbyters of Ephesus in terms of service and dedication:

> You know how I lived among you from the first day I set foot in the province of Asia—how I served the Lord in humility through the sorrows and trials that came my way from the plottings of certain Jews. Never did I shrink from telling you what was for your own good, or from teaching you in public or in private. With Jews and Greeks alike I insisted solemnly on repentance before God and on faith in our Lord Jesus . . . . I put no value on my life if only I can finish my race and complete the service to which I have been assigned by the Lord Jesus, bearing witness to the gospel of God's grace (Acts 20:18-21.24).[9]

The servant model of authority is historical and perennial; it is still of value today, even though our experience of servants is rather sporadic. Historically, the Church has assumed models from societies in which it found itself. Thus, we hear of Church leaders referred to as lords, princes, pontiffs, presidents, et cetera. But, these rarely capture the spirit of the gospel leader.

Other models of authority have been more successful, and some of them are still in use today. The shepherd theme is ancient and modern, taken up by Jesus himself to indicate his tender care and love for the flock, his knowledge of each sheep, and his sacrifice for the good of the whole flock. Jesus passes on the model to Peter and all who would follow him in guiding and caring for the flock. He also asks love for himself: "If authority is given, it must be based on love of Jesus. Moreover, Jesus continues to speak of 'my lambs, my sheep'. The sheep do not belong to Peter or to any human church officer; they continue to belong to the one who said 'I am the model shepherd; I know my sheep and mine know me' (Jn 10:14)."[10]

The model of teacher is again both ancient and modern, in use continually throughout the history of the Church in spite of the prohibition we find in Matthew's gospel: "Avoid being called teachers. Only one is your teacher, the Messiah" (Mt 23:10). Is this hyperbolic language? Can the leaders avoid being called teachers when they instruct people in the ways of the gospel? Saint Paul was not deterred from using the title: he counts teaching as one of the tasks of ministry (1 Cor 12:7).

Christian leaders are inevitably teachers, more by a way of life than by words, but without fail by words. The leaders are learners first of all, and even while they are teachers. But, they must also communicate the message of the gospel by choice words.

The model of fatherhood is also ancient and modern, again in spite of Jesus' prohibition of the use of the title father: "Do not call anyone on earth your father. Only one is your father, the One in heaven" (Mt 23:9).[11] Once more, Saint Paul was not deterred from using the title of father to depict his work and his relationship to the people he served (1 Cor 4:15).

The Christian leader as father is one who provides for his people, gives them correction, and oversees their growth from infancy to maturity. The father creates life situations in which the disciples can find new existence, growth, and adulthood. The father is protective of his children in faith, keeping the enemies at bay and forming a safe environment.

While this model is still attractive, some oppose it as carrying too many negative implications for those Christians who are, together with the leaders, equally disciples of Jesus and adult believers in the gospel. The leader who follows this model too closely becomes paternalistic and oppressive; he does not allow the believers room to grow and to become adult.

The image of mother is used less frequently because the ordained ministry has been closed to women. Even women religious today, at least in many congregations, tend to put aside the model of mother to describe their religious superior. The model carries with it too many implications of psychological and religious immaturity: the religious superior always remains the mother and the others remain children who need constant attention and guidance. Of course, the image still conveys a message of care and creation; as a mother creates life, so the religious superior creates the possibility of growth and new existence for the sisters in her charge.

Another ancient and modern image is that of prophet. One usually does not associate this image with the religious leader who is also an administrator. But, perhaps the reason for this is that we do not usually expect prophetic actions from top religious leaders. This is really unfair because prophetic words and actions should be part and parcel of religious authority, and, in fact, they are, though normally not in a stunning sort of way. One may think of those bishops who speak and act strongly for peace.

The image of the prophet suits many religious authorities of the Church, but it is not dominant in their thinking or in the thinking of believers at large. Prophecy in a religious authority seems to be a bonus; people are happy to discover it in their leader, but they do not expect it.

Another model of religious authority is that of administrator. People have mixed reactions to this model of religious leadership. They know that leadership involves stewardship of goods and personnel. They remember that some of the first references to the appointment of new authorities in the New Testament were to those who were chosen to care for the distribution of goods to the Greek-speaking widows (see Acts 6:1-6). They remember, too, that Saint Paul lists the administrator as one of the persons who build up the body of Christ (1 Cor 12:28).

The Church requires good administrators because the Church has many services and much of the earth's goods to convey to people of faith and to society at large. Religious authority can hardly avoid administering some goods and services. Indeed, some authorities should be content with the title and model of administrator; they are called to administration, and administration is the way in which they serve the people of the Church. One can cite here administrators of hospitals or non-ordained administrators of parishes and schools.

The Church needs administrators, but the image of administrator is not primary and does not serve to characterize the main aspects of religious authority. The image often carries the notion that a person is more concerned about buildings and objects than about persons and their spiritual needs.

The leader as steward is an attractive way of describing the work of religious authority. The model of stewardship makes it clear that the leader has received a responsibility from another; in this case, from the Lord Jesus. The leader also has a responsibility to the people he or she serves. The good steward is trustworthy and just; he or she is attentive and caring. The good steward makes available the riches of the gospel and oversees the goods that the community holds for worship services, for instruction, and for the poor.

All dioceses, parishes, and religious congregations have resources of goods and personnel. The leader is the one who knows the resources and wishes to put them to the service of the gospel.

Another image that is used of religious authority, especially in congregations of religious, is superior. This image indicates that a person is placed in higher position, a position of leadership. It also implies that the authority is living on a higher plane.

The image has its drawbacks since the opposite of superior is inferior. The fact that a person does not live his or her life as a religious leader does not imply that he or she is inferior as a religious person. In fact, the opposite may be the case. The nonleader could be more advanced in the Christian life than the leader.

It is not likely, outside of some congregations of religious, that this model of religious authority will become widely used or appreciated.

Contemporary society provides us with other images of authority, such as dictator, military general, president, and chairperson. The first two have no transfer potential to the religious scene, though at times some religious authorities are accused of acting as dictators and military officers, and perhaps some do. But, the images of president and chair have value for religious leaders. The title of chair is very close to that of president, except that one usually associates less power with the chair.

The one who presides is literally the one who sits before the religious group to ensure an orderly meeting of the group. He or she presides over meetings and activities that are carried on in large part by others. Decisions from the chair need to be made from time to time, but it is clear that much power remains with the group.

The image of president is used in religious circles; for example, in institutions of learning, health care, and social service. But, it is also used on the national episcopal scene. Since Vatican Council II, the bishops regularly elect a president to represent the National Conference of Catholic Bishops. He presides over their assemblies and speaks for them, even though he has little power over them as individuals.

Robert Murray, S.J., proposes the image of medical doctor. [12] The religious leader as doctor points up the task of healing and caring for the wounds of Christian believers. Everyone requires medical attention since we are all wounded in our human and Christian life. The doctor is professionally trained to care for the sick, and he or she is responsible to the profession and to the patient to exercise the office of doctor with care and intelligence.

Nicholas Lash suggests the model of orchestra director. [13] The director is professionally schooled in music and in the capabilities of many instruments. So, too, the religious leader needs to know the talents and capabilities of the people he or she leads. The director will be a point of focus for the work of the orchestra and will need skill to draw out the best from each player. One could do worse than seeing the religious authority as a director of harmonious activities of the people of God!

Some images that stem from Church law, such as rector and parochial vicar, leave much to be desired by way of resonances. They do not point to the preferred aspects of religious leadership.

Other titles, such as guardian and animator, which I do not see as catching on very widely, have more positive implications. The guardian is one who watches over the gathering of believers, protects it, and provides it with good counsel. The animator is one who stirs up the spirits of the people so that they remain committed to the gospel and carry out its mandates in today's world.

The words leader and leadership are quite popular today in spite of the fact that some fifty years ago they were associated with such political figures as *il duce* (Mussolini) and *der Fuehrer* (Hitler). The leader gives direction and sets the pace. He or she stands visibly at the head of the group and provides an animating spirit. The leader goes on ahead and blazes a trail for followers.

The image of leader is attractive for religious authority today. It has more positive than negative implications, though it might leave one with the impression that the followers are docile and that the leaders always have the right sense of direction. This is surely not the case.

Since models of authority vary in usefulness and change from age to age, the Church should not fix on any one model. Many models can be used simultaneously so long as one is aware of the strengths and weaknesses of each.

People of the Church are often less concerned about the title than about the style in which religious authority is exercised. They oppose instinctively the style that is authoritarian, autocratic, or impersonal. They do not want a distant and dominative type of authority. They want a style of leadership that is personal, close, consultative, and compassionate.

The style of leadership varies greatly from person to person, even among those holding the same office. Think of the dominative and badgering style of Pius IX, or the aristocratic style of Pius XII, the compassionate style of John XXIII, or the determined style of John Paul II. Many people, non-Christians included, were attracted to the style of John XXIII. A Maundy Thursday address of his, given a couple of months before he died, captures his compassionate style:

> It is the spirit that counts more than the gesture; and this lesson does not apply to the leaders of the Church alone: every position of power, every exercise of authority, is a service. The Pope gladly calls himself *Servus servorum Dei*; he is conscious of being, and strives to be, the servant of all. God grant that those who bear the burden of responsibility for the human community may take to heart this last great lesson of Maundy Thursday, and recognize that their authority will be all the more acceptable to their people for being exercised in a spirit of humble service and complete devotion to the welfare of all men.[14]

### D.  Episcopal and Priestly Leadership

The most visible religious authorities in the Roman Catholic Church are the bishops. It will not be possible to review all the dimensions of their religious authority in the Church, but the mention of a few aspects that have been stressed of late could be helpful.

The Lima document of 1982, *Baptism, Eucharist and Ministry*, includes a succinct description of the office of bishop: "*Bishops* preach the Word, preside at sacraments, and administer discipline in such a way as to be representative pastoral ministers of oversight, continuity and unity in the Church."[15] The theologians who prepared this document put preaching in the first place, for bishops are first of all proclaimers of the gospel message. They also carry on the task of *episkope*: overseeing the life and order of the Church. Of particular interest in this statement is the work of continuity and unity; bishops express in their persons and in their office the continuity of the current Church with the past, and they also form a point of unity for the present. People expect to hear bishops speak of the historical Church, and they expect to gather about their bishop as the central figure in a sacred drama—central from the standpoint of authority, not necessarily of holiness.

One other aspect of the bishop's office should be noted; it is the task of caring for the poor. Edward Schillebeeckx notes that one of the precious titles of the bishop, going back to the early centuries of the Church, is *pater pauperum*, father of the poor. Especially when other organizations failed, the bishop used his economic skills and his stewardship of resources to care for the poor in the area, both Christians and non-Christians.[16] It is in the best of traditions, therefore, that the bishops of the United States issued a pastoral on the economy.

A word about the special character that bishops need to function well. John Jay Hughes suggests that three specific episcopal virtues are prudence, courage, and compassion.[17] These virtues indeed sum up the fortitude it takes to be a bishop.

Since bishops oversee a whole city or a large territory, it is left to the priests to function as the principal persons of religious authority in parishes and institutions. Where is the Spirit moving priestly ministry today?

It is obvious to most in the Church that the number of priests has been reduced to a critical point. Parishes which enjoyed the services of two or three priests in the past are now reduced to one. Some parishes are now yoked with others and are served by a single, itinerant priest. Some few parishes are governed by non-ordained administrators and are served by priests a few times a month.

Now that the shortage of priests and seminarians is real, Church officials and researchers are putting extra effort into the study of the situation. Dean Hoge, sociologist from the Catholic University in Washington, D. C., finds that the priest shortage will not improve in the immediate future,[18] and yet he finds that the laity generally want the traditional services of the priest: "We conclude that laity will not easily accept any great reduction in priestly services."[19] Some laity, however, see the shortage of priests as an opportunity for more lay persons to get involved in the parish, even to the point of being innovative and reformative.[20]

It is acknowledged that priests have often been engaged in work that could be done by others: physical plant management, financial planning, catechetical instruction, et cetera. Today, such ministries as hospital visitation, marriage counseling, preparation for liturgy are managed by lay people, often professionals with the requisite education and degrees. The priest needs to change his style of leadership. His religious authority is expressed more directly in presiding at the Eucharist and other sacraments, in coordinating the ministries of all in the parish without wishing to duplicate them, in discerning what is needed for the parish or listening to others who surface the need, in supporting the works of other ministers in the parish, and in providing a leading spirit for the whole group of Christian disciples. In fact, he should be an animator of the parish and a center of focus.

Religious authority in parishes is being spread out to other ministers, generally non-ordained, though some work is being

assigned to permanent deacons. In a survey of adults and college
students, Dean Hoge found a surprising statistic: "...the major-
ity chose...restructuring parish leadership to include more deacons, sisters, and lay persons. This is a higher priority for laity
than recruiting many more priests to overcome the shortage."[21]
Catholics generally want more participation in their parish life;
in consequence, they want a greater share of the religious
authority of the parish.

The Spirit is bringing us to the realization that a multitude of
ministries exists in the parish community and that people generally want more participation in their parish and religious life.
They want to serve even as they are served. They want a larger
share of the religious authority that comes with ministry, and
they are willing to accept more lay leadership.[22]

In introducing Dean Hoge's book, which contains the afore-
mentioned studies, Richard McBrien states that, since Vatican
Council II, the Church has experienced "a weakening of its
authority structure."[23] The concentration of authority has
changed; so also the kind of unquestioning commitment that has
been given to bishops and priests. This may be called a weakening, but the Church is now in the process of adjusting its breadth
of religious authority. The authority is broadening out at the
base to include many more officially recognized, even if unor-
dained, religious authorities. Also, the Church generally
rejoices in the many ministries which are present in the community of disciples as a whole.

### E. Problems of Authority

Before looking at movements or changes in religious authority today, we need to mention some of the problems of authority.
Why is religious authority difficult today? What are some of its
difficulties? I realize that authority has always been difficult and
that some of today's problems have their roots in the past.

The first problem is as old as humankind. It is self-
centeredness, with which we are all afflicted since it is one of the
chief characteristics of the condition of sin in the world. Because
of self-centeredness, we find it difficult to accept outside guidance and direction. It seems like a compromise of self to be
subject to someone beyond the self. We acknowledge our debt to
others, but at the same time we find it limiting to depend on
outside directives, principles, and persons.

Self-centeredness in the American population is aggravated
by an emphasis on individualism. Our myths and our heroes
promote the rugged individualist who is able to manage on his
own. He (usually a he) is a law unto himself. The individualist

tames the forest and controls the forces of nature. Self-sufficiency is the ideal.

Our culture praises the individualist. Thus, the drive for self-sufficiency and self-centeredness combine to make subjection to religious authority very difficult indeed. Religious authority will have to take both obstacles into consideration as it goes about unifying the Church. Quentin Quesnell puts it well in this statement: "Moreover, modern concern with the individual, the person, fascination with the freedom aspects of christian faith, existential concern with the terrible responsibility of self-creation, self-determination—all this has led more and more within the churches to reflection on the question, Why? Why should I continue to submit? Can I as a christian abdicate decision-making power to another?"[24]

Related to self-centeredness and individualism is the suspicion of external authority, especially when no evidence or reason is provided for a command or a directive. The believer does not lose his or her intelligence and freedom when confronted with an authority situation. The believer wants an explanation, as often as it is possible to give one. If no explanation is possible but it is merely a matter of choice or intuition on the part of the religious authority, this should be frankly stated. The following of authority does not require full understanding; one also needs to trust in authority. But, authority becomes problematic when it demands mindless obedience and does not even attempt an explanation.

Religious authority becomes problematic if it is too centralized, that is, if regular governance is far removed from the actual life and place of the people. This is not to criticize the need for a point of unity in the Church, e.g., the Petrine function, but it is to say that normal exercise of authority should be much closer to the local community. Many matters can be left up to local control, e.g., certain hymns in the liturgy and certain manners of religious instruction. Some people feel the problem of authority today because they think the office or person of authority is too far removed from the local scene.

Another problem of religious authority today is the absolutizing of particular statements or institutions. In the words of Nicholas Lash: "...our hearing of the word of God will be distorted in the measure that we ascribe to any particular authority, to any particuar form of truth—any book, any proposition, any institution—the absolute authority of truth itself, the absolute authority of God."[25] In my home diocese, a fellow priest has absolutized the liturgical norms of Trent and of Pius V as well as a particular political movement today and thus has slipped into schism. I know of a parish that has absolutized the communion rail. Religious authority is not served when a particular item of the Church is absolutized. One problem of religious authority today is maintaining the proper tension between the dictates of authority and a reasonable evaluation of mandates in view of the whole Christian tradition.

Another problem of authority today is the perennial one of tension between the need for governance and discernment in the Church and the basic equality of baptized Christians who are gifted by the Holy Spirit. Any Christian may appeal to the presence of the Paraclete (according to the Johannine tradition) to support his or her own authority: "As for you, the anointing you received from him remains in your hearts. This means you have no need for anyone to teach you" (1 John 2:27). Raymond Brown cites this appeal to the Spirit to support one's personal authority in a controversy as one of the structural weaknesses of the Johannine tradition.[26] In any event, the tension will always abide, but it becomes excessively problematic if left unrecognized or if regarded as unacceptable.

Another problem today as in the past is the seeking of status in aspiring to positions of religious authority in the Church. Some seminarians seek the clerical state because of the honors and privileges it ensures, at least in some circles. Vatican Council II found it useful to warn seminarians of this temptation to authority for the sake of privilege: "Students must clearly understand that it is not their lot in life to lord it over others and enjoy honors, but to devote themselves completely to the service of God and the pastoral ministry."[27] Religious authority should make it quite evident to seminarians and others that high positions are not meant to be chairs of honor and privilege!

A final problem is one of language. Religious authority at times, less so today than it did in the past, phrases its language in pompous terms. On occasion, it will also attempt to justify itself, making sure that others understand its power. Finally, the language is often excessively male in tone, attending very little to the fact that half of the community of disciples is female. Everyone, religious authority included, needs to attend to the power that language has to set a tone and a mentality.

The language problem points up another issue which some discover in the Church; namely, that the authority is too dominated by men. Dean Hoge found some of this thinking in his surveys, more among women than among men.[28] This problem is also pointed up in the first draft of the pastoral letter on women of the bishops of the United States, "Partners in the Mystery of Redemption": "Women have suffered from profound as well as petty discrimination because of an attitude of male dominance

which, in any form, is alien to the Christian understanding of
the function of authority. . . . We intend, therefore, to insure
that women are empowered to take part in positions of authority
and leadership in church life in a wide range of situations and
ministries.''[29]

### F. Movements of Authority Today

Where is the Spirit moving us today in matters of religious
authority? What movements and changes are afoot in the midst
of the Church? I will take note of a dozen or more of them. Many
of them have become evident since Vatican Council II, and most
have roots in history.

I begin with one of the features of the communion model of the
Church. This model recognizes the necessary place of authority
in the Church, but it stresses the horizontal relationships of the
disciples of Jesus. The fact that all are brothers and sisters in the
Lord is the primary reality of the Church. Everyone is baptized
and is called to holiness and eternal life. Everyone receives gifts
of the Holy Spirit and is obliged to serve the community. Everyone has some authority which stems from these gifts as well as
from human qualities of mind and body. The ferment in the
Church today is the recognition that authority moves on many
levels, not just in the top echelons. Everyone is called to exercise
some religious authority in reference to the whole body of
Christ.

The communion model implies that religious authority is
shared more widely in the Church. We are beginning to see that
decisions are made on a cooperative basis; top religious authority receives the advice of other authorities in the Church. Consultation is becoming more widespread and normal before
important decisions are made that affect the local community.

In conjunction with consultation and power sharing, religious
authority also finds it important to persuade and to provide
reasons for a decision or a policy. People want to know the reason
certain directions are taken in liturgy or in doctrine. An adult
Church desires an adult approach to communication and understanding.

Many levels of the Church participate in the building up of
the Church. Ministry, especially administration, is becoming
increasingly participatory. No longer is ministry exercised by
one or two professionals, but many people now participate in the
service of others in Church and society.

Subsidiarity is also a factor in the change in religious authority today. Vatican Council II nudged the Church in this direction, and we are still in the process of testing out this feature of

administration. We have not come far along the road of subsidiarity, but many persons of religious authority have reason to take it into consideration.

The Spirit is also moving the Church in the direction of dialogue. This is not just dialogue with people of other Christian traditions, but it is also inner community dialogue. Dialogue takes place in bible studies, in prayer groups, in social action, in liturgy preparation, et cetera. Since more people are involved in the Church on the local scene, there is of necessity more dialogue. Serious differences appear in these dialogues, but at least the conversation is taking place, something that rarely happened on the local level before Vatican II.

The disciples of Jesus in the United States appreciate their democratic society. While they realize that the Church is not a democracy, they wish for more democratic structures in the Church. Already they elect a parish council and officers of various groups in the parish. They are also wont to let the bishop know what kind of priest they want for their parish, or they let the apostolic nuncio know what kind of bishop they want for their diocese. Some would like an election of both of these offices. The Spirit, it would seem, is moving the Church toward more democratic structures.

Since people understand that they are Church and that Church is not just the hierarchy, they take a deeper interest in the Church. It is *their* Church, and they assume ownership of it. They support it and build it up, not just financially, but by word and service. Ownership involves trust in the reality of the organization and its leaders. People trust themselves to others in the community of disciples, and at the same time they receive the trust of others.

The Spirit is also manifesting a greater participation of women in the religious power and authority of the Church. This movement, too, is in its infant stages, but it is quite evident for all to see. Women are taking degrees in theology, liturgy, canon law, and bible. They work in chancery offices and parish rectories. They assume more and more ministries in schools, hospitals, and parishes: visitation of the sick, care for the poor, instruction of converts, et cetera. Surely, the place of women in the Church of today looks very different from what it was fifty years ago or even at the time of Vatican Council II.

The power of the poor also manifests the presence of the Spirit in the Church today. Their demand for justice has turned the attention of all to the gospel teaching of concern for the poor. They have drawn to their side bishops, priests, religious, and lay people. The poor are teaching the Church, and religious authority is being shaped by their teaching and demands.

Base communities characterize the Church of Latin America where the priest shortage far exceeds that in the United States. The Church of the United States is not marked by base communities, at least not in their full expression as it is in Central and South America. Still, the Church of the United States gives expression to some features of the base communities, and it does this under the movement of the Spirit. Let me quote from Leonard Boff, and I would draw your attention to the features of the movement that I cited in the past few paragraphs:

> . . . the base ecclesial community . . . is a new and original way of living Christian faith, of organizing community around the Word, around the sacraments (when possible), and around new ministries exercised by lay people (both men and women). There is a new distribution of power in the community; it is much more participatory and avoids all centralization and domination. . . . The base ecclesial community is also the place where a true democracy of the people is practiced, where everything is discussed and decided together, where critical thought is encouraged.[30]

## G.  The Experience of Authority

I will close this section on religious authority with a few comments about the way in which the higher levels of authority are experienced. Most bishops, it seems to me, enter their office with a deep sense of the enormity of their tasks. They note the multiplicity of responsibilities that are concentrated in their office: the management of millions of dollars in buildings and lands, decisions about the assignments of priests, preaching the word to large crowds of people on a frequent basis, knowledge of liturgical theology and practice, correspondence with the many people who write to them, confirmation tours, meetings of the National Conference of Catholic Bishops, committee work in the same conference, the writing of articles for the diocesan newspaper, the arbitration of worker disputes, the handling of priests who are alcoholic or sexually deviant, and attendance at sundry social and business meetings. To be sure, the bishop works through all kinds of boards and committees in the actual performance of his tasks, but ultimately he is responsible, and he cannot fail to inform himself about issues so that he can make the proper decisions.

It is a wonder that bishops find satisfaction in their work, but most do. They feel a deep sense of responsibility to the tradition of the Church and to the people they serve. They are hard working people who are grateful for the confidence placed in them.

But, the burdens are not light, and some of them find that they need time off. Witness the recent "sabbatical" of Archbishop John Quinn. Other bishops have needed time off to take care of their alcoholism.

For many bishops the exercise of authority is a crucifixion, especially when they must discipline a priest, deal with sexual or financial scandals that come to their attention, answer irate people who are disturbed with liturgical practices or the preaching of priests, et cetera. Their headaches are many, but so too are their satisfactions in assisting the growth of the community of believers; and they often sense the tangible support of those who help them carry their burdens by a good word and by ready assistance.

Similar statements can be made of the experience of other religious authorities in the Church: priests, deacons, superiors of religious communities, youth ministers, teachers, et cetera. But, time does not permit a listing of their joys and woes. Ministry is not a paradise, but it prepares for it!

## III.  CHARISM IN THE CHURCH

This third and final section deals with the subject of charism. It is a short section, both because I wanted to spend more time on the subject of religious authority and because other speakers assigned the topics of Spirit and ministries will surely reflect on the workings of charisms in the Church.

In the two previous sections I noted the presence of power in the Church, power that stems from the gospel and the resurrection of Jesus Christ. This power is made available in the Church through the presence of believers and religious authorities. I noted the power in everyone who believes, a power that leads to the enhancement of the Church. I insisted that everyone has the authority to enrich the Church. Now, I will look briefly at the forms of enhancement. What is the Spirit giving to the Churches and where is the Spirit moving?

The post-Vatican II Church revels in the Spirit, partly because the Council itself promoted a reconsideration of the place of the Spirit in the midst of the Church. Its words are clear and instructive:

> Allotting his [the Spirit's] gifts according as he wills (cf. Cor 12:11), he also distributes special graces among the faithful of every rank. By these gifts he makes them fit and ready to undertake various tasks and offices for the renewal and building up of the Church, as it is written, "the manifestation of the Spirit is given to everyone for profit" (1 Cor. 12:7). Whether these charisms be very remarkable or more simple and widely diffused,

they are to be received with thanksgiving and consolation since
they are fitting and useful for the needs of the Church.[31]

Francis Sullivan sums up the teaching of Vatican II on the
charism with this definition: "A charism, then, as understood
by Vatican II, can be described as a grace-given capacity and
willingness for some kind of service that contributes to the
renewal and upbuilding of the church."[32]

Vatican II, which promoted the idea of the Church as the
people of God, noted the presence of gifts of the Spirit throughout all levels of the Church. The Spirit fills the whole people of
God, imparting gifts for the upbuilding of the Church. The
Spirit is not confined to pope and bishops, but is present to all
the people in order to make them effective believers and to
empower them for ministry in the Church.

Some of the charisms are extraordinary, and others are simple, but in either case they stem from the one Spirit and manifest
the presence of the Spirit. The Word becomes flesh in Jesus of
Nazareth, but the Spirit becomes concretized in the many charisms of the community. In the words of John Pilch: "They
[charisms] are by definition concretions or individuations of the
Spirit . . . intended solely for the service and upbuilding of the
community."[33]

I will not examine the various charisms listed in the New
Testament,[34] but I wish to indicate that some seem to be more
important than others; note, for example, that Saint Paul lists
tongues and interpretation of tongues in the last place. What is
important is to recognize that all of the charisms express the
favor of God, that all stem from the Spirit, and that all are for
service in the community, not for self-aggrandizement.

### A.  Charisms and Ministries

The words charism and ministry are interrelated and not
adequately distinct from each other. The word charism stresses
the idea of favor; God favors a person with gifts. However, the
gifts are not for self-service, but for service to the people of God.
Thus, they are gifts for the sake of ministry, and it is at this point
that charisms blend into ministries.

The 1982 Lima statement tries to clarify these terms, at least
for its own purposes:

> The word *charism* denotes the gifts bestowed by the Holy Spirit on
> any member of the body of Christ for the building up of the
> community and the fulfilment of its calling. The word *ministry* in
> its broadest sense denotes the service to which the whole people of

God is called, whether as individuals, as a local community, or as
the universal Church. Ministry or ministries can also denote the
particular institutional forms which this service may take. The
term *ordained ministry* refers to persons who have received a charism and whom the church appoints for service by ordination
through the invocation of the Spirit and the laying on of hands.[35]

It is noteworthy that ordained ministry is a charism, a gift of
the Spirit for the benefit of the Church, but yet an appointment
of the Church. The Church must recognize this gift of the Spirit
through a special rite of acknowledgment.

New Testament evidence and the writings of Vatican II make
it clear that no community is without the favor of gifts; no
community is without ministries. Charisms and ministries
belong to the nature of the Church. Without them there is no
Church.

Of course, the Church has not always attended to the multiplicity of charisms and ministries in the Church; sometimes they
have become repressed or coalesced into one office or person, at
least in official thought and practice. The post-Vatican II
Church has seen renewed interest in charism and ministry as
constitutive of the whole Church.

Francis Sullivan points up the close association of charisms
and ministries.[36] He cites in particular 1 Peter 4:10-11: "As
generous distributors of God's manifold grace, put your gifts
(*charisma*) at the service [*diakonountes*] of one another, each in the
measure he has received. The one who speaks is to deliver God's
message. The one who serves [*diakonei*] is to do it with the
strength provided by God."

Sullivan notes in the same place that Vatican II uses the word
ministry, not just for the work of bishops and priests, but also for
the faithful at large:

> The pastors, indeed, know well how much the laity contribute to
> the welfare of the whole Church. For they know that they them-
> selves were not established by Christ to undertake alone the
> whole salvific mission of the Church to the world, but that it is
> their exalted office [*munus*] so to be shepherds of the faithful and
> also recognize the latter's contribution and charisms [*ministra-
> tiones et charismata*] that everyone in his own way will, with one
> mind, cooperate in the common task.[37]

The Catholic bishops of the United States also use the word
ministry to refer to the Christian work and witness that lay
people do in the world. This statement is significant: "Baptism
and confirmation empower all believers to share in some form of
ministry. Although the specific form of participation in ministry
varies according to the gifts of the Holy Spirit, all who share in

this work are united with one another."[38] I single out this matter
for emphasis since recently there is a movement in some circles
for a restriction of the word ministry to the work of bishops and
priests.

Vatican II has moved us in the right direction: its emphasis on
the Church as the people of God and as a community endowed
with many gifts and ministries of the Spirit. It would be an
impoverishment not to recognize these widely distributed gifts.

The Lima statement indicates that charisms are both permanent and temporary: "While some [charisms] serve permanent needs in the life of the community, others will be temporary."[39] This statement implies that the Spirit will attend to the
needs of the Church by providing necessary gifts and charisms.

It should be noted, too, that someone gifted by the Spirit
cannot exactly pass the charisms on to the next person. The
charisms are personal, not used by proxy, and not passed on by
inheritance. They are special gifts of the Spirit. Of course, one
might inherit a disposition to receive them if one is exposed to
them continually in one's life; for example, one might be influenced by a teacher, preacher, or administrator.

We are tempted to draw up an exhaustive list of charisms and
ministries. But, this is not possible, especially since we do not
know the future needs of the Church. At one time the Church
needed to accept the gifts of musicians, ushers, professional
theologians, et cetera. What gifts will be needed in the future?
We do not know, but the Church must be open to the new
charisms of the Spirit.

## B. *Persons of Charism*

Up to this point we have been talking about charism as the
favor of God that is expressed in gifts of the Spirit and is carried
out as ministries for the benefit of the Church. But, now we
should look more directly at the person who receives the charism.

We assume that the person who receives charisms is made
different by them. Even though charisms are not meant for
personal honors, they certainly change the character of the person. Speaking in tongues is a dramatic way of being different in
prayer, but so is the gift of hospitality, the welcoming of people to
the household of faith. The person who assists the poor or the
stranger becomes different as a result of the ministry. Charisms
change people.

The person of charism is gifted by the Spirit, and this gift
shows. But, is it entirely evident that the gift is from the Spirit?
This can never be proved by argumentation or analysis. Who
can discern the God in our midst or the Spirit in our Church?
The discernment can take place only in a context of faith and the
Spirit.

What we observe is akin to what people observe in a so-called "charismatic person." We see a person with a style of leadership or hospitality. We note the attractiveness of the style. We note intelligence and prudence. We note love, compassion, and concern. These are charisms which people generally can recognize. Are they merely human qualities? I claim that their distinctiveness comes both from the human community and from the gift of the Spirit. Surely, the manner in which they are exercised stems from the power of the Spirit as well as from human society, or perhaps from family background. Charism has something to do with talent, but the gifts are released by the power of the Spirit and by the good will of the person.

The charismatic person is in touch with the Christian scriptures and with tradition. This is one way in which people test the spirits of the person who wishes to exercise a ministry. The community will support a person whom it regards as carrying on the gospel tradition; it will not accept the one who appears to deviate from the gospel.

Some whole communities are especially charismatic in the sense that members mutually recognize the various charisms of people, sustain them, and foster their development. Members of such communities listen to each other, to their leaders, and to their culture. The leaders themselves are open to a whole cluster of charisms. In fact, they reflect, represent, and mirror the charisms even as they govern them for the benefit of all the people.

Leaders and the whole community become involved in charisms because there is always the danger of sectarianism. Someone can insist on a work which is not a gift of the Spirit and which is destructive of the community. Someone, for instance, may insist that everyone should speak in tongues in order to belong to the community or that everyone should undergo psychoanalysis (or at least put one's whole psychological life out on the table for the sake of frankness in community). What is needed is a discernment of spirits. This accords with the Johannine tradition: "Beloved, do not trust every spirit, but put the spirits to a test to see if they belong to God, because many false prophets have appeared in the world" (1 John 4:1).

## C. Charisms Today

Where is the Spirit moving people today in the matter of charisms? The Spirit is making it evident that the whole Church is charismatic, that everyone has gifts of the Spirit for the well-being of the Church, and that the gifts need not be extraordinary.

The Spirit is moving people to greater collaboration in ministries. It is the Spirit who inspires people to work together for the
upbuilding of the Church and for the help of society. The movement of collaboration, of course, is not new, but it is being
stressed once again in our days. It is becoming more apparent
today that ministry, even ordained ministry, is a work of collaboration. In fact, the ordained ministry has as one of its principal
tasks the coordination of the many charisms and ministries that
are present in the Church today.

Finally, we find that people are recognizing the work of the
Spirit outside the Christian community. This, too, is a work of
the Spirit: the recognition that God's Spirit is effecting good
works of peace and justice in many communities, e.g., in the
Buddhists of Tibet seeking peace, in the native American seeking justice, in the farmer conserving the soil of the earth. The
Spirit is helping us acknowledge a wide range of God's work.

## CONCLUSION

The Spirit is moving in the Church today, making power,
authority, and charism effective for the upbuilding of the
Church. The Church needs all three realitities (power, authority, and charism) to unite the Church, to form community, and
to bring wholeness and peace to people of faith.

The three realities have always been present to the Church,
but each age has experienced them in a different combination.
In this essay I have tried to articulate the unique way in which
the three of them are present for us, or rather, the way in which
the Spirit is working through power, authority, and charism to
make us the disciples of Jesus Christ.

## NOTES

[1]See Thomas P. McDonnell, "An Interview with Thomas Merton," *Motive* 28 (October 1967): 41. Quoted by John F. Teahan, "Reason, Magisterium, Mysticism—and the Present Crisis in the
Church," *Cistercian Studies* 15 (1980): 426.

[2]Giuseppe Alberigo, "The Authority of the Church in the Docu-
ments of Vatican I and Vatican II," in *Authority in the Church and the
Schillebeeckx Case*, ed. Leonard Swidler and Piet Fransen (New York:
Crossroad, 1982), p. 141.

[3]For a discussion of various forms of power, see Franz Boeckle and
Jacques-Marie Pohier, eds., *Power and the Word of God*, in *Concilium*, vol.
90 (New York: Herder and Herder, 1973).

[4]Joseph Komonchak criticizes the idea of a one-directional flow of
power (from Peter, to bishops, to priests, to lay people) and calls it a
Christo-monism. See "Ministry and the Local Church," *Proceedings of*

*the Catholic Theological Society of America* 36 (1981): 78. Cf. Quentin Quesnell who makes a similar statement about authority: *The Authority for Authority* (Milwaukee: Marquette University Theology Department, 1973), p. 21.

⁵Ibid. p. 25. Another definition of authority puts even more stress on the persons who are subject to authority: "Most characteristically it [authority] stands for an invitation and a summons to men to exercise their freedom in ways indicated by the bearer of authority." [E. J. Yarnold, S. J., and Henry Chadwick, *Truth and Authority. A Commentary on the Agreed Statement of the Anglican-Roman Catholic International Commission: Authority in the Church. Venice 1976* (London: CTS/SPCK, 1977), p. 8.].

⁶John Futrell, S. J., *The Spirituality of Authority* (Ottawa: Canadian Religious Conference, 1985), p. 13.

⁷Ibid., p. 31.

⁸Raymond Brown, *The Churches the Apostles Left Behind* (New York: Paulist Press, 1984), p. 88, note 128.

⁹Cf. the whole passage (Acts 20:17-38) for an extended and moving account of the way in which Paul exercised his ministry to the people of Ephesus and others.

¹⁰Raymond Brown, *The Churches the Apostles Left Behind*, p. 93.

¹¹See Raymond Brown who suggests that Matthew takes precautions with regard to the rabbinic titles of rabbi, father, and master "lest the spirit of the Pharisees enter the church." (Ibid., p.135.)

¹²He is cited by Nicholas Lash, *Voices of Authority* (Shepherdstown, West Virginia: Patmos Press, 1976), p. 23.

¹³Ibid., p. 45.

¹⁴Cited by Y. Congar, *Power and Poverty in the Church* (Baltimore: Helicon, 1964), p.11.

¹⁵Faith and Order Paper No. 111 (Geneva: World Council of Churches, 1982), p. 26, no. 29.

¹⁶Edward Schillebeeckx, *The Church with a Human Face: A New and Expanded Theology of Ministry* (New York: Crossroad, 1985), p. 149.

¹⁷John Jay Hughes, "The Leadership We Need," *Commonweal* 106 (8 June 1979): 334.

¹⁸Dean Hoge, *The Future of Catholic Leadership* (Kansas City, Mo.: Sheed and Ward, 1987), p. x.

¹⁹Ibid., p. 28.

²⁰Ibid., p. 22.

²¹Ibid., pp. 24f.

²²See the results of Hoge's 1985 surveys on the subject of lay leadership, *The Future of Catholic Leadership*, pp. 186-190.

²³Ibid., p. vi.

²⁴Quentin Quesnell, *The Authority for Authority*, p. 16.

²⁵Nicholas Lash, *Voices of Authority*, p. 43.

²⁶Raymond Brown, *The Churches the Apostles Left Behind*, pp. 121f.

²⁷"Decree on the Training of Priests," in *Vatican Council II: The Conciliar and Post-Conciliar Documents*, ed. Austin Flannery, O.P. (Collegeville: The Liturgical Press, 1975), p. 714.

²⁸Dean Hoge, *The Future of Catholic Leadership*, pp. 124 and 191.

[29]*National Catholic Reporter*, 15 April 1988, p. 22.

[30]Leonard Boff, *Church: Charism and Power. Liberation Theology and the Institutional Church* (New York: Crossroad, 1985), p. 9.

[31]"Dogmatic Constitution on the Church," in *Vatican Council II*, p. 363.

[32]Francis Sullivan, *Charisms and Charismatic Renewal* (Ann Arbor, Mi: Servant Books, 1982), p. 13.

[33]John Pilch, *Galatians and Romans* (Collegeville: The Liturgical Press, 1983), p. 61.

[34]See 1 Cor 12; Rm 12:6-8; Eph 4:11-12; 1 Pt 4:10-11.

[35]*Baptism, Eucharist and Ministry*, "Ministry," no. 7, p. 21.

[36]Francis Sullivan, *Charisms and Charismatic Renewal*, p. 82.

[37]"Dogmatic Constitution on the Church," in *Vatican Council II*, p. 388.

[38]*Called and Gifted: The American Catholic Laity* (Washington, D. C.: USCC, 1980), p. 4. See also this statement on page 4 of the same document: "Christian service in the world is represented in a pre-eminent way by the laity. It is sometimes called the 'ministry of the laity' and balances the concept of ministry found in the ecclesial ministerial services. Because of lay persons, Christian service or ministry broadly understood includes civic and public activity, response to the imperatives of peace and justice, and resolution of social, political, and economic conflicts, especially as they influence the poor, oppressed and minorities."

[39]*Baptism, Eucharist and Ministry*, "Ministry," no. 32, p. 27.

# The Spirit in the Quest for Justice

## Sister Marie Augusta Neal, S.N.D. de Namur

Nowhere is there greater consistency with gospel roots in the Catholic Church than in its post-Vatican II social justice agenda. The gospel announces the good news to the poor: they will be poor no longer, but will dwell on the land, secure and content.[1] To the non-poor, it announces that they will be saved if they provide water, food, housing, and freedom to the poor.[2] Yet, no texts have received more convoluted reinterpretations in order to deny the simple reality to which they refer. Even though, in age after age, this promise had been set aside as Utopian, still in 1971 the Church announced it clearly as the gospel agenda for our day: a special option for the poor and the transformation of society to eliminate every oppressive situation.[3] What is it in this period of history that allowed the Church, with the conviction of the Spirit, to dissociate from established channels of action? What empowered it to make a special option to stand with the poor to transform the structures of society, according to long dormant principles of social justice?[4]

I believe that it has to do with the worldwide struggle for liberation among developing peoples and groups. In this essay, I will argue that, in our times, the worker population of the world, be it on the land or in the city, has reached a stage of development that makes all peoples peers in a way that has not previously existed. This development eliminates whatever right any group may have to speak for others without involving them or allowing them to speak for themselves. The good news of the gospel leads us to listen to the Spirit, as it speaks through the people in struggle toward their own liberation. It is this ferment which has emboldened the Church.

The task is new to all of us because the division of labor has changed radically. Teachers are becoming learners as well; interdependence and the sharing and analysis of information are becoming a world style. In 1988, for example, at its annual meeting, the Campaign for Human Development asked its members to consider the reason the Church had taken a "special option for the poor," and what it meant when it invited its members to participate in the "transformation of society." On regional levels, dioceses are setting up study days to examine the political, economic, and social conditions of society, in preparation for taking action to change unjust structures. The bishops have written pastorals on race, ethnicity, peace, and the economy; they are now working on one concerning women. All of this activity is a response to *A Call to Action,* that elicited response around the world in 1971, after the Bishops' World Synod declared:

> Action in behalf of justice and participation in the transformation of the world fully appear to us as a constitutive dimension of the preaching of the Gospel, or, in other words, of the Church's mission for the redemption of the human race and its liberation from every oppressive situation.[5]

This clarion call to action became the theme of the first national conference of Catholics in the United States in the Bicentennial year, 1976. The meeting was entitled: "A Call to Action." What has happened that stirs this national and international activity, focusing on social justice and urging participation on the part of all committed Christians? Those who speak to the new agenda take care to cite its biblical roots, its historical precedents in Church history, and its current response to the signs of the times. All these factors indicate that it is a movement of the Spirit.

   In the pages that follow, I will try to demonstrate the profound changes in our human situation that have called forth this new direction of life in the Church, the depth of the subtle resistance to it, and the evidence that it is indeed of the Spirit. Basically, for the first time in history, we have become one human community, struggling to recognize one another as peers. We are able to cope with the reality of our communal solidarity because the problems facing us are global and are no longer unsolvable. For many people, however, this call to global solidarity contradicts their definition of the situation so completely that they cannot consider it, despite the evidence that we are becoming an interdependent world. Consider, for example, the implications of this question: how many people are there in your community? Who of us will spontaneously answer, "five billion"? It is true that we are beginning to realize that in production, finance, and trade we are one world of competing parts, in which the more powerful and less powerful are in constant struggle. Still, many of us do not have to take one another's existence seriously any more than we did in the past. We see our jobs moving overseas as our technology changes; our former enemies, our trading partners; our creditors, non-English speaking.

   Although our global ties are made explicit through the United

Nations, they continue weak nonetheless, despite the fact that their base has been strengthened in the covenants of the United Nations Bill of Human Rights. Therein, we affirm the political and civil rights of all peoples, as well as their social, economic, and cultural rights. Further, we affirm "the rights of every people to self-determination and to enjoy and utilize fully and freely their natural wealth and resources."[6] This covenant of human rights, a twentieth century achievement, is the modern formulation of a biblical mandate. It is the Spirit moving in the Church; it points to the future of institutionalized altruism.[7] We will come back to this point later. But, is it the spirit of God which inspires this full realization of human dignity and the common good? I would submit that, for many, the God of history is still perceived as embodied in the nation state, where we are "one people under God," a people who can be called forth to celebrate national unity and to fight other peoples in the name of that God. Although we will expect, in some cases, to die in that effort to give our lives for our country, we are not ready yet to give our lives for our world. Nevertheless, the mandates of our religion call for that wider commitment beyond the nation state and inclusive of all peoples; human survival needs it today, and the social justice agenda of the Church prepares us for it.

The movement toward this one world commitment has already begun. Christianity has always identified with the poorest of the poor. It is not unexpected, then, that a strong sense of God's presence with the organizing poor, taking the initiative to change unjust structures which have victimized them, is characteristic of new liberation theology today.[8] The reality of liberation theology is strong in base Christian communities in different parts of the world. In these communities, deliberating the gospel and literally speaking in many tongues are directly associated with the living out of the social justice agenda of the Church universal.[9] There is a sense that God is with the dispossessed peoples of the world as they are reaching out to claim what is rightfully theirs. Some of God's more traditional allies, however, interpret the third world struggles as atheistic. These struggles are, therefore, to be crushed, violently if need be, either in the national political interest of those adversaries or in the private economic interests of more technologically developed organizations of finance or industry. This negative response to the efforts toward self-determination of Third World nations and of the organizing poor within developed nations is rationalized to be just among both committed Christians and others. They make this claim on the basis of their belief in a human incapacity to move beyond innate greed. Sometimes, this is equated with our proneness for sin; but, more often today, it is assumed to be part of human nature. I believe that this assumption of natural greed is a subtle political cooptation of religion and/or science. It is used to establish a credible base from which to enhance advantage in a struggle for ascendancy in First and Second World nations. Furthermore, it is a position that is not even practical any longer because of new initiatives coming from the Third World.

The development of initiative for self-determination in Third World countries, as well as the organizing of the homeless and the undocumented workers and welfare mothers for life-support legislation here in the United States, suggest clearly that the rights they claim are valid but, as yet, unprotected by law. They are, moreover, rooted in values still unrealized and relatively untaught in the current educational and social welfare programs. They are rights and values often ignored too in the university curriculum, and even in religious formation for preaching and for practice.[10] A world without God is conveniently created by the socializers to legitimate policies and programs that belie Scripture and theology. Subtle distinction is made between the spiritual and the material. Such a dichotomy obscures the centrality to the gospel of the social justice agenda and the urgency of its solution, beyond the love platitudes of reflection groups and the philosophical claims to the naturalness of self-interest. In such a world, are we in any sense a community of five billion people? A decade ago, Edward O. Wilson, in his Pulitzer Prize-winning volume, proclaimed that our genuine love of others, to the point of risking our lives for them, could not extend beyond our nearest relatives, and that God can be explained away by scientific naturalism, except for a possible final redoubt as creator of the universe.[11] After three centuries of dovetailing science, reason and faith, in the context of the Enlightenment, Western culture, including Christian churches, is now fairly comfortable with his thesis.

What are the implications of that thesis? They will sound familiar. According to Wilson, it is time we recognized, as a foundation for our social ethic, that our eternity is genetically programmed. He claims that we naturally act in our own self-interest and extend love of the other no farther than our nearest of kin, to ensure our chances of eternal life through gene replacement. He asserts that we live on in our progeny, for whom we are willing to die. Beyond this circle of very close relatives, he claims, kind behavior is characteristically reciprocal service of social contract; all the skills of guile can be fairly used in the political and economic arena (which life necessarily becomes) to

further one's own advantage toward the acquisition and reten-
tion of power and wealth.[12] In this competitive system, religion
explicitly becomes a major tool for getting what we want and
feeling justified in retaining it.

These premises comprise a pragmatism which is cruel but
acceptable to many. It is used to justify three centuries of acquisi-
tive action on the part of First World countries, which use liberal
capitalism to establish ascendancy in worldwide competition for
control of resources, including those essential for human survival. At the present moment, the powerful nations are the
United States and the Soviet Union. The struggle concentrates
on control over nuclear warfare and extra-territorial space mili-
tarization. This confrontation occurs within the political guiding ethic of national self-interest and aid to our allies. Politics in
this struggle is secular and firmly grounded in the assumption of
the rightness of nations' acting in their own self-interest. God,
where accepted, is assumed to be protecting the nation. Each
nation has its own ideas of God's functions. At the same time,
the economy, which operates beyond the bounds of the nation, is
secularized in its claims to seek personal profit as an ultimate
purpose. All this fits comfortably into a secularization theory
which incorporates a variety of religions, but no common ethic
that binds human behavior to any standard of right. There is,
however, a counter-movement that belies this easy trend to secularization.[13] Western theologians find it difficult to name and to
locate God. In the Third World, however, God's immanence is
not challenged. In fact, faith in God's presence is so strong that
officially atheistic communism is softening its strategic stand
against God, at the insistence of the practice of biblical religion
on the part of the organizing poor who know God's presence in
their midst.

Selfishness plays a major role in the conditioning of international and local politics, economics, family socialization, education, and all the other service institutions. But, it does so most
especially in religion, as it confronts the real atheism of modern
society, now embedded in class analysis and struggle. It does so
by narrowing the community of concern to people like ourselves. I use Wilson's *On Human Nature* to demonstrate the ideo-
logical use of science to affirm the structures of capitalist societies and their control over the resources of the world in their
current unequal distribution. There is, in this process as presented by Wilson, no intention to eliminate religion, but rather
to demonstrate as natural its adaptation to entrenched interest
groups. Social ethics is the field ultimately exploited, but the
social sciences are the place where this secular analysis is devel-

oped. The effects are resisting the initiatives of Third World
peoples, as they organize themselves to claim their rights, and so
managing the allocation of resources that poverty persists even
in affluent nations and does so with the support of Christian
communities within those nations. This is done by replacing
justice with charity.

The timing is right, I think, for examining the relationship of
Spirit to the shaping of world community. The self-interest philosophy that subsumes the rationale for First and Second World
hegemony is based on an assumption that is now obsolete: since
there are too many people in the world and not enough resources
to provide for them, we have to protect and care for our own
first.[14] We can demonstrate today, with facts and projections,
that these assumptions are false, even though still useful for
profiteers to justify the advantage of a powerful minority. We
need to address the ethic of self-interest, not only because it rests
on false premises, but also because of the pain and suffering its
application causes through the destruction of peoples. This concern, however, cannot be addressed effectively, so long as the
ethic of justified group interest holds in the teaching of the social
sciences and also in the teaching of religion. We will return to
this point further on.

On one level, the question of distributing resources is: who is
"our own"? To respond is to begin by appealing to the fact that,
in our times, there are sufficient resources for the survival of all.
What is this new evidence? Ever since Thomas Malthus hypothe-
sized, in the nineteenth century, that population would increase
geometrically while food supply would increase only arithmeti-
cally, ethicists have developed arguments for justifying hoarding
of resources to protect one's own progeny.[15] In 1950, when
calculations showed that the world population, that had taken
9500 years to reach one billion people, had doubled in just one
century, we were faced with fear of world starvation because of
the population explosion. In 1975, when the population had
again doubled and was then four billion in the interval of only
twenty-five years, that fear had become intense. Since 1980,
however, annual calculations, based on several variables and
projected through the year 2100, clearly indicate that the world
population will probably level off at 10.5 billion.[16] This does not
mean that specific nations do not now have an overpopulation
problem. It does mean, however, that countries with customs
and cultures very different by nation decrease in population rate
of natural increase as technology is introduced and as health care
and education develop. As a result, children survive, and people
live longer. In summary, we can say that as poverty declines, so

does population. If poverty is defined as low infant mortality rate, high life expectancy, and high GNP per capita, this pattern becomes quite consistent.[17]

Since 1984, scholars, studying world resources and trying to determine whether natural resources for food, shelter and other needs will provide for a population of the size predicted, have become cautiously optimistic. Serious studies of needed resources and their replenishment are underway. Reports are being made for scientists, scholars, and the general public to assess the situation in order to make judgments concerning the way to steward these resources to assure continuing supplies for human need.[18] Of course, it will take both planning and organization, intentionally addressed to this end. At this time, the possibility of supplying for the needs of all people can be assured, but the public will to do so is sorely lacking. It is my thesis that the lack of public will is a function of religious belief, as of other factors. New religions are rising up to seek immediate divine intervention for the solution of problems God has already provided for through human social action.[19] At the same time, the Church, responding to the movement of the Spirit, has been persistently moving to a new prophetic stance in spiritual guidance, directed to aid the structure of the social organization essential for the sharing of available resources. The form which the provision for human need takes today, however, is not the charity model of the recent past, intended to alleviate the results of poverty, but the justice model affirmed in Church assembly.

If implemented, this justice model will move us to social action for the elimination of the causes of poverty. These causes, to be found in the social structures, call for institutional change. First World peoples are increasingly aware that, in population size, they are decreasing while Third World peoples are still increasing. The new peoples in our cities are Latin Americans, Asians, and Africans. Just as, a hundred and fifty years ago, Irish, Germans, Italians, Poles and other southern and eastern European peoples came to America to escape famine and poor working conditions, so now the movement of peoples from the southern hemisphere is worldwide into centers of technology and development. In the previous century, most of the immigrants were Catholic; in the present century, it is the newly affluent Catholics, along with their Protestant and Jewish neighbors, who are receiving these new populations. The Church, through its missionary experience, has met the new immigrants in their places of origin and has heard their stories of struggle. Through its social documents, it has affirmed their rights to move to new lands and share in world resources, which have been expanded by the application of new technologies. Old ethnic groups often reject the challenge of hospitality from their Church and resist welcoming the new neighbors. Although a hundred years of Church teaching have been preparing us for a new openness to the stranger as neighbor and peer, traditions of hierarchy and control still blind us to this radical new direction of the Spirit.

In 1891, it was the industrial worker who was supported by the new encyclicals; by 1981, the city worker had joined with the farmer, and both now link with the developing peoples in the acclaim of their rights to share in the resources of produce and service.[20] The means of this sharing will be our tax monies, but the motivation for it will come from our transformation of consciousness. We are hardly prepared for this change. The Spirit moving in the Church finds us resistantly looking toward old models for the solution of new problems. We do so because our social ethics comfortably accept the inertia inherent in subtle assumptions of a gene-generated natural selfishness or sinfulness, eschewing the inspiration to change in a corresponding theology of conversion and/or resurrection.[21]

But, why is our faith concern centered now on material well-being? Surely, some protest, our faith transcends these material interests. Not so. Concern for material well-being has to do with God and love and faith. No one of faith doubts that altruism is the core biblical virtue. To love God with one's whole heart and mind and to love neighbor as oneself for the love of God — this is the fulfillment of the law and the prophets.[22] And, who is my neighbor? That, too, has a most familiar ring. We know the man on the road to Jericho who stops to attend the victim left to die by robbers. The altruist tends the victim's wounds, takes the trouble to bring him to the inn, and promises to pay all his expenses on his return, thus extending his service to see that all that is needed is, in fact, done. The message is clear. The neighbor is not just the family next door; no, the neighbor is the stranger with a need. The actor is not the priest or the person of status. Although these may even neglect their function, still the ordinary person, perhaps himself/herself an outcast, is expected to be altruistic. The disinterested love of the other, the giving of one's entire life in the service of those with a need, is what is asked of the ordinary believers in the Christian tradition. Sharing resources with those who have none and caring for the preservation of the life of the stranger are not only presented as behaviors to be emulated but also as behaviors to which is attached the promise of eternal life.[23]

The biblical evidence for equitable sharing is strong. In

Leviticus 25: 10-28, the jubilee and the sabbatical are designed
to assure that the land returns to the people, that any loss of the
ancestral rights to the land be restored every fifty years. The
sabbatical is given to reflect on our faithfulness to this duty and
to provide an environment for reform, if we have deviated from
it. Sin in the New Testament is repented by giving food to the
hungry and, if one has two coats, by giving one to someone who
has none.[24] If that constitutes repentance, it is quite clear that sin
is possessing abundance when others suffer from lack of
resources. The rich young man went away sadly, after asking
Jesus what he should do to be saved. The answer, "Go sell what
you have, give it to the poor and come follow me," was too much
for him because "he had so many possessions."[25] Jesus' reflection that "it is harder for a rich person to get into heaven than for
a camel to get through the eye of a needle" has been distorted
with much exegesis, but the message is clear: possessions were
meant to be shared.[26] In Deuteronomy, we read:

> If there is among you a poor man, one of your brothers in any of
> your towns within your land that the lord your God gives you,
> you shall not harden your heart or shut your hand against your
> poor brother but you shall open your hand to him and lend him
> sufficient for his need, whatever it may be.[27]

Later, Isaiah cried out against the landlord who accumulated
tenants' farms while the people went homeless.[28] For centuries,
we have managed to be inspired by these passages and, at the
same time, to gain wealth and power against our neighbors,
until the conditions have become so unjust that circumstances
cry out for reform.

Earlier, I cited a bias of self-interest in the teaching of the
social sciences, such that mistaken assumptions taught preclude
the achieving of their scientific objective: the understanding of
social order and social change. Ideology has preempted the analysis and control of culture. In sociology, these assumptions take
the form of presenting functional and conflict theory, as well as
symbolic interaction and exchange theory, as a smorgasbord for
the student to choose from in order to make interpretations of
social reality.[29] In economics, the reality of scarcity is assumed,
even though scarcity has to be artificially created by reducing
production to fit the model. Political science accepts the norm of
national self-interest as a given, not to be challenged, even when
powerful nations control survival resources in the less developed
nations struggling for self-determination.

New historical realities now move us to a conscious choice: to
share with all so that all can live or to continue to allow some to
acquire unlimited wealth and power by forcing others to die.

There is no scarcity to justify, on any level, the hoarding of accumulated wealth. There are no ethical grounds for the current continuing disparity between rich and poor. The poor and dispossessed of the world, through processes of conscientization, were coming to realize this in the 1960s, as literacy levels rose and media of communications radically extended awareness of the socio-economic inequities of existing conditions.[30] Once having become aware of their rights as human beings, the exploited peoples could no longer tolerate their subjugated situations. They began to speak out and to organize. The turning point on this ethic was becoming apparent in the civil rights movement, the Third World movement, and the women's movement in the 1960s. That three-fold emergence accounts for the confusion in the analysis of the student movements of that era. The university was not prepared for those conflicting but related uprisings of minorities, Third World peoples, and women. Students in Western societies were exposed to contradictory signals: They were told that it was movements of peoples claiming their rights and that these movements were being manipulated by atheistic communists. Yet, students felt the excitement and hope in the activities of the organizing poor. They were constantly warned against the atheism and violence of communism which was accused of competing for power with Western capitalism by proffering development assistance in the Third World. Yet, the students were being educated within the assumptions of an equally atheistic and secularized liberal capitalism, which, however, had come to terms with institutionalized Western traditional religions.

In the mid-seventies, the discipline of sociobiology captured the attention and interest of those who reflected on the human condition, when it proposed anew a strong genetic base to human selfishness. By claiming that scientific evidence would demonstrate the natural limitations of altruism, sociobiology justified narrowing the community of concern to "our own" progeny and programming social action to that end. It claimed that no cultural development, no matter how unselfish, could replace our natural struggle for personal survival because "genes have culture on a leash." It asserted that selfishness will prevail because all of culture, including religion especially, is but nature's way of protecting a gene pool from the land claims of strangers, seeking in competition the ascendancy of their own tribes in a natural warfare that can only be rationalized but never eliminated.[31] Sociobiologists argued, further, that the taming could be done only in a *quid pro quo* arrangement of realpolitik because the rules of the game are primarily and always based on deceit and lying.[32] Wilson, the main proponent of this thesis, argued from the premises of scientific naturalism. He claimed that three great myths guide our thinking today about human nature: 1. scientific naturalism; 2. Communism; 3. traditional religion. He predicted that the last two would be eliminated. Of Marxism, he said: "Although Marxism was formulated as the enemy of ignorance and superstition, to the extent that it has become dogmatic it has faulted in that commitment and is now mortally threatened by the discoveries of human sociobiology."[33] Of traditional religion, he says:

> But if Marxism is only a satrap so to speak, traditional religion is not. As science proceeds to dismantle the ancient mythic stories one by one, theology retreats to the final redoubt from which it can never be driven. This is the idea of God in the creation myth: God as will, the cause of existence and the agent who generated all the energy in the original fireball and set the natural laws by which the universe evolved. So long as the redoubt exists, theology can slip out through its portals and make sallies back into the real world.
> If this interpretation is correct, the final decisive edge enjoyed by scientific naturalism will come from its capacity to explain traditional religion, its chief competitor as a wholly material phenomenon. Theology is not likely to survive as an independent intellectual discipline. But religion itself will endure for a long time as a vital force in society.[34]

What role did Wilson expect religion to play as a vital force in society? He expected religion to be engaged in the "great new enterprise" of building a moral consensus, based on the assumption of our essential selfishness. That accomplished, we can structure all social relationships on a social contract of practicality and fairness, since the presumption would have prevailed that human nature is capable only of protecting its genetic fitness for survival in a highly competitive struggle for ascendancy. This is the way he expressed it: "If religion, including dogmatic secular ideologies, can be systematically analyzed and explained as a product of the brain's evolution, its power as an external source of morality will be gone forever . . ."[35]

According to Wilson's thesis: "Because natural selection has acted on the behavior of individuals who benefit themselves and their immediate relatives, human nature bends us to the imperatives of selfishness and tribalism."[36] Wilson's efforts are concentrated on accounting for religion as a product of the brain's evolution. In that case, it could no longer be treated as an independent guide to ethical behavior that might, on occasion, call a halt to trends which enhance "our" advantage over "theirs," that is, over that of the stranger with a need. This firm grounding of "our" advantage would then halt the threat of humanitarian trends. He says: "What I am suggesting is that the evolutionary epic is probably the best myth that we will ever have."[37]

If all that Wilson argues were true, then the myth of altruism would not be a realizable goal for a world religion. Even to suggest it is as such would be obstructive of the substitute human goal of refined social contract. Furthermore, by setting up unachievable ideals, religion becomes a liability for healthy psychic adjustment. He sought to substitute for it what he considered to be a healthy selfishness.[38] But, why did he devote so much scholarly effort to challenging "traditional religion" and trying to ferret it out even of its last redoubt? First of all, in his reference to traditional religion, Wilson is referring to Christianity in its Protestant and Catholic forms, and to Judaism and Islam, in so far as they treat of this same centrality of altruism over tribalism. He had already recognized that Marxism and Christianity proposed the same goal for our times: the liberation of the poor from a condition in which they lack food, shelter, education, health care, social security, and meaningful work. But, while Marxism rooted its initiative in a theory of dialectical materialism, traditional religion claimed God on its side. This created a problem, because, in the Western tradition, that God, perceived as a powerful ally of each state, was being called upon to inspire the people to national patriotism. This was done with some degree of success, because, for many, the ultimate institutional altruistic act has become that of dying for the sake of one's country.

Analyzing the sociobiological perspective, with its criticism of liberation goals, allows one to see more sharply both communism and traditional religion challenging the rights claimed by advantaged nations over other nations through military power, financial power, control of productive forces and of land. This new social science was proposing, unabashedly, a theory that legitimated, on scientific grounds, the maintaining of the military and economic ascendancy that western Europe and North America had achieved. By pursuing religion only as a dependent variable, the social scientist, in effect, was assisting to discredit the new religious life rising out of the Latin American base Christian communities, which were using the process of conscientization and biblical reflection.[39] This reduction of religion to a dependent variable confuses Christianity with communism. Wilson's analysis makes religion, as well as all of culture, epiphenomenal in the Marxist sense. For, even though the biblical mandate for the rights of the poor to share in the products of industry is very clear in Church documents, from his perspective it would have no divine inspirational imperative. From the viewpoint of Third World initiatives, such scientific studies, which sought to destroy the concept of altruism as a virtue and a human commitment, were clearly political and élitist in intent. It is to be recalled, however, that liberation theology, too, has been interpreted by many as playing a political power role, even by some Church functionaries.[40]

When we examine Church history, we frequently find sinners as well as saints. Almost every era portrays the way the Church has been caught up into the interests of established power and the way some of its ministers have, on occasion, succumbed to the enticements of wealth, sensuality, pride, greed, envy, anger, and power. Still, at the same time, we see, too, the prophetic function of religion entering into history, providing for reform and conversion, and influencing to altruism. We are still writing the books about the 1960s, trying to explain the rebellion of youth and their transition to yuppyism.[41] Each time, we miss the reality, however, that all of them did not become yuppies. Some went to work with the poor in the most neglected places. Some did this as a faith call. Others experienced what liberation theology records as God's presence with the organizing poor. They did this because they felt mandated by the Church's new spirit-filled option for the poor and commitment to the transformation of society, a mission of new direction and challenge of the very roots of its own institutional structure.

Consider, for example, the hypothesis that the upsurge of interest in altruistic behavior at mid-twentieth century was stimulated by the movement within the Church to make a radical break with societal establishment. It did so in order to call the world to a new structuring of its institutions, the better to realize the biblical mandates to share the fruits of the land with those who sit on it. Deciding to make an option for the poor, the Church responded to new possibilities latent in the new technology and population realities, which indicated that the time was right for a new interpretation of the gospel mandate to the rich and to the poor.

Can our human nature accept this new agenda? The fact is that it has already begun to do so. In Latin America, Africa, and now Asia, where new nations are rising through self-determination and claiming their rights to the resources of the land, a new spirit resides. Resistance to their efforts comes from more powerful nations that organize against their self-determination. The powerful nations do this to assure that the new governments will not challenge their established interests.

Accordingly, they set limiting conditions on the aid which they promise and which is so needed in the initial years of self-government and development. Mozambique, Angola, Zimbabwe, Chile, Brazil, Cuba, Nicaragua, El Salvador, and Haiti are cases in point. There are many others. As an example of the resistance to the Spirit, consider the case of Third World debt. The developing nations need either no-interest or low-interest loans, with long-term repayment arrangements. The peoples of those nations have been seriously wounded, like the stranger on the road to Jericho. What is offered, however, is not healing but punitive in the form of short-term, high-interest loans, to the profit of the loaning agency. The results are the current Third World debt crises.[42]

One of the altrusitic failures countenanced by the modern Church has to do precisely with the charging of interest on loans. By today's standards, we might scorn this comment, because, after all, business is business. But, in fact, in the high Middle Ages, charging such interest was considered sin and crime. Today, it is assumed to be natural. Max Weber did a brilliant study accounting for the rise of capitalism by asking: how did an action defined clearly as sin in the Middle Ages become high virtue? How did the pursuit of profit become a virtue in Protestant towns and then inspire the thrift, hard work and initiative that assisted in the accumulation of capital to invest in the effective development of Western style industrialization? He found the answer in the salvation doctrine of Protestantism, which took the ethic of the monastery, "to work is to pray," and applied it to the marketplace. Thus were supplied generations of faithful workers in a new productive force that supplied the necessities of life and promised salvation as well.[43] Today, we need to institutionalize another and equally vibrant ethic with the power to inspire the world's peoples to offer human services, as successfully, or more so, as the old ethic produced highly motivated workers and entrepreneurs. Current human deprivation calls for a new ethic of institutionalized altruism, a deeply held rule of human behavior that recognizes and realizes the right of every one to health care, education, social security, food and shelter, as well as to full participation in the decisions that affect their lives. The fact that communism has tried to realize this value without God is not a reason to prevent the Church's efforts to do so, but within a gospel mandate. A hundred years of Vatican social teaching attempts to move in that direction.[44]

Since 1891, the Church has been working on this new ethic. It was associated, at first, with the rights of workers to sufficient wages. Then, its focus moved on to the rights of the developing

peoples in the 1960s and in the 1980s, challenging unjust structures of capitalism and communism where they ignored human
want or curtailed human freedom.[45] That ethic is well on its way
into full being, through the acceptance of the United Nations
Convenants on Human Rights and the socialization of theology,
formalized as liberation theology. Serving as channels of its
implementation are Church-related groups, including religious
congregations of women and men in their statements of mission
and new lay perceptions brought to religious education.[46] But,
unfortunately, the churches are also, at times, the channels of
greatest opposition to the development of this ethic, because of
the historic tradition of acting for the poor instead of with them,
in the older Catholic Action tradition of élite leadership for social
causes.[47] In the past, there may have been scope for action by
dedicated élite, but certainly not now, especially not in the post-
Vatican II era.

The Second Vatican Council, convoked in 1963, brought
together an agenda that resulted in the announcement of a new
strategy for human development. That new strategy took into
account the fact that the dispossessed of the world, having heard
the message of the gospel, were experiencing themselves as
agents of their own destiny and were organizing to claim their
rights. The Church in the Council recognized that reality and,
choosing to realign itself, turned from working primarily
through the converted power élite to standing with the emerging
newly freed poor. Paulo Freire's method of *conscientization* is a
case in point. This process helps newly liberated peoples to
discover their rights to the resources of their land and to take
action to claim them.[48] From this perspective, it was not surprising that at the Second Vatican Council we were advised in
*Gaudium et Spes:*[49]

> God has meant the earth and all it contains for the use of the
> whole human race. Created wealth should be shared fairly by all
> human kind, under the aegis of justice and accompanied by
> charity. Whatever the form of property holding, we must not lose
> sight of the universal purpose of wealth.[50]

In 1971, *The Call to Action* was published, the encyclical of
Pope Paul VI on the eightieth anniversary of the first of the
papal letters on the conditions of the workers of the world. *The
Call to Action* mandated full political participation of all committed Christians to transform the structures of society according to
standards of social justice. Making that mandate more operative
became the task of the Bishops' Synod of 1971. It was there that
the doing of the justice agenda was stated in unambiguous terms
to be a "constitutive dimension of the preaching of the gospel."

Theologian Edward Schillebeeckx predicted, in 1978, that
implementing this mandate would be done at risk of life. He

wrote two years before Oscar Romero sought to effect the return of land to the people in El Salvador and was gunned down at the altar for so doing.[51] Romero himself sensed what his fate would be, if he attempted to implement the mission of sharing resources with the poor. He said:

> As a pastor, I am obliged by divine mandate to give my life for those I love—for all Salvadorans, even for those who may be going to kill me. If the threats come to be fulfilled, from this moment, I offer my blood to God for the redemption and for the resurrection of El Salvador. Let my death, if it is accepted by God, be for the liberation of my people and as a witness of hope in the future. A bishop will die, but the Church of God, which is the people, will never perish.[52]

Two months later, he was dead.

In 1988, on the twentieth anniversary of the publication of *Populorum Progressio,* Pope Paul VI's encyclical on the development of peoples as a central concern for social action, Pope John Paul II made a strong indictment of both capitalism and communism for confronting each other and holding the threat of nuclear annihilation over the whole world. He blamed liberal economics and collectivist communism in the two power blocs precisely for preventing the development of peoples. He called their economic and political structures of society structures of sin, when they prevent the production and distribution of goods and services needed for human development. Pope John Paul II states in *Sollicitudo Rei Socialis:*

> This determination is based on the solid conviction that what is hindering full development is that desire for profit and thirst for power already mentioned. These attitudes and "structures of sin" are only conquered—presupposing the help of divine grace—by a diametrically opposed attitude: a commitment to the good of one's neighbor with the readiness, in the gospel sense, to "lose oneself" for the sake of the other instead of exploiting him, and to "serve him" instead of oppressing him for one's own advantage (cf. Mt 10:40-42; 20:25; Mk 10: 42-45; Lk 22: 25-27) (#38).

This criticism of the "structures of sin" calls for the Church to dissociate itself from them and to identify with the poor as they organize to claim a just share of the resources of the world. Because his observations mandate some radical disassociations, it is useful to consider them in some detail. First, he says:

> Our daily life as well as our decisions in political and economic fields must be marked by these realities (i.e., the conditions of the poor of the world). Likewise the leaders of nations and heads of international bodies, while they are obliged always to keep in

mind the true human dimensions as a priority in their development plans, should not forget to give precedence to the phenomenon of growing poverty. Unfortunately, instead of becoming
fewer the poor are becoming more numerous, not only in less
developed countries but—and this seems no less scandalous—in
the more developed ones too.

Then he says:

It is necessary to state once more the characteristic principle of
Christian social doctrine: the goods of this world are originally
meant for all. The right to private property is valid and necessary, but it does not nullify the value of this principle. Private
property, in fact, is under a "social mortgage," which means that
it has an intrinsically social function, based upon and justified
precisely by the principle of the universal destination of
goods. . . . (#42).

and further:

The motivating concern for the poor—who are, in the very
meaningful term, "the Lord's poor"—must be translated at all
levels into concrete actions, until it decisively attains a series of
necessary reforms. . . . (#43).

The Pope includes among the structures needing reform: local
situations; the international trade system; the world monetary
and financial system; forms of technology and their exchange
(#53).

This labeling of the structures of our political economy as
structures of sin marks almost one hundred years of Vatican
teaching concerning the rights of the factory worker to a fair
share of the profits of industry and of landless peasants to ownership. We trace the movement over the years of Church teaching
on social issues: *Rerum Novarum* (1891), affirming the right of
workers to a fair share of the profits of industry sufficient to live
in simple dignity with their families; *Quadragesimo Anno* (1931),
*On the Reconstruction of the Social Order,* accepting the strike and the
boycott as tools to enhance the power of the organized workers
meeting managers and owners at the bargaining table; *Mater et
Magistra* (1961), chiding the Church of Latin America for its
close ties with state power and wealthy industry and urging a
realignment with the dispossessed poor; and *Octogesima Adveniens*
(1971), inviting all committed Christians to political action to
bring the institutions of society into conformity with principles
of justice and peace. In 1981, on the ninetieth anniversary of the
first of the social encyclicals recognizing the priority of labor
over capital in the development of rights to the land, Pope John
Paul II wrote the encyclical, *Laborem Exercens*. [54] We can perceive,
therefore, that the Church has gradually been moving to a new

position in world ethics. The World Council of Churches has initiated and joined in a similar movement.[55]

Historically, the Church's stand has been with the established structures of power and authority to reinforce civil laws in the common interest. The new position of the Church, therefore, is a prophetic one, since it denounces inadequate existing institutional arrangements and calls for new structures to serve the needs of all peoples. This action, praiseworthy in its intent, is disturbing to many, because it withdraws the ceremonial reinforcement of religious practice from its customary support of societal laws and customs. Will, then, such a progressive social stance divide the Church from within? Yes. Will it endanger the lives of some? Yes. Are Christians called to risk their lives in this agenda? Again, yes. Is it a true agenda for a Church, or is it merely a political diversion from "real" religion? The answer, once again, is that it is, indeed, an appropriate agenda. However, a caution is in order, since the possibility of co-optation is always present. Soft-heartedness can be accompanied by soft-headedness, as Sorokin noted so well in the 1950s.[56] That dual relationship, however, is not an inevitable one, as some would have us think. The direction preached by Jesus and witnessed to by the prophets long ago is now that of the Church, when it mandates its members to make an option for the poor and to work for the elimination of injustice in social institutions. What else can we interpret this to be but the Spirit active in our times and responding to new realities that do not fit into old institutional practices? This is truly a prophetic stance: the standing apart from what has become evil in its institutional form and calling society to a new set of customs and norms, in order to assure a just sharing for all in the planning, production, and distribution of goods and services.[57]

The associative relationship of Church and State is not creative fiction. Sociology of religion demonstrates, with ample evidence, the way religions do function to reinforce the power of the State. In Greek times, the *pietas* of Aeneas, as he packed his household gods on his back with his revered father and set out to found the city of Rome, made no distinction between faithfulness to religion and loyalty to the State. The Chinese emperors, Russian Czars, Japanese shoguns, as well as the heads of emerging European countries, claimed divine right. The medieval Church solemnly recognized that divine right in the anointing of kings. God spoke directly to the ruler, it was believed, and his anointing by the Pope or Patriarch assured the liturgical alliance and accommodation of Church and State. In its religious orientation, early modern Germany was Protestant; Austria, Catholic; France, Catholic; England, Episcopal. In the United States, Massachusetts started as Calvinist; Maryland, Catholic; and Virginia, Episcopal, because the founders assumed that State and Church went hand in hand. Max Weber distinguished the roles of priest and prophet, so that we could analyze the conditions under which the Church can justify standing against the law, in the interests of social justice.[58] In all of these questions of Church-State relations and issues of law and justice, the role of authority is often raised. Authority is the right to use power. It resides in the person who responds. Although it is expressed through the tradition, or in the charism of a new leader, or in the law itself, it becomes operative only when the people recognize it. If those for whom it has been written neither believe in the tradition nor experience its charism nor respect the law, none of those in administrative control can elicit the cooperative behavior essential for effective governance without using ultimate power; that is, violence.[59] "Taxation without representation is tyranny" was the definition of the situation that justified, for our civic forebears in the United States, a revolt against oppressive laws and customs. Our nation was founded on that dissociation of a new patriotism from established institutions. Yet, in our day, when other peoples strive to throw off tyrannical leaders, we, as Americans, often choose sides in their struggle, not on the basis of the justice of their cause, but on principles we hold with ethical assurance. We think and act in what we term our national self-interest. Therefore, when there is a problem relating to human need that is solvable, we do not always act justly. For example, we can produce more than enough food to feed the whole world, so much, indeed, that we pay farmers not to produce it, lest there be an imbalance in our trading system. Nonetheless, we concur with that curtailment, even knowing that one third of the world's people are going to bed hungry and 800 million are becoming chronically ill or even dying because of that decision.[60] Garrett Hardin chided us as a nation, when we let Cambodians into our country after the Vietnam war, lest our population exceed our resources. He advised a "lifeboat ethic," asking: "Our hearts bleed, can they also think?" That was in 1977.[61] There were then adequate resources, but still little public will to utilize them for all peoples.

Today, Pope John Paul II calls the present situation one of sin because of "desire for profit and thirst for power."[62] It is important to repeat that he is explicitly referring to the two power blocs of liberal capitalism and collectivist Communism. He finds the disparity between rich and poor intolerable, in view of the resources our technology could but does not provide. He is not

alone in this assessment. Our social consciousness is building in
that direction, despite our tolerance for billionaires and hostile
takeovers. Yet, the negative response of the Catholic establishment to the encyclical, *Sollicitudo Rei Socialis,* was instantaneous,
as William Buckley devoted two full sessions of his televised
"Firing Line" to conservative Catholic critique of the Pope's
social analysis. William Safire, of the *New York Times,* argued
that it was correct for the communist bloc but naive regarding
capitalism.[63] At the same time that the Church defines the greed
of affluent nations as structures of sin, it reaffirms that the action
of the poor who are driven to take from the rich when in dire
need is no sin at all. This is stated clearly in *Gaudium et Spes:*
"When a person is in extreme necessity he has the right to
supply himself with what he needs out of the riches of others."[64]
A footnote to this startling reference is to the *Summa Theologica* of
St. Thomas Aquinas which reads: "In case of need all things are
common property so that there would seem to be no sin in taking
another's property; for need has made it common."[65] These
references are not lightly quoted. What they tell us is that the
new direction of social justice teaching calls for a full review of
ownership and stewardship and the sanctions of the "thou shalt
not steal" command. Liberation theologians have contributed
significantly to the development of this theme: Gustavo Gutierrez, in *The Power of the Poor in History;* Charles Avila, in *Ownership;*
and Pablo Richard in *Idols of Death, God of Life,* are but a few who
attribute stealing to the group with excessive control over
resources that others need for survival.[66] As this ethic pervades
our consciousness, respect for the decisions made against the
interests of poor nations will be challenged. The challenge will
come from those very nations themselves.

What the social documents of the Church are developing, in
ever more persuasive form, is the original biblical claim of the
people, as people of God, to share in the resources of creation.
The hope that all peoples will struggle together to achieve
dominion over the land and, then, as stewards, continue to share
in its use is being expressed with ever clearer claims to authenticity in the twentieth century.

History recounts the way, in ancient times, work got done
throughout Western civilization by slaves, taken from conquered lands; by serfs, considered property attached to feudal
fiefs; by native peoples in colonized territories; and by exploited
free laborers, in seventeenth and eighteenth century industrial
centers. In each case, the workers were treated as outsiders;
recorded history lumped them together as the masses. Often,
they were of a different race from that of the dominant class

and/or of different ethnicity or religion. These differences were fostered to justify inhumane treatment. In the nineteenth century, social Darwinism became a convenient justification for this mistreatment as being suited to inferiors. It is still being used in the twentieth century; hence, the example of Wilson's work in this analysis.[67] This history reveals our human failure to recognize, in those of different race, religion, ethnic groups and social classes, our common origin. It reveals, too, our use of power and wealth to assure the continued production of goods and services in our own interests. In time, however, and after much struggle, awareness of the oppressive use of others was raised to consciousness, as we learned to reflect on the meaning and purpose of life and as the exploited peoples learned to organize to claim their rights.

The establishment of the United Nations was the single most powerful factor in deepening our understanding and appreciation of human worth in the twentieth century. The multinational community, which constitutes the body of the United Nations assembly, drew on their religions, philosophies and scientific methods, in concerted efforts to discover and proclaim our human rights to speak freely, to choose our work, to practice our faith, to gather together and reflect on our lives. Now, this vision has expanded to include other basic rights: to have food, shelter, health care, education, and recreation. These derive from our humanity and not from power and wealth. But, the lesson has not yet been assimilated by all people. Discovering that political and legal rights, on the one hand, and economic, social and cultural rights, on the other, are equally human rights is still a growing part of our understanding of our common humanity, with communist perceptions clearer on the second set and capitalist, on the first.[68] For both communists and capitalists, however, the acknowledgment that all peoples have the right to self-determination and to enjoy and use freely the natural wealth and resources of their own territory results from a new consciousness, raised through the United Nations, but only since 1967.[69] The rapid growth of skill and intellectual achievement among formerly oppressed peoples, as their opportunity for literacy expands, embarrasses previous judgments of ineptitude and incapacity. Misunderstanding with regard to what was considered inferior moral development was equally prevalent. This is not surprising. Until we can formally replace the basic assumptions of scarcity and natural self-interest with the more valid basic assumption that all have the right to a just share in the adequate resources and participation in planning for their use, we will be constantly chided by the spirit of the gospel, finding us wanting in providing for economic rights and in the analyses of political authority. The new ethic to be fostered could be called institutional altruism. It would mean that the rules are to be in harmony with human rights. The task would be to bring our failed conduct into line with these newly institutionalized norms. That will be difficult, but the Spirit of God is moving in that direction.

We are familiar with the tenets of this new ethic. They have been interspersed throughout this essay, serving as normative principles and motivating ideals. It is time now to assemble them and to summarize them briefly, in sharp focus on their significance and importance.

Four factors characterize and mark the future of institutional altruism, directionally. (1) There is a growing understanding that human rights are ours by virtue of our humanity and that they subsume all other law claims, over which they take priority. (2) This discovery is not the outcome of the efforts of an advantaged élite developing a greater consciousness of human gentility. It is, rather, that of the organizing poor, the marginal peoples, who, after reflecting on the oppressions of their lives, often in biblical context, have become fully aware that this world's goods are also theirs. (3) It has come to light, in the study of scripture and theology, that traditional religion has historically proclaimed those rights of the poor, and has judged that, if unjust laws prevent their realization, they are not to be considered binding. (4) Finally, the fact that the poor have organized to claim their rights adds a distinct dimension to the social justice activities of our day. In the past, the enlightened élite could give to the poor from their largesse, in order to alleviate the results of poverty. Today, they are being called to respond to the just demands of the poor to eliminate the causes of poverty. These are the foundation stones and these the building blocks of the new ethic.

This call to social justice comes, not from immediate divine inspiration in the depths of the individual conscience, in a setting of quiet meditation or of exultant religious revival, but rather from God speaking through the voices of the poor, as they organize themselves to make their claims. Faith is challenged by the ordinariness, the annoying insistence, the language of demand. Consider this statement of theological truth: "Inherent in our developing understanding of mission is the belief that God, who speaks to us in diverse ways, today, calls with special insistence through the voices of the poor as they organize themselves to claim their rights as human beings."[70] God's voice is no clearer in the poor than it is in any other way God speaks to people. It is a question of faith, of listening to the Spirit. What is clear, however, is that the gospel message to the poor is quite different from that to the non-poor. While the first group hear the news of their release from the effects of poverty, the latter hear that they will find liberation in release from excessive wealth. On the one hand, the poor are mandated to reach out; on the other, the non-poor to let go.

Who is neighbor? The production of goods and services is worldwide today. Raw materials, design of product, managers and planners know no culture boundary. The work force moves from state to state, country to country. The resources, workers, and needs touch every land. Everyone who has needs and responds to needs is neighbor. Then, who is enemy? It would seem there is none. Then, we have no target for weapons; hence, no need of weapons. But, if there be no need for weapons, how do we handle our differences and to what law do we give an account? Who does the work? Who gets the proceeds and who the profits? These practical questions are not rhetorical. They constitute our agenda. We have, in the past, personalized God; we have also nationalized God, and now we are invited to universalize God. That was what we thought we had done in the first place. Our social analysis points out that we have deceived ourselves in this regard. That does not mean we must continue the deception. So, where is God today? As we dismantle the structures of sin and participate in the construction of structures of justice, we stand with the poor as they reach out to take what is rightfully theirs. We find that what they need is what we have. But, they are not enemy. They are our progeny, We are a community becoming ten and a half billion people. We could begin with one principle: all social arrangements must stand the test of providing for the common good. We can decide to de-institutionalize self-interest as a principle of political action by challenging the use of it to justify unjust actions and by not accepting it as a rationale from public officers. This will require re-education, but this too we can introduce. The ground work is already laid in the *United Nations Bill of Human Rights*.

We acknowledge that the goods of this world are meant for all. We have not considered here the way we will reorder our lives so that this intention is realized. We have reflected on the reason it is timely that we do it, we members of a community of five billion people. Nothing short of this is authorized by the Spirit moving in the social justice agenda of the late twentieth century. Utopian? No longer so, but a problem with feasible solutions to be found. Our Church has made its decision to stand with the poor and to participate in the transformation of social structures. Some of us are trying to take back that decision with powerful manipulations. The Spirit resists this endeavor, and the Spirit is in the people who reach out to claim what is rightfully theirs.

## NOTES

[1]Luke 4:16-23.

[2]Matthew 25: 31-46.

[3]Synod of Bishops, *Synodal Document on Justice in the World* (Rome, Second General Assembly of Synod of Bishops, November 30, 1971; Boston: Daughters of St. Paul, 1971), p. 2.

[4]In 1951 William Ferree published a pamphlet entitled *The Act of Social Justice.* In this brief summary of his doctoral dissertation from Catholic University in 1941, he traced the history of the concept of justice as used in the Church, noting that the idea of social justice, i.e., a justice that calls even established law into question, is a very recent development in Church thinking. (Dayton, Ohio: Marianist Publication, 1951)

[5]Synod, *op. cit.,* 2.

[6]United Nations, *The International Bill of Human Rights* (New York: United Nations, 1978), p. 2.

[7]There is a striking similarity in the treatment of human rights in the United Nations' document and in the encyclical, *Pacem in Terris,* issued by Pope John XXIII in 1963.

[8]See especially Gustavo Gutierrez's *The Power of the Poor in History* (Maryknoll, New York: Orbis Books, 1983); Jon Sobrino, *The True Church of the Poor* (Maryknoll, New York: Orbis Books, 1984), and Elsa Tamez, *The Bible of the Oppressed,* 1982. Also from Orbis: Alejandro Cussianovich, *Religious Life and the Poor: Liberation Theology Perspectives* (Maryknoll, New York: Orbis Books, 1979).

[9]For an understanding of base Christian communities, see Phillip Berryman's *The Religious Root of Rebellion: Christians in Central American Revolution* (Maryknoll, New York: Orbis Books, 1984). To see a community in process, read Ernesto Cardenal's *The Gospel of Solentiname* (Orbis, 1976).

[10]There is a growing awareness of this deficiency. President Derek Bok of Harvard University has expressed his concern. See Derek Bok, "Ethics, the University, and Society," *Harvard Magazine* (May/June, 1988), pp. 39-50. See also Robert Bellah and Phillip E. Hammond, *Varieties of Civil Religion* (Berkeley, Calif: University of California Press, 1985), p. xiv.

[11]Edward O. Wilson, *On Human Nature* (Cambridge: Harvard University Press, 1978), p. 191.

[12]Ibid., Chapters 7 and 8.

[13]Research in sociology of religion in the 1980s has questioned the trend toward secularization that was assumed to characterize modern society in the early seventies. See, on this point, Richard K. Fenn's *Toward a Theory of Secularization,* Society for the Scientific Study of Religion Monograph Series, No. 1 (1978), and Phillip A. Hammond,

ed., *The Sacred in a Secular Age* (Berkeley: University of California Press, 1985).

[14]See Thomas R. Malthus, "An Essay on the Principle of Population," published originally in 1798 and reprinted in Gertrude Himmelfarb, ed., *The Modern Library* (New York: Random House, 1960).

[15]Garrett Hardin, "Living on a Lifeboat," *Bioscience* 24 (October 1974): 561-68.

[16]Elaine M. Murphy, *Food and Population: a Global Concern* (Washington, D.C.: Population Reference Bureau, 1984), p. 3.

[17]Peter Hendry, *Food and Population: Beyond Five Billion* (Washington, D.C.: Population Reference Bureau, 1988).

[18]See, for example, Frances Moore Lappe and Joseph Collins, *World Hunger: Twelve Myths* (New York: Grove Press, 1986); and World Resource Institute, *World Resources 1987* (New York: Basic Books, 1987).

[19]See Thomas Robbins, "Transformative Impact of the Study of New Religions," *Journal for the Scientific Study of Religion* 27 (March 1988): 12-31.

[20]The encyclicals referred to in this section can all be found in Michael Walsh and Brian Davies, eds., *Proclaiming Justice and Peace: Documents from John XXIII to John Paul II* (Mystic, Connecticut: Twenty Third Publications, 1984).

[21]A book that addresses this dilemma is Paul Steidl-Meier, S.J., *Social Justice Ministry: Foundations and Concerns* (New York: Le Jacq Publishing Co., 1984).

[22]Mark 12: 28-34.

[23]Luke 10: 29-37.

[24]Luke 3: 1-11.

[25]Mark 10: 7-23.

[26]Mark 10: 23-25.

[27]Deuteronomy 15: 7-8.

[28]Isaiah 5: 8.

[29]This assessment refers in general to introductory text books in sociology published since 1985.

[30]Paulo Freire, a Brazilian educator, is credited with the development of this literacy learning method that incorporates basic reading skills into organizing for action toward social transformation. See his *Pedagogy of the Oppressed* (New York: Herder & Herder, 1970).

[31]Wilson, *op. cit.,* pp. 167, 28, 165.

[32]Ibid., p. 156.

[33]Ibid., p. 191.

[34]Ibid.

[35]Ibid., p. 201.

[36]Ibid., p. 197.

[37]Ibid., p. 201.

[38]This emphasis on natural selfishness is shared by many other scientists and ethicists who sincerely seek a pragmatic basis for social justice within recognized human limitations. The concept, "Realpolitik," takes its name from this position. I am simply questioning its validity in view of other human realities related to religious belief and

practice, on the one hand, and the powerful political tool that thesis is
for those with power, on the other. Its political implications are being
exposed today. See Gregory Baum, *Religion and Society* (New York:
Paulist Press, 1987).

[39]Berryman, *op. cit.*

[40]Joseph Ratzinger, "Instruction on Certain Aspects of the Theology of Liberation," *Origins* 14 (September 13, 1984), pp. 193, 195-204;
"Instruction on Christian Freedom and Liberation," *Origins* 16 (April
17, 1986), pp. 713, 715-28.

[41]See, for example, George Katsiaficas, *The Imagination of the New
Left: A Global Analysis of 1968* (Boston: South End Press, 1988).

[42]Theodorlo Galdi, R. F. Grimmett, and Larry Q. Nowels, "For-
eign Assistance Overview: A Briefing for the House Appropriation
Subcommittee on Foreign Operations, Export Financing and Related
Programs," Congressional Research Service, Library of Congress
(March 1988). See also *A Journey through the Global Debt Crisis,* produced
by Debt Crisis Network, available through Washington, D.C.: Institute for Policy Studies, 1988, and "Perspectives on Revitalizing
Development, Growth, International Trade and Problems of the Least
Developed Countries," Recommendations of US NGO's to the Sev-
enth General Assembly of the UN Conference of Trade and Development (UNCTAD VII, 1987).

[43]See Max Weber, *The Protestant Ethic and the Spirit of Capitalism* (New
York: Charles Scribner's Sons, 1958).

[44]Donal Dorr, *Option for the Poor: A Hundred Years of Vatican Social
Teaching* (Maryknoll, New York: Orbis Books, 1984).

[45]Walsh and Davies, *op. cit.* See also the United States Bishops'
pastorals on the economy (1986), on peace (1983), on Hispanics
(1983), on race (1979), in the bibliography under United States Catholic Conference.

[46]See my *From Nuns to Sisters* (in press) and David Johnson, ed.,
*Justice and Peace Education: Models for College and University Faculty* (Mary-
knoll, New York: Orbis Books, 1986); Alice Frazer Evans, Robert A.
Evans, and William Beans Kennedy, *Pedagogies for the Non-Poor,* also
Orbis, 1987.

[47]See "Catholicism in the '80's *Quo Vadis?*," *Latin American Press:* a
weekly bulletin of news and analysis (July 16, 1987), pp. 1-2, 8.
Apartado 5594, Lima 100, Peru.

[48]See Paulo Freire's *Pedagogy of the Oppressed* (New York: Herder and
Herder, 1970), and *The Politics of Education: Culture, Power and Liberation*
(Massachusetts: Bergin and Garvey, 1985).

[49]In Austin Flannery, ed., *Vatican Council II: The Conciliar and Post-
Conciliar Documents* (Northport, New York: Costello Publishing Co.,
1975), p. 975, #69.

[50]*Gaudium et Spes,* #50.

[51]E. Schillebeeckx, "Liberation Theology between Medellin and
Puebla," *Theology Digest* 28 (Spring, 1980): 3-9.

[52]Placido Erdozain, *Archbishop Romero: Martyr of Salvador* (Maryknoll,
New York: Orbis Books, 1981), p. 751.

[53]Pope John Paul II, "Encyclical Letter *Sollicitudo Rei Socialis*" (On

Social Concerns) (Boston: St. Paul Books & Media), #38, #42, #43.

[54]Walsh and Davies, *op. cit.,* "Octogesima Adveniens," #48.

[55]Sodepax, "Rocca di Papa Colloquium on the Social Thinking of the Churches," Parts I, II, III, IV. *Church Alert,* Nos. 17-20 (Geneva, Switzerland: Ecumenical Center, 1977, 1978). See also Frederick Herzog, *The New Function of the Church in Christianity* (Maryknoll, New York: Orbis Books, 1980).

[56]Pitirim A. Sorokin, *Exploration in Altruistic Love and Behavior* (Boston: Beacon Press, 1950).

[57]Max Weber, *Sociology of Religion* (Boston: Beacon Press, 1964), pp. 46-59.

[58]Ibid.

[59]Max Weber, *The Theory of Social and Economic Organization* (Glencoe, Illinois; Free Press, 1966), pp. 380-86, 329-63.

[60]Hendry, *op. cit.,* pp. 23, 29.

[61]Garrett Hardin, *Boston Globe,* 14 July 1979, p. 11.

[62]Pope John Paul II, *op. cit.,* #38.

[63]See William Safire, *New York Times,* 22 February 1988, p. A19, for a commentary similar to Buckley's the day after the publication of the encyclical.

[64]Flannery, *op. cit., Gaudium et Spes,* #69.

[65]Thomas Aquinas, *Summa Theologica,* II, II, Q 66, a. 7.

[66]Maryknoll, New York: Orbis Books. All were published in 1983.

[67]The debate over Wilson's thesis and the political implications of racism, sexism and classism in Social Darwinism in general is continuous in the social sciences. See, for example, Arthur J. Caplan, *The Sociobiology Debate* (New York: Harper & Row, 1978); David Himmelstein and Steffie Woolhandler, eds., *Science, Technology and Capitalism, Monthly Review* (special issue) 38 (July/August, 1986).

[68]See Robert E. Drinan, *Cry of the Oppressed: The History and Hope of the Human Rights Revolution* (Mahwah, New Jersey: Paulist Press, 1988). See also "The Semantics of Human Rights," by Richard Schafter, United States Department of State, Bureau of Public Affairs, Washington, D.C., Current Policy No. 1041, 1988.

[69]This right to self-determination of nations was not included in the 1948 Declaration of Human Rights. It was formulated only later, when the covenants were prepared. United Nations, *op. cit.*

[70]This is Item 395 from the 1980 Sisters' Survey Retest. See *Probe,* National Association of Religious Women (NARW) (May-June, 1981): pp. 1-7.

# One Spirit — Many Ministries

Elizabeth Dreyer

## I. Introduction

One spirit, yet many ministries—the dialectic between the one and the many has been a topic of interest and puzzlement for the human race for as long as its members have been engaged in the philosophical process. The problem of Platonism, according to the master himself, was to build a bridge from the many to the one.[1] A multitude of questions arise. What does each term mean? What is its source? How do they relate to one another? How can both unity and diversity be present simultaneously? One is reminded of the trinitarian debates of the patristic period and the intense philosophical interest of the schoolmen in the one and the many.

Today, we address this issue again in the context of one Spirit—many ministries. In this volume—"The Spirit Moving the Church in the United States"—many perspectives are taken: the Church, the biblical understanding of the Spirit, the power of the Spirit as it is expressed in authority and charism, and the power of the Spirit in the quest for justice in our country and in our world. In the Christian community, this power of the Spirit becomes concrete action that is service to the world. We call this action ministry. In his recent book on ministry, Thomas O'Meara calls the power of the Spirit "the pulse of ministry."[2] If you would take a moment to feel your own pulse and reflect on what it means for your life, you will get some idea of the crucial value and intimate connection between what is producing your pulse and the action it makes possible. Pulse is what we check to see whether there is life or death in a human body.

In this essay, I will be talking about ministry in a very broad sense. I will be looking at ministry as part of the essence of the Christian community, as central to the baptismal covenant of that community, as a pivotal aspect of every Christian's life. My remarks will be organized in the following way: (1) reasons for the recent interest in ministry; (2) a review of some important books on ministry since 1970; (3) discussion of the primary ministry—ministry in the marketplace; (4) some qualities of a future renewed ministry and possible blocks to such a renewal; (5) final summary—one Spirit—many ministries.

## II. Reasons for a Renewed Interest in Ministry

For Roman Catholics, Vatican II was a watershed event. The Catholic Church presented a new face to the world, and the tone of the Council documents was fresh, open, collegial. One of the key shifts signaled by the Council was a realignment of the relationship between the Church and the modern world. Instead of focusing on fear and condemnation of the contemporary scene, the Church acknowledged its kinship with the world of the twentieth century, joined its ranks, and expressed solidarity and care for that world.[3]

This new attitude caused members of the Church at all levels to reexamine the Church's understanding of many of its ideas and practices. Ministry was one of hundreds of topics that called for such a reexamination. If the Church were to be open to and function in the modern world, if the Spirit were to be brought forth from the wings, if baptism were to regain its importance in the community, if the laity were to be raised up and encouraged to take their rightful place in the Church—then, indeed, our past ideas about ministry were in need of a far-reaching overhaul.

In addition to ecclesial factors, there have been some general sociological changes that have motivated or, perhaps more accurately, mandated a renewed examination of ministry. These include: a growing number of American Catholics who are involved in the institutional Church at many levels; a high degree of education; a growing sense of theological maturity; the growing influence of Roman Catholics within the power structures of our society (economic, educational, political, legal, et cetera); and the growing financial stability of so many Catholic laity.[4] Let us now look more closely at several specific reasons for the recent interest in ministry.

## A. Ministry's Inability to Respond to Needs

Ministry is linked intimately with the needs of people. In order to determine what such needs are, one has to pay close attention to experience. With a new and open stance toward the world, the Church began to see that too often it was responding to needs of another time, or imagined needs, or needs that would merely help to keep the superstructure in place. As we continue to look with care and reverence at modern experience, the needs of people today may become clearer. To the extent that people are invited to speak about their needs, the Church will continue to grow in knowledge and appreciation of these needs. The more we discover ways in which the Church's ministry fails to meet society's needs, the more we feel called upon to reexamine the very foundations and structures of the way we perceive and practice ministry. When something is not working, we sit down and try to figure out what is wrong in order to remedy it.

## B. Ecumenical Dialogue

Second, a greater focus on ministry has grown out of recent ecumenical dialogue in the World Council of Churches, between Protestant and Catholic Churches, and among other groups in search of union. A surprising amount of common theological understanding about ministry is emerging from these efforts.[5]

## C. Gap between Theory and Practice

A third reason for the renewed interest in ministry is the gap that exists between ministerial theory and practice. This gap may be especially pronounced in the United States—a land of pragmatists, problem solvers, "doers." Americans naturally bring gifts of efficiency and creativity to problem solving. In many instances in the American Church, ministerial practice moved forward quite rapidly as needs were uncovered and responses sought. Our inherited theory, however, was left behind, and, as the gap grew, theologians felt compelled to reflect on contemporary ministerial practice in light of the scriptures and the tradition. We felt the need to broaden our ideas of ministry in order to keep up with the steady expansion we have experienced in the practice of ministry since Vatican II. In large measure because of the shortage of ordained clergy, the range of persons involved in ministry has grown, and the activities we call ministry, while not without some debate, are growing in kind and scope. Instead of an exclusive association between ministry and formal sacraments, we now take for granted that religious educators, psychologists, home visitors, distributors of Eucharist, musicians, parish administrators, teachers, hosts and hostesses, bookkeepers and social workers, advocates of justice, may be regarded as ministers, directly or indirectly contributing to the building up of the community.

## D. Diversity of Gifts in the Community

Fourth, the growing awareness of and appreciation for the many gifts in the community and the knowledge that many of those gifts have been left untapped are forcing us to look at our structures in order to understand the way they nurture or block these gifts. Excluding or ignoring gifts is a stance that we can no longer afford to maintain. And, we are unsure about the way to realign structures in such a way that they call forth and encourage the many and diverse charisms in the community.

## E.  Gap between Theology and Ministry

Finally, we are seeing the need to address dichotomies that may exist between theology and ministry. There is an element of élitism in the theological academy that looks down on ministry as watered-down theology. Workshops or publications centered on ministry are sometimes regarded with disdain as being less "intellectually rigorous" than academic theology. Over the past fifty years, the study of ministry has been dominated by the teachers of pastoral care.[6]

Recent theologies of ministry by leading theologians have been a major step in overcoming this dichotomy. We are beginning to realize that theology and ministry must go hand in hand and that our theology will change as theologians begin to reflect on ministerial praxis today. Theology has the crucial task of reflecting on the community's experience in light of the biblical and theological traditions. It has the tools both to support new practice in light of the tradition and to critique those elements that are not true to the best in that tradition.[7]

Let us turn, then, to a survey of this literature. I will examine several major theologies of ministry written since 1970.[8] The choice of texts has been guided by the theological/spiritual interests of this essay rather than by the more practical concerns of ministry. These particular authors seem to me to have figured prominently in recent discussions on ministry, exerting a noteworthy influence on contemporary thinking on the topic. With the exception of Edward Schillebeeckx, all of these authors are North American or, in the case of Henri Nouwen, have had extensive experience here.

## III.  Survey of Recent Theological Literature on Ministry

## A.  George Tavard

In 1967, George Tavard wrote *The Pilgrim Church,* in which he brought into relief the post Vatican II turn to a new way of doing theology. Tavard presents what he terms a serious theological reflection on the text of *Lumen Gentium.* From our perspective twenty years later, it appears as a cautious book in which Tavard walks the tightrope between a well established ecclesiology and some sweeping changes in the way we conceive of the Church. He is a pioneer, presenting a new language and a new vision of theology, all the while struggling to respect and preserve the best of the past.

Tavard signals an attitude toward Church that will have important ramifications for the ways in which we understand ministry. He uses the image of a New Pentecost to note the new awareness and desire for oneness in the Body of Christ and the renewed attention to the working of the Holy Spirit among the faithful.[9] He suggests that thought in the Catholic Church is "passing from the letter, from the body, from the external forms, from the institutions, from the routine, to a new sense of the Spirit, to a new conviction that Tradition is a living process, to a renewed faith that the body of Christ leads to his Spirit" and that we will succeed only if we allow ourselves to be drawn by that Spirit.[10]

In 1983, Tavard produced another work, *A Theology for Ministry*.[11] In this volume, he continues what he sees to be a pressing need for serious, theoretical, theological reflection on the realities of Church and ministry. His point of departure is concern about the nature of ministry and its possible reorganization to meet the needs of modern times in a better way.[12] Evident in his remarks are his on-going commitments to preserve the tradition and to enhance ecumenical cooperation. He chooses catholicity and eucharistic communion as the theological bases for ministry. By catholicity, he means the goal of wholeness, of totality, of an all-embracing vision that must undergird our ministry. He offers a fourfold structure for ministry: mediation, proclamation, service and education.[13] This fourfold structure, he posits, belongs to the essence of the Church and, as such, must be preserved. What can and perhaps should be changed are the specific forms each of these elements assumes.

While Tavard eschews an out-dated understanding of the relationship between ministry and culture, he lays a significant amount of blame on that culture as a cause of the present crisis in ministry. He paints a picture of *fin de siècle* malaise, a culture at the end of its tether.[14] He advocates what might be termed a "renewed return" to the basic theological underpinnings of ministry. He says he is not afraid of a cultic emphasis (as many seem to be today) and disagrees with Küng and Schillebeeckx who propose leadership as the primary function of ministry.[15]

Tavard seems especially concerned to maintain past foundations of ministry, even as he heralds and appreciates newness in our understanding. But, his discussion of ministry remains firmly within Church structures and over against contemporary culture.

## B. Henri Nouwen

In the 70s, we have books by Henri Nouwen, Urban Holmes and Bernard Cooke. In 1971, the Dutch theologian/pastor, Henri Nouwen, wrote *Creative Ministry*.[16] His stated concern is the relationship between professionalism and the spirituality of the minister.[17] The style is a mix of theology and meditative reflection, aimed at responding to a perceived over-emphasis on the professional preparation and competencies of the minister. While Nouwen clearly supports such preparation and presumes it, he is more interested in the minister's personal life and spirituality, things beyond professional skill training.

He names the functions of ministry as preaching, teaching, caring, organizing, and celebrating. If one sees ministry as a way of life (as opposed to a 9-5 job), it must be possible to "find the seeds of this new spirituality in the center of Christian service." Nouwen stresses that spirituality cannot be outside the limits of one's ministry. "Prayer is life; prayer and ministry are the same and can never be divorced."[18]

Nouwen broadens the discussion of ministry from a strictly theological interest to the spirituality of the minister. And, while there is a hint of universal ministry in his statement, "Prayer is life," he has in mind the ordained professional minister, not the person in the pew.

## C. Urban T. Holmes

Also in 1971, Urban T. Holmes, episcopal priest and Dean of the School of Theology of the University of the South in Sewanee, Tennessee, from 1973 until his death in 1981, wrote the first of three volumes on ministry, entitled *The Future Shape of Ministry*.[19] In 1976, he published *Ministry and Imagination*,[20] and in 1982, *Spirituality for Ministry* was published posthumously.[21]

In *The Future Shape of Ministry*, Holmes acknowledges the abundance of literature on ministry, but points to three deficiencies: few address the historical or theological dimensions of ministry, and none approaches what might be called a comprehensive study of ministry. These, he thinks, are needed to complement the more sociological and psychological analyses.[22] This he attempts to do in this volume.

According to Holmes, the task of ministry is to serve the purposes of the Church, the *Ursakrament,* or primal means of encounter with Christ.[23] Ministry is a function of offering the

sacramental presence of God to others.[24] It follows, then, that
the minister is primarily a sacramental person, with ritual and
preaching as central functions. Holmes harkens back to the first
three hundred years of the Church's ministry and identifies
eight ministerial functions: (1) cultic preaching, (2) evangelism,
or missionary preaching, (3) teaching, (4) prophecy, (5) ritual,
(6) discipline, (7) care of the poor, and (8) administration.[25] The
formation of the doctrine of ministry, he says, was the result of
theological reflection on pastoral needs,[26] a task he considers
urgent today.

Holmes is critical of the churches' ministry in this regard. He
thinks the Church should ask, "In what language is God's revelation to be understood today?"[27] For him, "the question we
must continue to ask is whether our ministry effectively confronts us in this present culture with the transcendent power of
God in a form that has promise for man [and woman] as he
perceives reality."[28]

Awareness of the culture is a key element in any authentic
ministry. Holmes offers four characteristics of contemporary
Western society—loss of universal coherence, a different model
of knowledge, a renewed sense of freedom and the future, and
the impact of technology. Happily, he does not take a condemnatory or demeaning stance toward society.[29] His point, rather, is
to highlight the importance for ministry of being intimately
connected with culture in order to speak meaningfully to it. His
assessment, on the whole, is that the churches have failed, and
the reasons he offers are a lack of imagination and courage and
the temptation to idolatry.

A solution to this problem lies in the careful balance of offering service that is both transcendent and immanent. The future
of this service, if it is to be effective, needs to be fueled by an
imaginative openness of heart.[30] He speaks of the minister as
artist, as one who loves enough and is creative enough to ask,
"What would it be like if . . . ?" In contrast to Tavard's position, Holmes invites us to embrace secularity—to speak the
Word and do our ritual in the midst of the marketplace.[31]

These seminal ideas on the role of the imagination became a
full-length book in 1976, *Ministry and Imagination*. Whereas *The
Future Shape of Ministry* was chronological, general and comprehensive, this book seeks to be more analytical and focuses on a
particular dimension of ministry. Holmes turns to some of the
issues treated by Nouwen—opting, however, for the term
"piety" rather than "spirituality." Holmes holds that a renewed
piety "will go a long way to vivifying all other aspects of ministry

inasmuch as they are the expressions of the salvific work of the body of Christ."[32] He also acknowledges the past, the environment, and the internal life of the Church as important issues for ministry, but focuses his attention particularly on the way God, Christ, and the Holy Spirit are present in the community now.[33]

Holmes has gotten more pessimistic about society since 1971 (also more creative about ministry's response to its problems), emphasizing the growing sense of God's absence and the failure of ministry to mediate transcendence to the world. He still has the same question: "How can you and I know God as he speaks to our world today?"[34] But, his response is more specific, inasmuch as it addresses what he sees to be the cultural causes of the present crisis in ministry. He lists four: (1) a tendency to reduce experience to logical categories and the control that comes from organizing material in a syllogistic way; (2) the dissolution of the natural communities in which ministry was done—an outcome of the Industrial Revolution; (3) the disestablishment of the Church and clerical roles; (4) the disenchantment of our culture. His articulation of the crisis sets the stage for his response: "The fundamental issue in ministry today is the recovery of a sense of enchantment and the ability to be enchanting."[35] He calls for a long-term conversion of the Church's ministry somewhat on the order of the personal conversion chronicled by Carlos Castaneda.[36]

A nexus of this conversion, for Holmes, is the imagination. The minister, he says, is more than a skilled professional. A wholistic anthropology demands that we employ the totality of our being, especially the neglected, intuitive, right brain functions. The minister has got to be "mana-person," "clown," "storyteller," "wagon master."[37] These qualities are required in order to keep in healthy tension living together in an orderly, structured way *and* moving out into the "antistructure," a consequence of paying attention to the transcendent, with its attendant threat to the *status quo*. The imaginative person, together with his/her symbols gathered in ritual and story, is the *open* human being.[38] The appropriation of images in the Christian tradition has the potential to lead us to the meaning of the Church's experience and to discern the transcendent in our present world.[39]

Holmes' final book on ministry, *Spirituality for Ministry,* attempts a more empirical approach. He has gathered material from parish clergy from five denominations, both in informal listening sessions and from more formal questionnaires. His formal research sample is small—twenty-two persons (two women and twenty men). All are ordained and considered by their superiors to be "spiritually mature" persons.[40]

Holmes' interest here is to discover the contours of the spirituality of active parish clergy. This is one of the more empirically oriented books on ministry, but the sample is so small that it can have but very much limited conclusions. The text is anecdotal, using examples from the sample and from Holmes' own life. He takes the reader into the daily warp and woof of the lives of a few ministers, revealing the sublimity of the call, the loneliness, the temptation to sin.

Holmes' focus on culture and on the needs of people in today's society suggests a wider horizon than one with an exclusively inter-ecclesial preoccupation. But, he still sees the primary function of ministry to be service to the Church through preaching and ritual, even though service to the poor is included. The minister he has in mind, as with the other authors we have seen, is the ordained or professional minister.

## D. Bernard Cooke

In 1976, Bernard Cooke published *Ministry to Word and Sacraments*.[41] Citing the prevalence of attention to the broadening aspects of the ministry of the People of God after Vatican II, Cooke perceives a need for a more in-depth historical and theological treatment of the specialized ministry of the ordained person.[42] He organizes his material under five headings: (1) ministry as formation of community; (2) ministry to God's Word; (3) service to the People of God; (4) ministering to God's judgment; (5) ministry to the church's sacramentality. In fact, because of the inevitable connections he sees between specialized ministries and the broader ministries of the People of God, Cooke ends up treating both in a thorough way.

He makes a major contribution to the conversation about ministry by delineating its theological connections with soteriology, pneumatology, ecclesiology, and biblical and historical considerations. Cooke weighs carefully and in a balanced way the many values on all sides of the various questions about ministry. But, his own position is clear inasmuch as he points the way toward a ministry that aims at overcoming the opposition between sacred/profane, clergy/laity, *docens/discens,* tradition/ change, and static/dynamic ways of understanding and acting within Christianity.

Perceiving an abundance of attention to the broader understanding of ministry, Cooke consciously chooses to narrow his focus to the ordained ministry. But, by confronting the dichotomies between sacred/profane, clergy/laity, et cetera, Cooke is indirectly laying the groundwork for a more universal kind of ministry as well. I would also suggest that the widespread discussion of the broader ministry of the People of God that he sees is located primarily in Protestant communities and that, even there, statements as to its importance are made without further in-depth discussion of what such a ministry entails.

## E.  David N. Power

The focus on the ministry of the laity resumes with the 1980 publication of David N. Power's *Gifts That Differ: Lay Ministries Established and Unestablished.*[43] In response to an invitation to write a book on the rites for the installation of the minor orders of acolyte and reader, Power situates these two "official" ministries for laity, set up by Paul VI in 1972, within the broader context of past and present practice of lay service in the Church. He also offers a theology, drawn from this practice, that might guide new development in the ministry of the laity. Such a theology, he says, needs to examine the place of the laity in the Church, the specific character of their ministry, and the process of reorganizing lay ministers.[44]

While the focus of this volume is ostensibly the rather insignificant offices of acolyte and lector, Power uses their new status as a touchstone from which to discuss the truly important issues of lay responsibility and lay service in the Church, most of which go beyond the boundaries of the liturgical assembly.[45] He notes that pressing questions about ministry today emerge, not from Church documents, but rather from the actual practice that is constantly evolving in the Church at the present time. He seeks to relate the question of ministry to our experience of community renewal rather than to any abstract notion of Church.[46]

While Power examines specifically lay ministries, and even emphasizes the ministries outside the liturgical context, his viewpoint remains inter-ecclesial, reinforcing the impression that ministry is exclusively connected with official Church functions of one kind or another.

## F.  Edward Schillebeeckx

In 1981, Edward Schillebeeckx wrote the first of two volumes on ministry, entitled *Ministry: Leadership in the Community of Jesus Christ.*[47] Four years later, he produced a second volume, *The Church with a Human Face: A New and Expanded Theology of Ministry.*[48]

In the first volume, this giant of theological thought reviews the first ten centuries of ministry in order to compare it with the second Christian millennium. His historical interest is not solely in the beginning because, as beginning, it is intrinsically valuable, but rather in the whole of history. Our ideas and practice of ministry have to be formed, according to Schillebeeckx, from theological reflection on new human and cultural situations.[49] He emphasizes the constantly changing circumstances in which Christian identity must be preserved and sees this as the task of ministry. Along with many of the authors we have considered, Schillebeeckx reiterates the need to reestablish the links between ministry and community, to eliminate sharp distinctions between laity and clergy, and to allow trust in the gifts of the Spirit to take precedence over presbyteral Church order.

Schillebeeckx also addresses the issue of experimentation. While it is the right of the Christian community to do everything necessary to be a true community of Jesus, e.g., to have leaders, he suggests that the official Church, although accepting this truth, acts on decisions which have been made at an earlier time and are no longer adequate to the new situation.[50] Since ministry has been more or less in a state of change since the beginning of Christianity, he sees no reason to label as heretics those who continue the process of adapting ministerial practice to changing contemporary situations. He tries to bring understanding to the many practices in the Church today all over the world that fall outside of the strict limits of the law (non-acceptatio legis).

In The Church with a Human Face—written in large measure to respond to critiques of the first book—Schillebeeckx develops in a more nuanced way the aims of Ministry. The sharp opposition he drew between ministry in the first and second Christian millennia becomes more sophisticated and detailed. He acknowledges the continuities and overlap of practices throughout history and, to accommodate this reality, identifies several turning points that were significant in the development of ministry.[51]

Second, Schillebeeckx counters the criticism that he is doing historical/sociological research at the expense of a faith perspective. He maintains, persuasively I think, that the datum of experience is one datum among many and confronts those who protest against a theology that takes history and the social setting seriously. (Such authors maintain repeatedly that ministry is not only a sociological or historical fact.) He strongly objects to any position that puts grace alongside or above its socio-historical context.[52]

Finally, Schillebeeckx defends his hermeneutical process, especially in response to the critique of Pierre Grelot.[53] Schillebeeckx's methodological starting point is the concrete experience of discontent in the Church. It is this experience that moves him to ask questions, to seek understanding, and to search for ground upon which to judge the rightness or wrongness of the new practices that have arisen as a result of the inadequacies of ministry today. He approaches the texts of the tradition with the questions and experience of today—and wonders about such authors as Grelot, who seems to admit the possibility of a "neutral" reading of the past. Schillebeeckx asks: Are the specific forms of ministry given in history liberating or enslaving and alienating for the believing community?[54]

The broad strokes of this discussion—historical, cultural, theological and hermeneutical—make it potentially helpful in the quest for understanding *any* ministry. Schillebeeckx offers a perspective that can enlighten the discussion of all forms of ministry, whether within the Church or within the larger society.

### G. Thomas F. O'Meara

Thomas O'Meara, in *Theology of Ministry,*[55] approaches the topic of ministry from a fundamental theological perspective. He describes his book as a cultural metaphysics of ministry, a cultural history of ministry and as a theology of grace, since it is God's presence in the world that is the source, milieu and goal of ministry.[56] O'Meara covers much of the same historical ground as Schillebeeckx, Tavard, Cooke and Power, organizing his material a bit differently in line with his systematic interests. He wants to explain what is happening in ministry today, i.e., crisis, change and broadening, so that our theology can begin to catch up with our practice. The book has two main sections—biblical and theological—joined by a chapter on the major incarnations of ministry in history.

O'Meara's analysis is clear and provocative, raising questions that will occupy us for years to come, but his goals do not include sustained attention to or analysis of the ministry of ordinary believing persons.

### H. John Macquarrie

Finally, I take note of an Anglican perspective on ministry, John Macquarrie's *Theology, Church & Ministry.*[57] As the title indicates, Macquarrie considers ministry in the context of theology and Church. In the section on ministry, he treats the nature of ministry and then discusses three controversial aspects of it: the theological responsibility of the bishop, the question of women priests, and the issue of political ministry which he considers a lay, not a clerical, activity.[58] In continuity with his earlier treatment of ministry in *Principles of Christian Theology,*[59]

Macquarrie takes a cautious stance. He seems fearful of the recent crises in ministry, viewing them as a threat rather than as an opportunity to legitimate further change. He admits that, while the Church is a human institution and, therefore, susceptible to sociological analysis, he wants to emphasize (perhaps not, one hopes, in the way of Schillebeeckx's despisers) that it is also more than a *merely* human institution.[60] He is wary of blurring the distinction between clergy and laity and does not want to use the diversity of the early Church as an exclusive norm for diversity today.

Macquarrie includes a political dimension in his concept of ministry and sees it as a realm distinct to the laity. Since he addresses only three very specific problems in this text, one cannot draw from it general conclusions about ministry. But, his division of labor approach would allow for the development of either a specifically clerical or a lay ministry. However, one would still need to address the questions of lay ministry beyond the political realm and of the relationships among the various ministerial functions.

## I. Briefly Noted

Before bringing this review to a close, I want to mention two other volumes worthy of note. The first is *Ministry: Traditions, Tensions, Transitions* by William J. Bausch, a scholar/pastor from New Jersey.[61] This book makes available in clear, concise, simple language the fruits of more detailed, analytical, theological scholarship for the person who has not the expertise or the time to read the longer works. The second volume of note is James C. Fenhagen's *Ministry and Solitude*.[62] This volume presents a spirituality of ministry that is concrete, yet broad enough to appeal to all serious Christians. The author places ministry in the context of one's whole life, begun in Baptism and nurtured by a growing sensitivity to the Spirit that allows one to use his/her gifts on behalf of others in the human community.[63] The use of the term "solitude" in the title is a bit misleading, since equal emphasis is placed on service in the community as the fruit and source of solitude. This last text, perhaps more than any of the others, begins to address or could readily be applied to a wider understanding of ministry—what I am calling "ministry in the marketplace."

## Elements of Consensus

While there are differences of approach and opinion among some of these theologians, one is more struck by the commonalities among them, six of which I would like to mention.

(1) All acknowledge a crisis in ministry, a crisis that is seen by most as an opportunity, and for some as a mandate, to reflect theologically on the Church's mission. This crisis is the result of a new and open attitude toward society and culture. In the wake of this openness has come confusion about many ecclesial issues, primary among them being the substance of ministry and the identity of the minister. Questions have arisen about how effective ministry has been in the task of calling attention to the transcendent in today's world; about how well the Church understands and responds to the real needs of people today; about the tension between the laity and the clergy; about the shortage of ordained clergy, and about the real pain and suffering that are being experienced by many in the Church today as a result of these changes.

(2) In their historical analyses, most theologians have traced a narrowing trend in the nature and functions of ministry from the early years of Christianity. Some point to one event or period as more significant than another, but most agree that, in the beginning, a minister arose out of a given community of believers and was intimately related to that community. Gradually, this connection was weakened and in the medieval period disappeared altogether. The concept of the ministerial power of the Spirit operating in and through a community moved instead toward that of the personal power of an office holder to celebrate Eucharist.

In contradistinction to this trend, the term used consistently to describe what is happening today is "broadening." This broadening includes many more functions considered as ministry; laity considered as true ministers; a focus on baptism rather than on ordination; and an awareness of the presence and need of a variety of gifts in the Christian community.

(3) Vatican II signaled a change of emphasis from the cultic to the diaconal in the understanding of ministry.[64] Many of the authors in our sample (Tavard and Macquarrie being exceptions) agree with the direction set by Hans Küng in *Why Priests? A Proposal for a New Church Ministry* that emphasizes the charism of leadership over liturgical function.[65] The conviction that ministry must be reconnected in a primary way with the needs of people has led to the position that a variety of gifts are required in order to respond to the diversities of needs in the world. There is a visible struggle not to oppose ministry as charism to ministry as office, but, in view of our past and our present situation, there is a clear expression of the importance of a correcting emphasis toward the charismatic dimension of ministry.

(4) A constant complaint in this material points to a lack of critical, historical, theological reflection on ministry. In fact, most of these authors have written to remedy that lacuna, the result being that we are well on our way to having a significant body of serious theological literature on ministry. There is great concern on the part of these theologians to understand contemporary culture and ministerial practice and to connect these with the biblical, theological and ministerial tradition, even though the specific method or application may differ depending on one's bent toward more liberal or conservative positions. However, all agree that there is a distinctive grass roots newness to our present situation that prohibits any kind of definitive statements about ministry. They see their work as tentative and probing and supportive of new ministries, but a great deal more experience is needed before we will be standing on more solid ground.

(5) A fifth common trend worthy of mention is the importance of the larger context in which a theology of ministry must be placed. Individual theologians may have one or the other focus, but all agree that one cannot do a theology of ministry in isolation from history, anthropology, pneumatology, christology, ecclesiology, biblical studies, a theology of grace, and eschatology, to name the most important.

(6) A final point has to do with the role theologians give to ever-changing cultural realities. I do not want to oversimplify or shortchange the at times deeply felt divergences here, but I do sense that many theologians writing on ministry stress the importance of experience, of our present and social/cultural realities, in their discussions on ministry. As we have seen, Edward Schillebeeckx addresses this issue most directly in response to criticisms of his work.[66]

It is not possible here to go into the many issues at stake in this discussion, but I would say that the most convincing position is one that eschews a kind of divine/human dualism that places anthropology, history, sociology, and cultural analysis in some "theological storm-free zone" (to use Schillebeeckx's phrase). Such a dichotomy belies the truth of history, belittles the truth of our experience, runs the risk of turning grace into magic, and ignores the theological ramifications of the Incarnation. It gets the Church into the kind of situation in which it now finds itself, with a ministry that fails in significant ways to give meaning to and re-present the presence of God in our historical situation. I often wonder about the fear of having a God who is involved in and working through our changing human experience. Why are some so ready to see in this a reduction of God or of theology or of ministry to the *merely* human?

After sketching some of the major contours of recent theologies on, of, and for ministry, I would like to call attention again to an element I did not find in this literature in any developed way—a theology of what I shall call "ministry in the marketplace." One can read all of this material on ministry without finding a satisfying answer to the question: What are the specific contours, theological foundations, language, and ways of understanding the ministry of the believing Christian in her/his everyday life? While the attention to the role of baptism, the analysis of culture, and the condemnation of false dualisms and hierarchies all contribute to the discussion, none of the authors takes ministry in the above sense as a primary focus. What follows is intended to be an initial step in that direction.

## IV. Ministry in the Marketplace

Ministry in the marketplace is implied in many statements that speak of the expanded role of the laity and the common priesthood of the people of God. It is even explicitly stated on occasion, but never with any extended discussion about the specifics of the way we are to think theologically about such a ministry, or what it would look like or feel like to engage in it, or the way to teach or nurture it—or, for that matter, the way it might relate to other forms of ministry in the Church.

This is the ministry that takes place wherever people find themselves—on the job, at home, at leisure. And yet, in many of the regional consultations that took place in this country in preparation for the 1987 Synod on the Laity, the issue came up repeatedly, even though often in a vague way. People have heard about this understanding of ministry and sense in some way that it is important, but are not clear about what it means:

> As with the spiritual life, these faithful recognize that ministry includes secular activity, but they are not sure what this means or how to accomplish it. Most often they mention social services and charitable activities. Almost never are efforts toward structural change cited or opportunities to influence society through work, political involvement or civic organizations.[67]

Some of the reasons for this are obvious. Few of those writing on ministry are employed full-time at a bank or a record store, or selling insurance, or raising children, and so do not have the benefit of that kind of experience and the light that is shed on it by Christian commitment. A corollary to this is the vested interest ministers and theologians may have in keeping the focus and, to some extent, the power with ordained ministry. Second, the

focus on formal, ordained ministry has been exclusive for so
long that few of us know the way to think in other categories. In
addition, the growing number of laity in formal ministry has
tended to keep us in this mindset. Third, formal ministry is a
more obvious kind of ministry and, therefore, easier to discuss.
It is more circumscribed and identifiable and has more set structures in history than does ministry in the marketplace. The
pluriformity of the latter can be overwhelming and resist efforts
at systematization.

Finally, the dualism of which I spoke earlier contributes
mightily to the problem. The radical disjuncture we have known
between sacred and secular makes the marketplace an unlikely
place to look for the activities and fruits of the Church's
ministry—even though the Church has said that this is the distinctive realm of the laity.[68] In spite of the best intentions on
behalf of the laity (and in the midst of a great deal of genuine
affirmation), several authors speak of the differences between
laity and clergy in ways that will suggest value judgments of
"higher" and "lower" or "good" and "better." Holmes seems
to link the gift of prophecy exclusively with the clergy:

> It is apparent, however, that the clergy not only have a different
> outlook from the laity's, but that this is necessary. It comes with
> the role of prophet, which is indissolubly linked to the pastoral
> function.[69]

Macquarrie holds that the primacy of ministry belongs to the
ordained, not to the People of God, and that the differences are
essential:

> This finds echo in the Anglican-Roman Catholic agreed state-
> ment on ministry, where we read that the ordained ministry "is
> not an extension of the common Christian priesthood but
> belongs to another realm of the gifts of the Spirit." Similarly the
> dogmatic constitution on the church (*Lumen Gentium*) of Vatican
> II declares that while the common priesthood of the faithful and
> ministerial priesthood are interrelated, "they differ from one
> another in essence and not only in degree."[70]

In many cases, the terms, "special" or "fullness" or "higher
intensity," are used of the ordained ministry. Bishops and priests
are said to share in a special or fuller way the priesthood derived
from Christ. Such language implies, I think, that other ministries are lesser or shallow in their participation in the ministry of
Christ. There is also the suggestion that, since the ordained
ministry is the most visible form of Christian service, we need
simply to talk about *it*, since it applies automatically to all other
kinds of service in the Church.[71] Indeed, the result of such

writing *is* the creation of an invisible ministry, a ministry, therefore, that is not that important to the Church's life—at least as
we express it. David Power captures the tone of ambiguity still
present in our thinking about ministry:

> On the bottom rung, the one that is most down to earth, there is
> the daily Christian involvement in temporal affairs, called by the
> rather generic term of "witness," but obviously involving much
> sweat and tears if a person is to take unfailing cognizance of the
> gospel in all things. It is this which is rather constantly and
> consistently pointed to in magisterial documents on service and
> ministry as that which constitutes the basic function of lay Chris-
> tians and the most important part of their Christian service,
> rendered in the name and in the love of Christ. In one mouth,
> this can sound like an admonition to the laity to keep their place.
> In another, it is a cry of anguish, lest Christ be absent from the
> affairs of the world.[72]

Mindful of these difficulties, let us launch out into these
uncharted waters in order to continue the conversation and to
offer some tentative viewpoints on ministry in the marketplace.

## A.  The Cosmos as the Locus of Ministry[73]

If one wanted to stretch "marketplace" to its furthest reaches,
and I do, one arrives at cosmos. My thesis is that the primary
locus of ministry is the cosmos. This position flows directly from
our belief in the event of Incarnation which has sacralized all of
reality in a definitive way. We are true to the model of Jesus to the
extent that we attend with care and reverence to the world in its
fullness and to that particular piece of history before us with its
joys, challenges, opportunities, problems, suffering, injustices
and needs. And, since ministry has to do with needs in a special
way, being a minister involves discerning what these needs are,
listening and responding to them in the light of the gospel. This
means that nothing, *a priori,* is excluded from the realm of ministry. It includes the needs of economics, politics, social structures
of all kinds, our intellectual and affective life, business, ecology,
personal relationships, medicine, and religious experience, et
cetera. It means nurturing life and goodness and combatting
death and evil in any of these spheres.

The existence of a sacred/profane dualism alluded to above
impinges on the way we understand the various ministerial
functions. An easy (and, I would add, grossly inadequate) solution we have often espoused is to assign "secular" activity to the
laity and "sacred" activity to the clergy or to say that the clergy
minister to the Christian community and the laity minister to
the world. While a fully satisfying response to this difficulty may

be elusive, any solution must take seriously the effect of creation and incarnation upon all of existence. Bernard Cooke speaks to this issue: "If anything is new in our present situation it is the realization in the church that the matter cannot be solved authentically by divorcing Christianity and 'the secular.' This realization has been and is one of the most powerful influences in forcing a reconsideration of Christian ministry."[74]

If ministry is a response to the needs of the world, it may be helpful to distinguish at least two different kinds of needs. One is the need that is overtly oriented toward the transcendent. Rahner and others speak of an openness to God in the human person that strains toward the totality of reality whether we are conscious of it or not. A second kind of need is less overtly religious or transcendent and has to do with becoming fully human, i.e., able to live in freedom and dignity with access to food, housing, work and education. The first need requires hearing about God and discovering the way God is present in one's life. The second need might involve fighting for a just wage or lobbying to save our diminishing rain forests. However, we need not separate these needs in any substantive way. God's unbounded, unconditional love for the world includes both the desire that God be known and loved and that we live as full human beings.

## B. Ministry as a Matter of Intention

This leads to a second thesis—that ministry is a matter of intention. James Fenhagen speaks eloquently to this issue.[75] If we have a vision of ministry that encompasses all of life and empowers us to bear witness to the presence of Christ at every point of existence, then our being, our actions and our words can be an expression of ministry. Ministry is the term we use to describe the ways in which we live out the implications of our baptism. If the meaning of who we are and what we do is connected with the grace of Christ, then that being and doing become ministerial. It involves what we understand to be the purpose and meaning of our lives.

In order for us to have this kind of intention, we need to continue the work that has been started in the Church since Vatican II—teaching, preaching and giving witness to a renewed sense of the meaning of Baptism and Confirmation as invitation and affirmation of our Christian vocation. Vocation belongs to everyone and cannot be limited to clergy, religious or, in the secular sphere, the trades.[76] Until we begin to speak of ministry as a normative reality in the Church, it will continue to be seen as something that is highly specialized and "churchy" in connotation.[77] The call to every human being is to nurture life, i.e., freedom, justice, and self-transcending love. For Christians, this call to belong to and feel responsible for the world is seen in terms of giftedness in the Spirit.

## C.  The Call to Be in the World

Third, entering into the cosmic ministry requires that we disabuse ourselves of the common and age-old practice of equating the term "the world" with the forces of evil. Today, the term "world" connotes the environment in which all of us find ourselves—whether we are laity, clergy, religious, atheists or agnostics. Quite simply, there is nowhere else to be; thus, it makes no sense to designate "being in the world" as a distinctive quality of any group in the Church. This way of speaking is not intended to diminish our awareness of sin and evil in ourselves or in our world, but merely to clean up our language about it. Ministry is service to, not escape from or condemnation of, the world.

The past practice of equating "world" with  sin prevents us today from entering into, identifying with, loving, celebrating, and feeling proud about being in the world and about being human. It can also prevent us from owning and taking responsibility for the sinfulness that we know is in us and all around us. If we experience our humanity and our life in the world as a gift of unparalleled magnitude, we are much more likely to feel at one with the world and those in it, to empathize with its suffering and discern ways in which to alleviate it. The all too human Jesus can be a model here and can prompt us to ask whether our understanding of ministry is based primarily on the humanity of Jesus or on the divinity of Christ?

## D.  Ministry as Public

If we choose to turn, as I think we should, to the primacy of a cosmic ministry, we need to address the issue of the public aspect of ministry. Thomas O'Meara deals with this aspect of ministry most directly, making it one of its six characteristics: He says:

> When we say ministry is public, we mean that the ministry normally takes on a visible and public form in words and deeds . . . The communication of the Gospel has not been done mainly through uncertain signs, such as justice in commerce or casual neighborliness although these may be part of Christian life.[78]

I agree strongly about the importance of a Christian ministry that is clearly interpreted and articulated as gift and fruit of the grace of Christ. I also acknowledge the inner dynamics of human experience of all kinds toward clarity and self-interpretation.[79] But, this quality of publicness usually applies only to official ministry—and is often given an inordinate value. In fact, a great deal of ministry is public—from Catholic Charities to Church sponsored relief programs too numerous to mention—all giving overt witness to the Spirit of God active in the world. What is needed is a complementary analysis of the way we are to understand actions that are ministry, but not in a public sense.

Our earlier discussion of intention is relevant here. One thing that makes action ministry is that we *intend* it to be that. But, I want to ask a further question: How important is it that persons who are the beneficiaries of ministry *know* the motivation behind the action? In a similar vein, Bernard Cooke raises the question: "What difference does it make whether a certain agent of salvation or a certain course of saving action is 'official'?"[80] In some situations, action for the good of others may cause an overt inquiry—Why are you doing this? Or, we have all had the experience of having something dawn on us years after the event that then becomes a catalyst for new or renewed faith. Or, in more intimate relationships, it frequently becomes known that one's actions flow in a significant way from one's religious commitments.

But, in the interest of a more universal ministry, we need to ask to what extent it should be a goal of ministry to tell people about our motivations? Should it be of primary or ultimate significance or, rather, a hope, a desire that can be celebrated when given? At the least, we should examine the reasons behind any compulsion to divulge our motives, uninvited. Perhaps too much of our ministry in the past has been tainted with arrogance and self-aggrandizement in this regard. As we become attuned to the mysteriousness of God's action, we may be freed from worrying about whether people know the reason we are acting and free to concentrate on making this planet a better place to live for all people.

In support of giving full value to what we might call "anonymous ministry," I point to the stories from the New Testament. The first is the story of the Good Samaritan (Luke 10:25-37). It is set up as an explication of the great commandment: love God and love your neighbor. But, in the story, there is no talk of God. Rather, the story answers the question at the heart of ministry— who is my neighbor? We also note that the one who proves to be neighbor is not the one we might expect to perform well because of office. Rather, it is the Samaritan *who is moved to pity,* and *who shows the wounded man kindness.*

The second story is part of Matthew's eschatological discourse in chapter 25:31-46. At the separation of the sheep and the goats at the end of time, the Son of Man explains the reason the sheep are to enter into the kingdom. They fed the hungry, gave drink to the thirsty, clothed the naked, et cetera. *But, they did not even know they had done this.* And, the well-known reply, "Anything you did for one of my children here, however humble, you did for me." These stories challenge us to acknowledge, value and celebrate all kinds of ministry—the ministry that is publicly named, the ministry that is named in the heart of the minister, but not by the beneficiaries, and even the ministry that is not so named by the ministers themselves.

## E.  The Ministry of Telling the Story

For Christians, the source of these gifts is the Good News, the freedom and love offered by God through Jesus Christ. Therefore, another kind of ministry—overt, official ministry—is needed to insure that the story continues to be told, that we hold ourselves accountable to its message, that opportunities be provided to come together to celebrate the cosmic ministry in the marketplace, to lament our failure to minister well and to open ourselves to the kind of hope that insures creativity and perseverance in the marketplace. While we do know that often lofty aspiration, peace, insight, or a desert struggle are experienced during periods of quiet prayer or meditation, and that the works of grace are celebrated in our liturgical ceremonies, we also know that often the really decisive encounters with grace commonly occur elsewhere, often when we are not expecting anything momentous to happen.[81] What has become skewed since the early centuries of Christianity is the way we understand the relationship between cosmic ministry and sacrament. Thomas O'Meara speaks of it in terms of a need for reversal:

> The reversal is a move from symbol to reality, from church building to world, from liturgy to service. The reversal is: affirming the liturgical side of ministry to be only one side of ministry— the symbol-sacramental side and source of ministry—and recognizing ministry to be more than liturgy, preaching is more than preaching during the Eucharist, love more than the kiss of peace. . . . Sacrament presumes reality . . . sacraments and worship were intended to confirm and nourish their ministries in the world.[82]

Seen in this light, such a reversal can only enhance both our service to the world and our sacramental celebrations.

With our growing ability to acknowledge and celebrate the diversity of ministries in the Church, let us turn now to name some important qualities that might characterize a future, renewed ministry.

## V. Characteristics of a Renewed Ministry

If we agree that the question (in two forms) pertaining to ministry is: Does it effectively enhance awareness in this present culture of the power and love of God in a form that has promise for human beings as they perceive reality?[83] and, What should we do to further human history, to alleviate the oppression and suffering of most of the human race, to foster the movement towards freedom and dignity?,[84] we still would produce a list of qualities characterizing that ministry that would be as diverse as there are persons in the Church. My list is avowedly eclectic, and the elements have been chosen because they respond in some direct way to specific needs as I perceive them today. They are five.

## A. Sense of the Corporate Priesthood of the People of God

There is a frequently voiced desire to return to an earlier understanding of priesthood as it was applied corporately to the whole Christian people.[85] This desire for a communal center is supported by recent discussions on the destructive aspects of what some consider to be rampant individualism in the United States.[86] If anything, Christianity is a community affair, and in our time there is a longing to bring this dimension back into the center of the picture once again. We have seen that ministry emerges out of the community and not vice versa, and we struggle for ways to re-establish this community connection.

In addition to allowing official ministry to be called forth more recognizably from the community, we want to enhance the awareness of every baptized person of her/his own priesthood. How can we offer the invitation to all Christians to translate their own faith into whatever course of service seems desirable? What kind of invitation should be extended? What things would motivate us to enhance our sense of being minister wherever we find ourselves? What tools do we need in order to do this? Most importantly, how can we communicate the good news that much of daily life is already ministry—simply unrecognized because of the narrow parameters we have placed around ministry?

Images have a distinctive and enjoyable way of enhancing an idea, in this case that of corporate priesthood. I offer two—one

of the more literal variety, "holy people," and the other a bit
more imaginative, "the marsh reed."

A theology of ministry needs to explain the way baptism
constitutes a call to share in the mission of the Church as well as
give proper acknowledgment to the role of orders. David Power
suggests that the image of a "holy people" has the potential to do
this.[87] For Power, "this symbol stands out to best advantage
when it is applied to the people who have been initiated into the
church through baptism and gather together for the celebration
of the eucharist."[88] It is a symbol that can integrate the images of
covenant, kingdom, worship, mission, prophecy, and Spirit.
And, the symbol of a people implies a history, with all its images
and sub-plots and meaning.[89] I affirm this understanding of the
symbol, but would extend it in the sense of a people sent to be in
the world. Being a member of the Christian people is connected
with being a member of the human community, with *its* history,
images, sub-plots and meaning.

Holiness may involve a relatively more profound experience
of being human, but need not, and should not, imply the excep-
tional or the extraordinary. We can understand holiness in terms
of the wholeness of human life and see it in "the normal, the
typical, the ordinary, the generic, the exemplary."[90] I suggest
that Christian ministry will never be effective if we have an
esoteric sense of holiness or a weakened sense of belonging to the
human race, which is also a "holy people."

The second image—the marsh reed—is taken from Robert
Capon[91] and may be more difficult to evoke. But, I am committed to try and will rely heavily on his own eloquent rendering.
Capon speaks of a conversion to walking that gave him a new
sense of place, e.g., he rediscovered what a hill is. Walking also
caused him to rediscover the small town in which he lived, Port
Jefferson—and, by metaphoric extension, the world. In that
town, through what was once a marsh, flows a small creek lined
with reeds. Marsh reeds, he tells us, "when full grown, vary
from five to ten feet in height, and the tassels on the ends of the
good ones are thicker than squirrels' tails." Capon invites his
readers to try something the next time they walk past a bank of
reeds—ideally in reality, but, in the case of the unavailability of a
bank of reeds, at least in their imaginations. "Pick out the tallest
one you can reach, and cut it off as close to the ground as
possible." Ostensibly, he says, perhaps even to yourself, it will
seem that you are cutting it down to carry home to your children:

> But in the carrying of it, you will make a discovery. Keep a record
> of your reactions: *It is impossible simply to carry a marsh reed.* For how

will you hold it? Level? Fine. But it is ten feet long, and plumed in the bargain. Are you seriously ready to march up the main street of town as a knight with lance lowered? Perhaps it would be less embarrassing to hold it vertically. Good. It rests gracefully in the crook of your arm. But now it is ten feet tall and makes you the bearer of a fantastic mace. What can you do to keep it from making a fool of you? To grasp it with one hand and use it in your walking only turns you from being a king into an apostle; to try to make light of it by holding it upside down is to become a deacon carrying the inverted crozier at an archbishop's requiem. Do you see what you have discovered? There is no way of bearing the thing home without becoming an august and sacred figure— without being yourself carried back to Adam, the first King and Priest. . . . If you ever want to walk your native ground in the sceptered fullness of the majesty of Adam, I commend the marsh reed to you. Whatever embarrassment it may cause you will be an *embarras des richesses.*

Let us contemplate the image of the marsh reed and allow it to wash over us and fill us with a sense of what it means to be a "holy people."

## B. Uncovering God's Presence

A second characteristic of a renewed ministry involves changing some of our language and understanding about ministry so that it more accurately reflects its true reality. Too many theologians discussing ministry use verbs like "bringing," "offering," "giving," "mediating," "helping," even "confronting" the world with God's power. Within a certain important, but limited, horizon this kind of language has a place—we need to continue to tell the story—but, it does not get at the deepest reaches of the reality of ministry and, in fact, may involve presuppositions that are inimical to it.

The truth to keep before us as ministers in the cosmos is that God is already in the world in more ways and more intimately than we can imagine. Granted we abuse, reject and are blinded to this presence also in more ways than we can imagine. But, this failure cannot obliterate the primary task of ministry which is to "uncover," "evoke," or "re-present" this presence. There is a profound sense in which talk of "bringing God to the world" smacks of an arrogance too bold to contemplate. From this vantage point, then, an important task of the minister is to see not only needs of people, but ways in which grace is present in our world. The ability to recognize, name, affirm, and celebrate goodness is an unparalleled gift of ministry—a gift that can be used to build up the people and give glory to God.

## C.  Belonging to the World

This third quality, belonging to the world, needs little further discussion. We have spoken at length about it above and want only to underline its importance here. There is a capacity to be moved to pity and a quality of showing kindness, as exemplified in the story of the Good Samaritan, that can come only from a genuine identification with the world and its people. It comes from the knowledge of both the head and the heart that we are one with the human race, that our true identity comes from belonging to and not setting ourselves apart from others.

Fenhagen sees the task of the Church today as engaging the world at every level with the claims and values of the gospel. At the heart of this understanding is something he calls a "holy worldliness"—a commitment to participate in the struggle of the world as one who knows the Lord: "Holy worldliness is life-affirming rather than pleasure-denying. It calls people to faith, not out of guilt or fear, but out of a vision of God that *evokes* response rather than commands it."[92] This can be done effectively only from *within* the community of the world.

## D.  Needing Each Other

The variety of gifts in the community is called forth most persuasively when the call comes from a genuine, felt need. We can talk theoretically and convincingly about the many needs we have within the Christian community and in the world, but one wonders at times about whether the call for gifts to respond to those needs comes from an experience of true need—if, indeed, the call comes at all. It is easy, I think, to by-pass the stage at which we allow ourselves to acknowledge and feel the ways in which we do need each other. There is an enormous difference between enabling the charisms of others to come forth because people will complain or think me odd if I do not and nurturing gifts simply by voicing the awareness that I need others to survive and prosper as a human being and as a Christian.

It is easier for a hungry person to feel need than it is for one who has her/his larders full. It is easier for the powerless to experience need than it is for those in power. It is easier for the poor to feel genuine need than it is for the wealthy. It is easier for the person in the pew to know the need of official ministers than it is for official ministers to feel the need of the gifts of the person in the pew. When genuine need is felt, true invitations are proffered to each other, and the community is enriched by the breadth of charisms within it. The acknowledgment of genuine need can foster an active imagination. An active imagination can nurture creativity, and then we have the possibility of a whole new way of understanding ministry.

## E. Evaluation

A final note, and one much less exalted than the others, is the need for evaluation in our ministry. We do not do enough of it, and often when we do it, we do not know how, and so do not do a very good job. But, there are resources in many disciplines available to us as a Christian community, and it behooves us to make use of them. We also have access to a *sensus fidelium* as to what is truly good for the communities to which we belong, and we have or can acquire tools that will help us evaluate how we are doing. Not to ask how we are doing is to be self-satisfied in a way that is repugnant to the struggle and pain of our world. If an unexamined life is not worth living, then an unexamined ministry is not worth doing.

## Obstacles to a Renewed Ministry

It is evident from the foregoing that we need to examine ourselves individually and as a community to discover what may be blocking the gifts in the community. Certainly, claims to élitism, status, personal power, arrogance, and ministerial hegemony would be major obstacles. Theologies or institutional structures that prove divisive or nurture a hierarchy of good, better, and best need to be abandoned. A magical sense of grace that ignores the instrumentality and goodness of the human will prevent the calling forth of ministerial charisms in the cosmic sense spoken of above. We need to identify and evaluate the things in our past that have caused us to have a growingly narrow sense of ministry. Urban Holmes thinks that "it is a very bad theology that makes a doctrine of ministerial office the center of the 'good news', and we can be thankful for a growing maturity in this regard."[93] Global awareness today challenges us, indeed requires that we broaden our horizons with respect to ministry.

Let us return now to the place from which we began: One Spirit — Many Ministries.

## VI.  One Spirit — Many Ministries

The debate about the one and the many has been "the battle of the giants concerning being."[94] From a religious perspective, we speak of unity as an attribute of God, as a goal toward which the human spirit strives, as a mystery to be glimpsed and celebrated, as a discovery to be uncovered. John's gospel records Jesus' desire that the disciples' unity be like God's unity (17:11). Plurality, on the other hand, is a constant element of our experience, an inescapable dimension of our spatio-temporal existence. It is the stuff of life's endless complexity, richness and variety, providing an interest and a challenge without which we can imagine only eternal boredom. It is hard to fathom one without the other, but also elusive to speak coherently about their co-existence. Plurality can be attested to in a way that unity cannot. But, it is possible to talk about unity in a teleological sense, as unfinished business, as a goal to which we are open, and we can raise the question about what it is like when we do have an experience of what we call unity.

## A. One Spirit

During the centuries-long evolution of the Church, unity has always been a goal. But, the meaning of unity and the ways of achieving it have varied greatly from one historical period to another. In the Roman Catholic tradition, unity has been closely allied with institutional structure and uniform liturgical expression. There is no doubt that the faith community can and should take action that will nurture the unity, but it is not something one can create on demand. We also need to attend to the gifted dimension of oneness. We can pray for it, be open to it, hope for it, and pay attention to these life experiences of unity we do indeed have. I offer some suggestions to tease out further reflection on the question, How do we experience the one Spirit?

1. Theological anthropology attests to the unity of the human race. We believe in a radical inter-relationship among all humans and between each person and humankind.[95] Our experience of the global village as an economic, political, cultural, and ecological web provides an opportunity in which we can allow ourselves to be connected with all other peoples. Scientists tell us that they have found the geographical origins of our birthplace as the human race. We are all descendants of a single African tribe, making all persons brothers and sisters, or at least very distant cousins. This is the forum for ministry.

2. Today, we have a growing sense of relationship with persons of all faiths. The East and the West are in dialogue. Persons like Thomas Merton and Raimundo Panikkar lead the way toward common understanding with those who share similar ministerial goals of building up the community and uncovering God's presence in the world.

3. As Christians, we share a common story whose hero is Jesus Christ. And, although far from perfect, we do have a common language, common symbols, and participate in a common journey. From this base, we struggle to become ever more inclusive and welcoming. James Fenhagen notes that "we will discover our mutuality not in our differences but in the solidarity that comes in the recognition of a common pilgrimage."[96] This pilgrimage is fuelled by the power of the Spirit in the world, and its elements include faith, hope, love, the breaking of one bread, patience, long-suffering, and a generous heart. Above all, the minister on this journey is one who knows the way to repent and forgive.[97]

4. Although the gifts of the Spirit are many, the acknowledgment that they are indeed gifts of the Spirit unifies. Where and how do we experience ourselves as a gifted people? How do we nurture a response of gratitude that has the power to bring us together? How can we be so sensitive to the Spirit that we will recognize our giftedness and use it on behalf of others?[98]

5. Finally, we may experience one Spirit in our common ministerial intention of building up the communities to which we belong. Although we often disagree on what this means and on the way to work toward this goal, and although we fail repeatedly because of our indifference and sinfulness, we have access to the means by which we might continually purify our hearts and align ourselves with that intention of God that wishes us well without qualifications. We can always keep alive the desire for purity of intention and a single-minded heart.

As we continue to break down a false opposition between sacred and secular, we will be more able to look at all kinds of life experiences in order to discover there the contours and meaning of unity. Such experiences run the gamut from the affective experience of oneness between black and white Americans as we listen to the words of Martin Luther King in a crowd in Washington, D.C.—to the uncomfortable and inconvenient decision to be with an ill or dying person day after day—to the joy of a simple birthday with family and friends. We will not know the way to nurture unity until we recognize where we are embracing a pseudo-unity and until we know something about authentic unity. This knowledge can be had, in part, by being open to and paying attention to our lives with others and the ways in which we already know one Spirit.

## B. Many Ministries

Pluralism is more readily available to us. Our country struggles with tolerance and diversity. As individualists, we are aware of the differences in each person, and psychology instructs us about the uniqueness of each personality and its history.

The Roman Catholic experience has been an anomaly of sorts. Outsiders have the impression of a kind of uniformity that has never existed when its history is looked at from close range. But, our idea and practice of ministry has indeed become too monolithic, making the task of allowing many ministries to emerge a difficult one. The control and narrow categories that have been maintained work against us, and we are threatened by new, more inclusive ideas about ministry. In many ways, we need a theological and ecclesial rethinking of ministry of wide proportions. Allow me to make two comments.

1. If ministry's task is to make grace concrete in word, sign and personal meeting,[99] then plurality is an inevitable outcome at the very heart of that ministry. The ideology of unity has been so strong and so pertinent in our spiritual tradition that it is not easy for us to notice and celebrate diversity as a value in itself and not as a result of sin—something to be tolerated and fled from. We need to discover ways in which we can enhance our ability to value different contributions to ministry.

Thomas Aquinas offers a theological base for such a position. In the *Summa theologiae,* in the treatise on creation, Aquinas places the origin of the diversity in creation in the intention of the Creator. The cosmos was created in order that God's goodness might be communicated to it, and because this divine goodness could not be adequately represented by one creature alone, God created many and diverse creatures. Hence, "the whole universe together participates in the divine goodness more perfectly, and represents it better than any single creature whatever."[100]

2. As a community, we need to ask whether or not we are free enough to allow the Spirit to blow where it wills. This requires, of course, a willingness to be open to the art and practice of discernment *as a community.* The power of the Spirit is quite obviously alive and well in the Church today, and the variety of its expression is infinite. We can apply to ministry our knowledge of the dignity, value and uniqueness of each person and grow to appreciate and celebrate the many, different gifts the Spirit is offering to the community.

## VII. Conclusion

The recovery of the ministry given to each person in baptism cannot take place without a growing understanding and acceptance of the many gifts the one Spirit gives. The needs of our world require it; the integrity of our faith and the dignity of each person invite it; the power of the one Spirit allows it to flourish. Paul, spokesperson for the goodness of the variety of gifts, says to the Corinthians:

> I am always thanking God for you. I thank God for the grace given to you in Christ Jesus. I thank God for all the enrichment that has come to you in Christ. You possess full knowledge and you can give full expression to it, because in you the evidence for the truth of Christ has found confirmation. There is indeed no single gift you lack. . . . It is the very God who called you to share in the life of God's son Jesus Christ our Lord; and God keeps faith (1Corinthians 1:4-7, 9).

There is no gift we lack. Trust in this promise and the joy that comes from the many gifts we have been given at the hands of a loving God and a life-giving Spirit must be the hallmarks of our ministry today. What if ministry were to become the commission and the glory of all the baptized[101] to all the world?

## NOTES

[1]Charles Cochrane, *Christianity and Classical Culture* (London: Oxford University Press, 1940), 428.

[2]Thomas O'Meara, *Theology of Ministry* (New York: Paulist Press, 1983), 34.

[3]This attitude is reflected throughout the documents, but especially in *The Church in the Modern World*.

[4]See recent studies by Andrew Greeley and the University of Notre Dame. See also Rembert G. Weakland, "The Church in Worldly Affairs: Tensions Between Laity and Clergy," *America,* 18 October 1986, 201-202. There is evidence throughout history that lay involvement and a high level of education go hand in hand. See Stephen Charles Neill and Hans-Reudi Weber, eds., *The Layman in Christian History* (Philadelphia: Westminster Press, 1963).

[5]For a summary of many of these dialogues, see Bernard Cooke, *Ministry to Word and Sacraments* (Philadelphia: Fortress, 1976), 2-8.

[6]Urban Holmes, *The Future Shape of Ministry* (New York: The Seabury Press, 1971), 167.

[7]See Edward Schillebeeckx, *Ministry* (New York: Crossroad, 1981), especially Chapter V, "A Brief Hermeneutical Intermezzo," 100-104.

[8]It is important to take note of the challenges offered by process theology, liberation theology, Black theology, and feminist theology. Our understanding of ministry must be situated within these broader contexts, even though such an analysis is not the specific topic of the present essay.

[9]George Tavard, *Pilgrim Church* (New York: Herder & Herder, 1967), 40.

[10]Ibid., 41.

[11]George Tavard, *A Theology for Ministry,* Theology and Life Series, no. 6 (Wilmington, DE: Michael Glazier, Inc., 1983).

[12]Ibid., 7.

[13]Ibid., 80-86.
[14]Ibid., 27.
[15]Ibid., 93.
[16]Henri Nouwen, *Creative Ministry* (New York: Doubleday, 1971).
[17]Ibid., xiv.
[18]Ibid., xx.
[19]Urban Holmes, *The Future Shape of Ministry* (New York: Seabury, 1971).
[20]Urban Holmes, *Ministry and Imagination* (New York: Seabury, 1976).
[21]Urban Holmes, *Spirituality for Ministry* (San Francisco: Harper & Row, 1982).
[22]Holmes, *The Future Shape,* iii. Examples of such authors include William Clebsch, Charles Jaekle, John T. McNeill.
[23]Ibid., 203.
[24]Ibid., 5.
[25]Ibid., 32.
[26]Ibid., 96. Holmes is citing Killian McDonnell, "Ways of Validating Ministry," *Journal of Ecumenical Studies* 7 (1970): 260.
[27]Holmes, *The Future Shape,* 212.
[28]Ibid., 113.
[29]Ibid.
[30]Ibid., 217f.
[31]Ibid., 228.
[32]Holmes, *Ministry and Imagination,* 2.
[33]Ibid., 28-34.
[34]Ibid., 8.
[35]Ibid.
[36]Carlos Castaneda, *Tales of Power* (New York: Simon and Schuster, 1974).
[37]Holmes, *Ministry and Imagination,* 263.
[38]Ibid., 264.
[39]Ibid., 58.
[40]Holmes, *Spirituality for Ministry,* 4.
[41]Bernard Cooke, *Ministry to Word and Sacraments* (Philadelphia: Fortress Press, 1976).
[42]Ibid., 1-3.
[43]David Power, *Gifts That Differ: Lay Ministries Established and Unestablished, Studies of the Reformed Rites of the Catholic Church,* vol. VIII (New York: Pueblo Publishing Company, 1980).
[44]Ibid., 10.
[45]Ibid., 31.
[46]Ibid., 159.
[47]Edward Schillebeeckx, *Ministry: Leadership in the Community of Jesus Christ* (New York: Crossroad, 1981).
[48]Edward Schillebeeckx, *The Church With A Human Face: A New and Expanded Theology of Ministry* (New York: Crossroad, 1985).
[49]Schillebeeckx, *Ministry,* 2.
[50]Ibid., 76.
[51]Schillebeeckx, *The Church with a Human Face,* 4.

[52]Ibid., 5.

[53]Pierre Grelot, *Église et ministères. Pour un dialogue critique avec Edward Schillebeeckx* (Paris, 1983).

[54]Schillebeeckx, *The Church with a Human Face,* 11-12.

[55]Thomas O'Meara, *Theology of Ministry* (New York: Paulist Press, 1983).

[56]Ibid., 1.

[57]John Macquarrie, *Theology, Church & Ministry* (New York: Crossroad, 1986).

[58]Ibid., 201.

[59]John Macquarrie, *Principles of Christian Theology,* 2nd ed. (New York: Charles Scribner's, 1966).

[60]Ibid., 156.

[61]William J. Bausch, *Ministry: Traditions, Tensions, Transitions* (Mystic, CT: Twenty-third Publications, 1982).

[62]James C. Fenhagen, *Ministry and Solitude* (New York: Seabury, 1981).

[63]Other books of interest on ministry include: H. Richard Niebuhr and Daniel Day Williams, eds., *The Ministry in Historical Perspectives* (New York: Harper & Row, 1956); Daniel Day Williams, *The Minister and the Care of Souls* (New York: Harper & Row, 1961); John V. Taylor, *The Go-Between God: The Holy Spirit and the Christian Mission* (Philadelphia: Fortress Press, 1972); Dennis Geaney, *Emerging Lay Ministries* (Kansas City: Andrews and McMeel, Inc., 1979); Murray Steward Thompson, *Grace and Forgiveness in Ministry* (Nashville: Abingdon, 1981); Helen Doohan, *The Ministry of God: Effective and Fulfilled* (New York: Alba House, 1986); Leonard Doohan, *Laity's Mission in the Local Church* (San Francisco: Harper & Row, 1986); Anne Rowthorn, *The Liberation of the Laity* (Wilton, CT: Morehouse-Barlow, 1986); Edmund Flood, *The Laity Today and Tomorrow* (New York: Paulist Press, 1987).

[64]Cooke, *Ministry,* 12. Cooke refers to documents on the priesthood produced at the last session of Vatican II: *Christus Dominus, Presbyterorum ordinis,* and *Optatum totius,* and the ensuing commentaries. See S. Ryan, "The Hierarchical Structure of the Church," in *Vatican II: the Constitution on the Church,* ed. K. McNamara (London, 1968), 163-234.

[65]Hans Küng, *Why Priests? A Proposal for a New Church Ministry,* trans. Robert C. Collins (Garden City, New York: Doubleday, 1972).

[66]Schillebeeckx, *The Church with a Human Face,* 4-12.

[67]Robert Kinast, "A Consultation with U.S. Lay People," *Origins,* 2 April 1987, 733.

[68]See *Gaudium et Spes* and *Lumen Gentium.* Also Paul VI, *Evangelii nuntiandi,* 1975. English translation: *On Evangelization in the Modern World* (Washington, D.C.: USCC, 1976).

[69]Holmes, *Spiritual Ministry,* 157.

[70]Macquarrie, *Theology, Church & Ministry,* 158.

[71]Nouwen, *Creative Ministry,* xxi.

[72]Power, *Gifts That Differ,* 54.

[73]Other resources for a broad sense of theology in a cosmic perspective include the works of Teilhard de Chardin and the theology and

liturgy of the Eastern churches, e.g., those that see Christ as Pantocrator.

[74]Cooke, *Ministry to Word and Sacraments,* 190.

[75]Fenhagen, *Ministry and Solitude,* 18.

[76]William Stringfellow speaks of vocation as "the name of the awareness of *that* significance of one's own biography [that it yields knowledge of the Word of God incarnate in human life]. To have a vocation or to be called in Christ means to discern the coincidence of the Word of God with one's own selfhood, in one's own being, in the most specific, thorough, unique and conscientious sense." *A Simplicity of Faith* (Nashville: Abingdon, 1982), 21. See also Leonard Doohan, *The Lay-Centered Church: Theology and Spirituality* (Minneapolis: Winston Press, 1984), 112-19.

[77]Stringfellow, *A Simplicity,* 14. Thomas O'Meara underlines this same point: "The church is ministerial. Ministry is not a rare vocation or a privileged office but belongs to the nature of the new covenant. As with its universal source, baptism, ministry exists in the churches as an aspect of every Christian's life." *Theology of Ministry,* 209.

[78]O'Meara, *Theology of Ministry,* 137.

[79]Ibid.

[80]Cooke, *Ministry to Word,* 191.

[81]Eugene Hillman, "Spirituality Beyond Words, Where Action Is," *National Catholic Reporter,* 13 February 1987, 11.

[82]O'Meara, *Theology of Ministry,* 199. See also David Power, *Gifts That Differ,* 29: " . . . time seems to indicate that worship can only be true worship if it is part of a more broadly based community life. Hence the community under its lay leadership looks to matters of the temperal order, inclusive of mutual care within the community and of its responsibility in the social, political and cultural arena."

[83]Urban Holmes, *The Future Shape,* 113.

[84]Cooke, *Ministry to Word,* vii.

[85]Some examples include John Macquarrie, *Theology,* 157, and George Tavard, *A Theology for Ministry,* 97.

[86]See Robert Bellah et al., *Habits of the Heart: Individualism and Commitment in American Life* (Berkeley: University of California Press, 1985).

[87]Power, *Gifts That Differ,* 121.

[88]Ibid.

[89]Ibid., 122.

[90]William Stringfellow, *The Politics of Spirituality* (Philadelphia: Westminster Press, 1984), 30.

[91]Robert Capon, *An Offering of Uncles: The Priesthood of Adam & the Shape of the World* (New York: Sheed and Ward, 1967), 11-28.

[92]Fenhagen, *Ministry and Solitude,* 89.

[93]Holmes, *The Future Shape,* 4.

[94]Plato, *Sophist,* 246A.

[95]Tavard, *A Theology for Ministry,* 22-23.

[96]Fenhagen, *Ministry and Solitude,* 38.

[97]Eugene Hillman, "Spirituality Beyond Words," 11.

[98]Fenhagen, *Ministry and Solitude,* 38.

[99]O'Meara, *Theology of Ministry,* 33.

[100]I. q. 47, a. 1. resp.
[101]O'Meara, *Theology of Ministry,* 3.

# Living in the Spirit

## John C. Haughey, S. J.

Living in God's Spirit means living off of powers that exceed our human powers. The ordinary means Christians use to receive these extraordinary empowerings are the sacraments, the Scriptures, personal and communal prayer.

We will proceed in the usual manner in order to understand the empowerings of the Spirit. Although much of pneumatology emphasizes the theme of power, the Spirit is unlike any power we know. It operates in the human order and in the areas wherein human powers are being generated just as easily as it does in spiritual contexts. We will, therefore, examine some of the more frequent ways in which human powers attempt to show their relationship to the power of the Spirit.

Another oddity about the Spirit and, therefore, a second methodological presupposition that will shape this essay, is the conviction that the Holy Spirit is better understood with and through Christological data than it is with pneumatological data. We will use pneumatological data, of course, since Jesus could have said not only that "he who sees me, sees the Father," but also, "he who sees me, sees the Spirit." The Spirit is revealed to us through Jesus. Reflection on the Holy Spirit, therefore, in this essay, will be rooted in reflections both on human empowering and on the Spirit of Jesus.

There are many ways we experience power. We will examine only three here. The power of indignation, the power of solidarity, and the power of love will each be examined as experiences of the human spirit, then as experiences in Jesus' life, at least as the Gospel communicates them.

## I. THE POWER OF INDIGNATION

It is obvious in observing the human scene that indignation generates considerable energy. People who otherwise give very little evidence of energy can become overnight zealots and activists if and when they are brought to indignation. Indignation erupts where dignity is violated. The indignity might be subtle or blatant, personal or structural.

The combinations are many. The point that is important here

is that psychologically, sociologically, and politically indignation creates power or generates energy. When indignation is due to some personal affront, the degree of power will obviously not approach the degree of power that erupts when a whole people or nation feels a sense of indignation. Witness modern day Israel and the power in the Palestinian people. Indignation can even reach the point where death is preferable to acquiescing in the ongoing indignities.

Indignation leads to action. Even those who might see themselves as ordinarily non-reactive or reserved can become very confrontative when provoked by the violation of the norms of fairness that at least implicitly govern social life. But, even more than individual action, indignation has the power to create communities of people who, although not of one mind before, become so when they suffer some violation of human dignity or see one inflicted on some members of a community with whom they identify. Indignation generates solidarity. Relationships of solidarity are themselves a new source of power. What was latent before is catalyzed by indignities.

If one were to read the four Gospels simply looking for instances in which Jesus is indignant, one would begin to see the relationship between power and indignation. And, since "Spirit-led" fits him better than it does anyone who ever lived, we can also see the way the Spirit can be behind righteous indignation. Examples abound. Think of his indignation when the relief of people's plight on the sabbath is considered less important than observance of the sabbath behavior codes. Or, think of his indignation at the phoney piety that would proscribe some goods by sacralizing them through a process called Korban (Mark 7,6-13). This practice would keep younger members of the family from having to allocate some things or their monetary value to their needy mothers and fathers. He did not hesitate to reprimand these younger family members for their hypocrisy because they paid lip service to God while their hearts were far from God. Think of the indignation that seized Jesus at the mess he witnessed in the Temple area. "Get out of here! Stop turning my Father's house into a marketplace" (Jn.3,16). His indignation led him to toppling the money changers' tables.

Jesus' indignation has a few idiosyncracies to it. It seems that it is not triggered by affronts to his own dignity. Rather, it is occasioned by all the kinds of injustices done to those with whom he identified himself. Empathetic indignation, it might be termed.

A large movement began to form around Jesus. Their numbers and their coalescence began to unsettle the entrenched religious establishment. "If we let him go on like this (performing signs), the whole world will believe in him. Then the Romans will come in and sweep away our sanctuary and our nation" (Jn.11,48). Threatened entrenched power was up against the inchoate power of indignation. In the short run, the former form of power had its way; in the long run, the latter form of power triumphed.

Jesus' message was at least in part a message about human dignity. It was in direct line with the whole thrust of the inbreakings of God in the Hebrew Scriptures, which called people away from their bondage. The hearers and followers of Jesus were not being called out of a bondage devised by foreign despots, but one devised by their own leadership. That leadership did not convey to people a sense of their dignity in God's eyes. It managed to make them feel unworthy, guilty, blameworthy. The parable of the two men who went up to the temple to pray is a good example of this. The one humbled himself while the other exalted himself and disparaged the bowed down man, reminding God how unlike him he was. "I give you thanks, O God, that I am not like the rest of men—grasping, crooked, adulterous—or even like this tax collector" (Lk.18,11).

This self-exalted, self-congratulatory dignity was foolish. It was subtly closed to transcendence while acknowledging the Transcendent. It was auto-salvific, even though it claimed to be awaiting a saving Messiah.

In what does living in the Spirit consist? So far, it should be clear it means living in the truth, first of all the truth of oneself, one's dignity, power and powerlessness. To Jesus, the Spirit was the Spirit of Truth. He described it as able to indwell the human spirit. "The Spirit of truth whom the world cannot accept . . . remains with you and will be within you" (Jn.14,17). This indwelling Spirit could guide the human spirit into the truth about everything. "When he comes, being the Spirit of truth he will guide you to all truth" (Jn.16,13). Three of the things the Spirit has to teach about are sin, justice and condemnation. They are the very things about which religious people can most easily be in error. But, to be in error about them jeopardizes the sense of self esteem the Spirit would convey by knowing the truth about being a person.

The context we live in makes us live in error. It is "the world" in the heart and mind of the believer that keeps him or her from the truth. The world in the Gospel of John symbolically encapsulates all the forces of secularization that seduce people into trying to be something they are not by imagining they can live in ruthless independence from God. The real world is full of the

glory of God. The worldly world refuses to accept this truth. It
attempts to be its own source of truth, a counterfeit truth it
conveys to everyone, believer and non-believer alike.

Three matters that the world would teach the believer go to
the core of this matter of Spirit-inspired self esteem. The world
would teach believers either that there is no such thing as personal sin or that we are so sinful we are hopeless. But, the Spirit
"will prove the world wrong about sin . . . in that they refuse to
believe in me" (Jn.16, 8-9). Unpacked, this cryptic sentence
means that the believer needs to learn the Spirit's teaching about
Jesus' triumph over sin. This would rid believers of a false, self-
attributed sense of rectitude that did not know repentance. Or, it
would free them of a destructive guilt that did not know the
peace that comes from God's unconditional love and infinite
mercy.

Secondly, "about justice—from the fact that I go to the Father
and you can see me no more" (Jn.16,10). Again, the errors the
world puts in the hearts of believers about justice are, first of all,
that they can make themselves just in God's eyes or then that
they can make the world just. Both of these are untrue, even
nonsense. The One who has gone to the Father has won justice
for us. Our own efforts will never justify us. Justice is always a
gift won by Jesus for us. And, the justice we would do in this
world is a responsibility related directly to the gift of being
justiced by God. The justice God does and will do in this world is
incommensurate with both our ability to know and our ability to
succeed at being just or in making a just world. We know the
initial forms of justice, such as human rights. These are enough
of an agenda to occupy a lifetime. But, the fuller, further forms
of justice are still enfolded in the unseen and unknowable ways
of God.

Unreal aspirations about justice in this world, those that are
scaled too high, are a constant source of frustration, discourage-
ment, and mututal recrimination. But, there is the other population of believers, unfortunately much larger, whose sights are
scaled too low. They believe in the gift of justification, but do not
see that it is intimately connected to the tasks that derive from
the gift, tasks of justice and freedom and reconciliation. Both
those who grow discouraged about justice and those who do not
see it as a part of the Christian task in the world, together these
populations probably do more to create doubts about God's
presence in the world than all the efforts of atheistic materialism
to prove it is the true philosophy of life.

And, finally, the Spirit will prove the world wrong "about
condemnation—for the prince of this world has been con-

demned" (Jn.16,11). The world tries to get the followers of Christ to judge others and condemn themselves. The Spirit, on the other hand, teaches believers that judgment is not their province and that personal condemnation is not possible for one who is in Christ. In him there is no condemnation. Condemnation, therefore, is germane only for one who refuses the light emanating from his or her conscience, a light whose Author is God. Such people condemn themselves, in fact. They condemn themselves to the lot of those who do not know God and, therefore, do not know love and life, truth and beauty. In biblical terms, these people are seen to have a leader, the prince of this world. This prince is a personification of all those energies which have built up over time in those who would formally live without God, beyond God and against God. John's Jesus insists that his followers can successfully resist the world and its prince: "Take courage! I have overcome the world" (Jn.16,33).

## II. THE POWER OF SOLIDARITY

There is a whole other side to this living in the Spirit than the one mentioned above. What we have been looking at is the human and Christian experience of the individual person. What we must examine now are the social effects of many individuals who have a common experience and who are living in the Spirit. These effects can be summed up in one word: solidarity. The Hebrew Scriptures teem with the evidence that this solidarity was what God meant to be the centerpiece of the divine plan from the beginning. It is expressed sometimes in terms of common worship, with all peoples streaming towards Jerusalem, doing homage to Israel's God. It is expressed sometimes in terms of *shalom*, which was interpersonal or inter-nation peace on earth. It is expressed sometimes in terms of justice. Biblical solidarity in any and all of these expressions is always eschatological in tone and contents. We will return to this later in the essay.

In the New Testament, some of the old symbols are repeated, but some new ones are also employed. Consider Jesus' depiction of himself, for example, as Shepherd who intends to pasture one flock. The source of its unity is to be the Holy Spirit. Before this eschatological unity is realized, lesser solidarities will be possible because of this outpoured Spirit. People's relationships with one another can give evidence of the gift of the Spirit by the behavioral fruit it produces. The fruits of the Spirit are: "love, joy, peace, patient endurance, kindness, generosity, faith, mildness and chastity" (Gal. 5,22).

The key symbol of solidarity in both testaments is the Kingdom of God, or even better, the reign of God. This eschatological symbol describes the definitive future awaiting those who are upright in God's eyes. But, it is also a description of what the present can be and is meant to become. The present inchoate reign of God is characterized by relationships of justice and, therefore, peace. What we can be now is a people, each of whom gives to both God and to one another what is due them, given who we are.

In his recent encyclical, *Sollicitudo Rei Socialis*, Pope John Paul II has highlighted solidarity as a virtue that has "many points of contact with charity which is the distinguishing mark of Christ's disciples (Jn. 13,35)."[1] He envisions solidarity as a quality in the whole network of relationships, from the most intimate to the most remote. In the most local or intimate of structures as also in the most global, the Pope sees persons having to take responsibility for what goes on in their lives and in their society. Unfortunately, their interactions are often insensitive, even exploitative, leaving in their wake "structures of sin."[2] These structures are the main obstacles to relationships of solidarity. While he points up the role played by liberal capitalism and Marxist collectivism in creating these structures of sin, he does not let individual Christians or their faith communities simply lament such things and assume the role of victim. Structures of sin are the products of many personal sins. Hence, their removal can be attained by an accumulation of many acts of solidarity.[3] What we have perversely made we can unmake and graciously recompose.

The virtue of solidarity presumes people recognize the interdependence they have on one another, both as persons, as groups, and even as nations. That interdependence has already arrived at every level of life, economic, political, cultural, religious, even without our planning it. But, its recognition lifts interdependence to a "moral category," calling for a response.[4] This response is acts of solidarity. Solidarity as a virtue is "a firm and persevering determination to commit oneself to the common good; that is to say to the good of all and of each individual because we are all really responsible for all."[5]

Although he does not refer to him, one of the Pope's sources and inspirations in this whole development of his thinking about solidarity has been a Polish priest/theologian, Jozef Tischner. His book, *The Spirit of Solidarity*, makes several points about this virtue, worth noting here. Solidarity is a "feeling for those who have been struck down."[6] The pain need not have been. It was devised by someone for another: "Nothing enrages one more than a gratuitous wound."[7] The conscience of persons is the deepest source of solidarity. It is in conscience that God speaks

most clearly. If they hear that voice, they can join with others
who also have heard it. "What happens then is that one person
joins with another to tend to the one who needs care. I am with
you, you are with me, we are together—for him . . . 'For him'
comes first and 'we' comes later."[8] Ignoring conscience and
condoning indignities or structures of sin, on the other hand,
tighten the noose around one's own humanity. But, rebelling
against these structures is the same as refusing to participate in a
lie.

There is a clear relationship between the Spirit and the human
experience of solidarity. The Holy Father speaks of the need we
have for the Spirit to give the world a new vision of itself, with
solidarity as the new criterion for interpreting it.[9] In both his
1986 encyclical on the Holy Spirit and in this recent one, he
connects the process of humanizing the world with the gift of the
Holy Spirit.[10] He acknowledges that our efforts at solidarity will
not fully succeed in history, but that Christ will make them part
of what is gathered up, cleansed and transfigured into the eternal and universal kingdom.[11] This eschatological trans-
figuration is possible because of the presence in history of "the
efficacious action of the Holy Spirit which fills the earth."[12] In
fact, every person born in time "is placed under the permanent
action of the Holy Spirit."[13] It is the inner gift character of the
Holy Spirit to persons that insures an outer authentic solidarity.

Counterfeit kinds of solidarity are usually collectivist. Most
socialist ideologies are collectivist. By collectivism I mean an
infelicitous aggregating of people that removes their ability to
function freely, at least in some ways. The price people pay for a
collectivist vision of the common good is their individuality. This
kind of solidarity is inauthentic because it does not develop from
within people, but is imposed upon them from without. The
intention will not be totalitarian, but somehow or other it is the
effect. When an ideology, rather than the convictions and virtues
and gifts of the people, is relied on to create the collectivity and
have it pursue its purposes, a distaste for true solidarity
develops.

One of the experiences of the first Christian communities was
the great variety of gifts that flowed from the same Spirit, each
affecting the community as a whole and upbuilding it (I
Cor.12,4-7). These gifts made for considerable fecundity in the
Ministries the Christian communities exercised both within
their own ranks and in the world. These gifts also guaranteed the
community that it would not become sodden with a uniformity
or with a collectivistic disfigurement of the kind of unity the
Spirit would give.

The New Testament notion that comes closest to the idea of the solidarity we have been examining here is that of *koinonia*. It can be translated only partially by such words as communion, partnership, bond, community or fellowship.[14] It is a favorite term of Luke and Paul in the New Testament. For example, "The grace of the Lord Jesus Christ, and the love of God and the fellowship (koinonia) of the Holy Spirit be with you all" (I Cor. 13,13). The follower of Christ is brought into the fellowship of the Holy Spirit. The *koinonia* of the Spirit is like a milieu inhabited, so to speak, by Father, Son and Spirit.

But, this same concept has its counterpart on earth. The first communities are described by Luke in the Acts of the Apostles in terms of *koinonia*. "They devoted themselves to the apostles' instruction and the communal life (koinonia), to the breaking of bread and the prayers" (Acts 2,42). The community came to be so closely knit that the explanation of their communion or fellowship could not be given in terms or causes that were intramundane. In a very real sense, these communities were brought into the eternal, pre-existing *koinonia* of Father, Son and Holy Spirit by the Holy Spirit.

When *koinonia* is enjoyed or experienced and the gifts of the members of the community are exercised, *koinonia* becomes *diakonia*: "service." The exercise of the gifts upbuilds the ecclesial and the wider human community. Something new enters the world when this combination of *koinonia* and *diakonia* is operating. The sacraments, especially the Eucharist, are the ordinary way the Spirit forges and deepens the bonds between the people of God. Paul describes the cup we drink at the table of the Lord as "a sharing in (koinonia) the blood of Christ" (I Cor.10,16). And of the bread of life the eucharistic participants share, Paul asks, "Is not the bread we break a sharing in (koinonia) the body of Christ?" (I Cor.10,17). Every Eucharist causes the *koinonia* we already enjoy to be even more tightly knitted together.[15]

There is real merit in subsuming the elaboration of the notions of solidarity into this more biblical concept of *koinonia*. It would serve to deepen the notion and insure its continuance as a valuable part of the Catholic tradition.

### III.  THE POWER OF LOVE

A third experience of power is the one we associate with love. To fall in love is to fall into a powerful and mysterious energy. One who has not known the thrall of it is truly pitiable. That thrall has much to do with freedom, joy, and self-transcendence. While it is highly personal or, to be more precise, interpersonal, the experience can start off or end up self-enclosed and in an unfortunate individualism. This would make it the opposite of love, its contradiction, in fact. Counterfeit love encloses the other in oneself. Real love loses its life; it does not gain another's.

Love has to make judgments in order to express itself. It does not have a good record in this regard. It is not always wise, in other words. Sometimes its misjudgments are amusingly wrongheaded. The sight one has through rose-colored glasses is famous for its distortion. Sometimes these judgments are nothing short of tragic. The world is full of children who were conceived and born of a mistaken judgment about love's presence. Those whose existence was terminated before birth are no less a sign of the fallibility of the judgments that are made from the power of this affect.

Affectivity is a grand term to describe the mysterious lair where love assumes ascendency. The heart is the best and, yet, the blindest part of everyone. To be wise, this blind part of us needs more than it has going for it. Judgments of affectivity, to be wise, must be informed. By reason, of course. But, where does that leave us since, as we know, the heart has reasons that reason cannot fathom? Love has an uncanny reluctance to be subservient to reason, and rightly so. Love will never be reducible to categories of intelligibilty. It will always have more folly and foolhardiness in it that it has rationality.

There is much more to love than romantic experiences. No less a part of love is patience, forbearance, trust, hope, perseverance. If we were to take love's analogue to be not romance but the love of mothers or fathers for their children, these other substantial characteristics would stand out in bolder relief. With this different measure of love, there is still folly, but it is more sober. There is still foolhardiness, but it is more heroic. There is the non-rational, but it is not of the adolescent variety. It can be killed, but it dies more slowly. It lives much longer without response than romantic love does. It can be spontaneous or a highly deliberate act of the will.

Love grows where there are actions that express it. The actions may be simple gestures or heroic deeds or any of the in between ways of symbolizing the inner reality. Words are never as sure as deeds to prove that love is really operating. Words may commit much, but they cost little of themselves. Voiced love is on its way to somewhere, hopefully real love. It does not always arrive.

These are incontrovertible reflections on the ordinary experience of human love. The privileged, authoritative disclosures of God that we learn about and receive from God complete and complement these human experiences of love. The entry of God's love into the realm of authentic human love can be purifying and corrective, but it should not be condemnatory. Divine love does not eschew human love, but opens it out to the transcendent with which it is in a continuum.

Jesus was born of the Holy Spirit and of Mary. The Spirit is the Spirit of love. It is instructive to see the effect of this love in his life. It explains his birth; it also explains his everyday dealings, at least as these were portrayed by the evangelists.

It would seem that he lived in love. That love was noted again and again in his interactions. To cite a few. The evangelist who wrote the fourth Gospel never names himself, but refers to himself again and again as "the disciple whom Jesus loved." It seems that this experience of being loved was more central to his sense of himself than his own name. Sometimes Jesus is explicitly described as loving someone. Think of the rich young man, or of Martha and Mary, and their brother Lazarus.

Even greater evidence that he lived in love is in the highly charged energy field that develops from his interactions with the populace. This is the energy of love that is released when people feel love pouring out of him for them and respond with love for him. Zacchaeus is a good individual example of this response. He promised to give half his money to the poor and pay fourfold if there was anyone he defrauded. This largesse erupted spontaneously once Jesus affirmed him before his neighbors by inviting himself into his house.

Jesus' love for God comes through the Gospels as clearly, if not more clearly, than his love of his neighbor. Being Jewish, he obeyed the great commandment of Deuteronomy, except that he did so to the fullest. "You shall love the Lord, your God, with all your heart, and with all your soul, and with all your strength" (Dt.6,5). For Israel, loving God with all of one's heart meant with one's "innermost being, the center of one's thoughts, will, feelings, instincts."[16] And, loving God with all your soul meant "even if God requires that you face death for his sake you are not to renounce the good and proper allegiance God demands in order to escape it."[17] And loving God with all one's strength, according to the scribes and rabbis, meant with all one's mammon; namely, with all the things one had going for oneself. These would be material and financial resources and the things that usually accompany them: power and status.[18]

Even the most cursory perusal of the Gospels will uncover any number of instances of Jesus' love of God having this rich dimensionality to it. His attunement of heart with his Father is attested to throughout, especially in the Gospel of John. "I do

nothing by myself. I say only what the Father has taught me"
(Jn.8,27). The full-souled way he loved his Father had him
accept the cup which meant his own death, although everything
in him resisted this: "My soul is troubled now, yet what should I
say—Father, save me from this hour? But it was for this that I
came to this hour. Father glorify your name!" (Jn. 12,27-28).
And, the commitment of all his physical, material, relational
resources to loving God is best symbolized by his death. "Now it
is finished," he said, "Then he bowed his head and delivered
over his spirit" (Jn. 19,30).

Peter's love for Jesus is even more illustrative than Jesus' love
of God to understand this continuum between human love and
the love of God that has the Holy Spirit as its author. On the one
hand, Peter's love was unlimited. "I will lay down my life for
you," he vowed before Jesus entered into the agony of the
garden. On the other hand, his love was very limited, as Jesus
knew: "You will lay down your life for me, will you? . . . the
cock will not crow three times before you have disowned me"
(Jn.13,38).

Human love is energy and power. Its fullness, its transcendence, its efficacy can be explained only by the gift of the Spirit
of God, the Love of God outpoured: "The love of God has been
poured out in our hearts through the Holy Spirit who has been
given to us" (Rom.5,5). Human love is only part of the explanation of Peter's love for Jesus. Of itself it proved ineffective. It
could not measure up to its own aspiration to lay down his life for
his friend.

Peter is sometimes ludicrous before Pentecost. The Spirit is
needed for the affectivity of Peter to come into order. With the
arrival of the Spirit, Peter begins to fill the shoes Jesus had
meant him to wear. Or, perhaps it would be better to say Pentecost allowed Peter to unfurl his sails to catch the wind that took
him whither he would not have otherwise been able to go. Before
the Spirit-gift, Peter's is an impetuous and unwise affectivity.
After it, he has the wisdom to hear and obey the Spirit's upbuilding of the nascent Church.

If love is power, the Spirit of Love is a transcendence of the
limitations of this power. The Spirit is also a bearer of ancillary
powers. Even before there is a theological doctrine of the gifts of
the Spirit, there is a biblical elaboration of them by Paul in
Corinthians. Most of these gifts center on wisdom, or the need
for the young Church and its members to be wise and able to
distinguish one spirit from another (I Cor. 12,8-10). This seems
to be a felicitous nexus between love and the wisdom-gifts since

the one thing human love was most likely to be deficient in was, as we have seen, wisdom.

## IV.  REASONS IT DOES NOT WORK

So far, we have examined the continuum between the human experiences and the gift of the Spirit that completes them. But, we now have to ask ourselves the reason the Spirit seems so seldom to break into the undergirding of human experiences if there is such an affinity between the two. Here, we will examine five attitudes that impede the inbreaking Spirit.

The first is pragmatism. This is a characteristic that runs deep in the American culture and coarsens the people's spiritual and cultural sensibilities. The economy's two dynamics of production and consumption or the business of business are a major reason for this very pragmatic approach to the expenditure of energy and resources. This pragmatism is not sufficiently kept in check by other values and cultural interests, as they seem to be, for example, in many of the nations from which the American people came to this county. The result is an American over-concern with dividends: how is this or that effort going to cash out? In a word, a commodity consciousness builds, even towards the deepest values, such as love.

But, love is not a commodity. Once it is so treated, we are beyond the pale of love. Love of a person, another's love for us, God's love of us, our love of God—none of these dynamics flourishes in an atmosphere of pragmatism. We cannot relate to another, whether the other be God or neighbor, in terms of his/her usefulness to us. God is not a commodity. Neither is neighbor. Love is its own reason for being given and received. If it has to have an angle to it, if it is given in order to get something, it is an impure kind of love, if it is love at all.

God, the love of God, the Spirit of God, is the pearl of great price: "The kingdom of heaven is like a merchant's search for fine pearls. When he found one really valuable pearl, he went back and put up for sale all that he had and bought it" (Mt.13,45). We do not seek to acquire this pearl for purposes or pearls beyond it. It is its own reason for being acquired. Love is its own reason for being. In fact, reason for being is love. Love is what it is all about. Everything else is a means for attaining to this condition of being. Being in love is what being human is for.

There are, of course, many good Christians who cannot be considered coarse, but who develop a kind of pragmatic faith that is slightly off center. It misses the mark. This near-miss Christianity seeks to receive the Spirit, not in order to love, but to conquer or to join a cause. There is near-miss Christianity because it is true that the Spirit has a mission, is on mission, sent by the Father and the Son. That mission is "justice to the nations" (Is.42,1). Justice done from love and justice done with love and justice done with love as its goal are all very different from justice as a cause and an absolute. The manner of the Servant who was chosen to bring justice to the nations never ceases to be instructive: "A bruised reed he shall not break, and a smoldering wick he shall not quench until he establish justice on the earth" (Is.42,3-4).

The second obstacle that makes the gift of the Holy Spirit difficult to receive in any degree of power is the one that has grown cynical about love or is disillusioned with love. This generation has come to be referred to as the post-romantic 80s that has supposedly wised up about love. Love words are now heard with suspicion, whether these come from the lips of paramours or preachers. A popular tune in recent times laments: "Love is strange." Cynics would attest the older one gets the stranger it becomes.

One of the weaknesses of our culture is its propensity to use the measure of romantic love to judge all other manifestations of love. If one has had nothing but sour romantic experiences, other kinds of love will suffer proportionately. The mistake is with the measure that is used, not with love itself. Romantic love does not have to be the measure by which we judge love. For most of us, the way we start off in life has the love of a mother or a father as our initial measure of love, its authenticity and power.

To argue the above point: God is revealed in the Scriptures as Love, with much of the manner of God's love manifested after the fashion of a mother for her child/children or a father for his child/children. The love of a lover for a lover is not lacking in the inspired books of the bible revelation; for example, in the Song of Songs, but this kind of passionate love is given a lesser place than the parental love analogy.

Expectancy about love, that it happens and will happen in greater degrees, that one is loveable, that one's love is desired— these human dynamics make one a good candidate for the gift of the Spirit. A lack of expectancy about God's desire to show love to us or a lack of realization that this love is there without measure and unconditionally—these attitudes seriously thwart the entry of God's love for us, in power, into our hearts, souls and consciousness. Non-expectancy about love inevitably has one expect something else to satisfy one's thirst. It will not, and the results of the error are not simple, as those with drug addiction, alcoholic dependencies or sexual compulsions can attest.

There is a third obstacle to receiving the renewing Spirit of God that is certainly as subtle and pervasive as the first two. It is a kind of defense that uses the intellect to fend off anything beyond one's control. It is as if the intellect tries to function as a sentinel who requires that anything that would enter the heart has to pass muster at his checkpoint. Since love is not analyzable, it is turned away. Since it is not understandable, intelligible or controllable, it is not allowed in.

The intellect or mind is well used if it weighs what is already in the heart. It is ill used if it disregards the data of the heart or disdains what would otherwise impact the heart. An intellect so positioned will leave one impoverished, since the most important things in our lives are matters of the heart. They will never be fully understood or controlled by the understanding. Efforts at reducing love to intelligibility will never be successful.

Love is not rational. If this is true of human love, it is all the more true of Divine Love. Paul taunted Greek listeners who avidly sought wisdom with the absurdity of God's way of loving; namely, Christ crucified. Here was both "the power and the wisdom of God. For God's folly is wiser than men and his weakness more powerful than men" (I Cor. 1, 24-25).

The fourth unpromising attitude in a Christian for the renewing power of the Spirit is a revivalist bias. This associates the Spirit with fireworks, hype, the bizarre. The more fireworks, the greater the Spirit—or so the bias goes. Sects that preach this kind of doctrine are constantly under pressure to incite and maintain enthusiasm. The Spirit rescues those who receive it, or so the doctrine implies, from the world of the humdrum and the everyday.

God's love, however, does not rescue us from our humanity and all its ordinariness. It anoints us, so to speak, with the oil of gladness in and through the everyday things that bedevil, bewitch and immerse anyone. Since human love does not know everyday fireworks nor does it require these, why should divine love be required to deliver that kind of kick?

The fifth and final impediment to God's Spirit's filling the human spirit with the love and power that transcend human power is a kind of unilateralism that knows the way to give but does not know the way to receive. In this case, love. Some people learn to give of themselves and serve and look out for and care for others, but are very much unprepared to admit they are in need of this same kind of love and care to be shown to them. When love is initiated by another towards them, they are not comfortable. They feel undeserving of love or of being loved for who they are. Presumably, because they have a sense of self that cannot take in an appreciation of themselves.

Apart from the psychological explanation of this phenome-

non, there is the spiritual malady that has internalized a personal disesteem of self that must constantly merit worthiness by
what one is doing for others or doing to become righteous in
God's eyes. This kind of malady plagued the first Jewish Christians as it had Judaism before that. They had learned the way to
observe the commandments and the statutes and, thus, they
thought they knew the way to please and earn the favor of God.
When they saw that the Holy Spirit was being poured out gratui-
tously on the Gentiles who had not known or observed the law,
they were astonished (Acts 10, 34-48).

One does not come to merit the gift of God's Spirit any more
than one comes to merit God's Love. Merit has nothing to do
with it. One could never come to merit God's love or the gift of
the Spirit of God. God does not love us when we come to be
worthy; God loves us notwithstanding our unworthiness. The
reason one experiences the Gift of the Spirit and another does
not is much more difficult to know. In fact, it is impossible to
know. One surely false assumption would be to expect that the
action of God is based on a partiality. In the context cited above
in which the first Christian community was puzzed at God's
beneficence towards the Gentiles and seeming lack of discrimination, Peter comments: "I begin to see how true it is that God
shows no partiality." Peter had not finished these words when
the Holy Spirit descended upon all (the Gentiles) (Acts 10,34 &
44).

## V.  THE WAY IT WORKS

It would be incorrect to conclude from the above section about
the obstacles to receiving the Spirit that there are some validly
baptized Christians who have not received the Spirit. The reception of the Spirit is coextensive with the conferral of the sacrament of baptism. Everyone who is validly baptized is baptized in
the name of the Father and of the Son and of the Holy Spirit.
The point of the above exercise, which is an examination of
consciousness, is to see whether there are obstacles to a growth in
degrees of the Spirit's power. Baptism begins this growth in the
Spirit. It is not meant to be the end of the outpouring. If we need
bread daily—"Give us this day our daily bread"—do we not
have to drink daily also?

How does one grow in the power of the Spirit? Ask to! Seek to!
Knock! and it shall be opened unto you. How? Where? Of
whom does one ask? I believe the best answer to these questions
can be found in John 7, 37-39:

On the last day of the festival Jesus stood up and cried out: "If anyone thirst, let him come to me; let him drink who believes in me. Scripture has it: 'From within him living waters shall flow.'" (Here he was referring to the Spirit, whom those that come to believe in him were to receive. There was, of course, no Spirit as yet, since Jesus had not yet been glorified.)

There are three keys to both this text and the questions we have posed about receiving the Spirit in greater degrees. The three keys are all verbs: thirst, believe, and drink. Most people thirst; many fewer believe. Some who believe do not thirst, at least not consciously. They have settled for satisfactions that have dulled their deeper thirsts. Many who drink do not believe. They know their thirsts and have embraced some form of transcendence that is not Christ. And finally, the most important group of all: those who know they thirst and who believe in Christ, but do not go to him with their thirst because they do not believe going to him will give them drink. There is no expectation here. They have no experience of having their thirst slaked by Christ. Or, no one has ever taught them to have recourse to him.

He slakes thirsts by giving of his spirit. His death came about when and because he "delivered over his spirit" (Jn. 19,30). It was, of course, delivered over to his Father, but with his followers in mind. The Ascension came about because he wished to prepare his followers for his presence to them in a wholly new way, in and through his spirit. Pentecost or the outpouring of his spirit came about to complete the whole process of redemption that began with the Incarnation.

A deeper examination of the context should help us to appreciate the significance of this text about Jesus and the Spirit. Two things had shaped the liturgy of the feast of Tabernacles, which is the liturgy referred to here.[19] The first was the great need Israel had for rain in early autumn when the feast was celebrated. The whole economy suffered or flourished, depending on the downpouring or its absence. The second was the dedication of the temple of Solomon centuries before. The feast of Tabernacles had its origins in these two moments.

The feast lasted seven days. Every day, the priests and people would process to the fountain outside the temple that fed the pool of Siloam. The main celebrant would fill a gold pitcher with the fountain's water, and the people would then follow him into the temple, waving willow, palm or myrtle branches. The choir would sing: "With joy you will draw water from the springs of salvation." The priest would pour out the water over the altar of the holocausts, and it would pour onto the ground. The congregation would have been reminded of Zechariah 9-14. This

eschatological scene described the outpouring of Yahweh's spirit
of compassion over Jerusalem, with its cleansing stream stretch-
ing to the Mediterranean and the Dead Sea. Peoples from all
corners of the earth would eventually stream into Jerusalem to
worship the God of Israel.[20]

The Spirit and water were very often linked in the mind of
Israel. Part of this might be explained by the fact that the soul,
which can also be translated spirit, was considered the seat of
thirst. Moses' striking of the rock from which water poured forth
and Ezekiel's vision of water flowing out from the temple were
among the most frequently used images in Jewish prayer. They
nurtured the memory and shaped the expectation of Israel about
its future Messiah.

It is this apperceptive background that the reader of John or
the hearer of Jesus would have had when he stands up and cries
out that he has the capacity to assuage their thirsts. "From
within him" these living waters shall flow. Literally, from his
belly or from his guts. According to the exegetes, this phrase is
used infrequently, and it is meant to convey stong emotions
when it is used. This water, which is the Spirit, will tumble from
his gut because in a real sense it is his gut or his own spirit. The
long-awaited water of the Spirit will come from me, so come to
me with your need for this outpouring, Jeus is saying here.

## VI. THE PARADOX OF POWER

It will surely come as no surprise to reflective Christians to
hear that the power of the Spirit works like no other power in the
world. It is not of the world. Though it is in the world, it is the
complete antithesis of power that is of the world. The Gospel
says as much everytime it affirms childlikeness or vulnerability
or humility. If we want to let the power of the Spirit invade us,
one of the things we have to allow for is an intellectual and
affective conversion of our notions and desires for power.

No one savored the paradox of this new kind of power more
than St. Paul. For example, he went to the heart of the paradox
by his choice of the focus of his preaching: "We proclaim Christ
crucified . . . (who is) the power of God and the wisdom of God"
(I Cor. 1,23-24). Of all the scenes to display the power of God,
St. Paul chose that of the crucifixion! He invited his hearers into
the same conversion of concepts that everything in the Gospels
and, for that matter, everything of God requires: "As high as the
heavens are above the earth, so high are my ways above your
ways and my thoughts above your thoughts" (Is.55,9).

Some will seek the power of the Spirit to escape their
straitened condition or intolerable situation. If this would-be

escape is tantamount to seeking moral probity and integrity, the power of the Spirit will eventually succeed in bringing about the sought-for change. Living in the Spirit in Paul's language means "crucifying the flesh with its passions and desires" (Gal.5,24-25). The fruits of an uncrucified flesh are: "idolatry, sorcery, lewd conduct, impurity, licentiousness, hostilities, bickering, jealousy, outbursts of rage, selfish rivalries, dissensions, factions, envy, drunkenness, orgies and the like" (Gal.5, 19-21). Uncrucified flesh has any number of powers, all of them destructive and capable of bringing one into further grief than what he/she experienced in an already fragile situation.

In beseeching the power of the Spirit, however, one is hopefully not attempting to escape from the human condition or not looking for some kind of circumvention of the ills our flesh is heir to. The power of the Spirit will not deliver these effects. The Spirit's power is given so that everyday-things, everybody-things, can be lived through in a different way. What way? After the manner of the one whose spirit it is. The gift of the Spirit takes the three powers of faith, hope and love with which the Christian is endowed at the time of the sacrament of Baptism and enlivens or emboldens them. Their frequent exercise will become a way of life, a different way of living human life, a way of living that is redolent of the way Jesus lived.

In what way can it be said that everyday things that are done in the Spirit are powerful things? We will take only one example here, that of daily work. Work itself is a participation in the activity of the Creator. Howsoever humdrum it seems, our work picks up where God leaves off and perfects what God has already begun. This is not a successive process in the sense that God has finished "his" work, and now it is up to us. It is, rather, a compenetrative process since "Christ is now at work in people's hearts through the power of his Spirit...(which) animates, purifies and strengthens those noble longings by which the human family strives to make its life more human and to render the whole earth submissive to this goal."[21]

The Second Vatican Council was anxious to cite a second sense in which human labors are powerful. They are already part of what will compose the new heavens and the new earth:

> When we have spread on earth the fruits of our nature and our enterprise—human dignity, fraternal communion and freedom—according to the command of the Lord and in his Spirit, we will find them once again, cleansed this time from the stain of sin, illumined and transfigured, when Christ presents to the Father an eternal and universal kingdom.[22]

The eschatological nature of the power of the Spirit is what undergirds this insight. We will come back to this later.

There is a third sense in which the daily work we do in the Spirit can be powerful. The Eucharist is what makes them so. "The kingdom of God becomes present above all in the celebration of the sacrament of the eucharist. In that celebration the fruits of the earth and the work of human hands—the bread and the wine—are transformed mysteriously but really and substantially through the power of the Holy Spirit."[23] The encyclical goes on: "The Lord through his Spirit takes (the goods of this world and the work of our hands) up into himself in order to offer himself to the Father and to offer us with himself in the renewal of his one sacrifice which anticipates God's kingdom and proclaims its final coming."[24]

We can see in each of these three different ways that faith is necessary to see the way there really is power here. It is power in a different sense from the one we are accustomed to. It is power from another world but for this world, transformed into the new heavens and the new earth.

I said above that the power of the Spirit is meant for everyday things and everybody things. By the latter I meant the things that everyone must endure. To take just one example, death. The power of the Spirit is given the believer in order to undergo death, but to undergo it in a different way from others who have no faith. The best example of a death undergone in the Spirit of Christ is Christ's own death.

Without an elaborate theologizing about this complex and rich subject, I will take only one biblical theme from the Gospel of John. The theme is "the hour." The paradoxical nature of power stands out in bold relief in this theme. The Synoptics advert to the theme. Luke, for example, sees it as the hour of the power of darkness (Lk. 22,53).

John goes deeper. Throughout the Gospel, Jesus comments that the hour has not yet come. When it does come, it is no less a process of going to his death, but he does so almost majestically. The shame and death are in the background, and the way of the cross is suffused with glory and power. John's Jesus ascends to the Father through the whole ordeal. The glory is not at the end of the tunnel, as it is in the Synoptics. It is throughout the whole process of his diminution that he is in command.

Instead of the hour being an hour in the power of darkness, Jesus announces: "Now has judgment come upon this world, now will this world's prince be driven out, and I—once I am lifted up from earth—will draw all men to myself" (Jn. 12, 31-32). This being lifted up from the earth obviously means more than one thing. The most obvious is the action by which he was crucified. The less obvious is the action by which he was raised from the dead by the Father. And, finally, there is the action by which he redeems persons and draws them up out of death in all its senses.

The primary reason the power of the Spirit is paradoxical is the eschatological character of that power. It is next world power for this world. It is then power that begins now. It is power that gives us hope for this world while at the same time we know this world is passing away. It is power to act in this world and on it without knowing in any great detail what it is that we or it will become.

Growth in the power of the Spirit is more and more capable of accepting the powerlessness endemic to being human. Growth in the power of the Spirit is a growth in our ability to know less and trust more. The hoper begins his or her Christianity with a sense of vision about what the world should become and what his or her role is in bringing this about. But, the hoper matures to pray with the Psalmist, "You are my hope, O Lord"(Ps.71,5). This does not mean any less zeal for the world's transformation, only less belief in one's own vision or version about what God is doing in and intending for this world.

The biggest paradox of all we save till the last. The less one presumes to know about the power of the Spirit, the closer one is likely to be wise about it. Possibly Jesus was saying as much when he observed how like wind it was. Recall the scene! He no sooner tells Nicodemus how essential it is for entering the Kingdom of God that one be begotten "of water and the Spirit" than he likens the Spirit to the wind: "The wind blows where it will. You hear the sound it makes but you do not know where it comes from or where it goes" (Jn. 3,8). Possibly, Jesus was implying that he himself did not presume to speculate about the Spirit. He was certainly telling Nicodemus that being begotten by the Spirit was essential but largely myterious.

The Spirit in the Old Testament is always associated with very unusual happenings. And, certainly, the New Testament Pentecost had its share of unusual phenomena accompanying it as well, tongues of fire and glossalalia, for example. But, the kind of power this New Testament Spirit gives differs considerably from many of the Old Testament augurs of it (Joel 3,1-5). The fact that the Spirit indwells the Christian is a major reason for this difference. It is not sporadic and infrequent and bizarre and awaited; it is here and constant, the stand-in in the soul of God's faithfulness. It takes its place in the life cycle of the person which is always becoming, yet is slow to change and slow to grow, as befits the nature of life, vegetable, animal and human.

Wrapped around the person from the beginning of Christian

life is this Spirit Gift. One's baptism in the Spirit, not to mention the Father and the Son, is never accompanied by the extraordinary, preternatural if you will, phenomena that occurred at the outpouring of the Spirit at Pentecost. A Christian's Pentecost is at the time of the Christian's baptism. One cannot be validly baptized without being baptized in the Spirit.

In a sense, the rest of one's life consists of a dramatic though quiet interaction between this "guest of the soul" and the soul itself. The welcome is not assured nor is it automatic. This guest is unusual. If you give this guest an inch, it will not satisfy him or her or it(?). The prayer of the Christian, "Come Holy Spirit," should be prayed with an awareness that the Holy Spirit has long since come and is desiring to come in greater measure by being allowed into a heart that really welcomes it. A more sincere prayer might go something like this: "Come Holy Spirit, make me want to welcome you more than I do; I give you permission to take over territory that hasn't welcomed you and is afraid to let you nearer."

There is some reason for apprehension. This Spirit is other than my spirit. It has an agenda that is not mine. It is a center of subjectivity other than mine. Jesus implied as much when he described to Peter what his growth in the Spirit of Love was going to cost him. Recall that this scene on the shores of the Sea of Tiberias takes place after the Risen One had breathed the Holy Spirit into the Apostles Easter night. He tested Peter about whether he had received the Spirit by asking him whether he loved him, and this three times. This Spirit of Love would be in Peter if, in fact, he could profess his love for Jesus. He does this, and Jesus proceeds to describe what this will eventually mean to Peter: "I tell you solemnly: as a young man you fastened your belt and went about as you pleased; but when you are older you will stretch out your hands and another will hold you fast and carry you off against your will" (Jn.21,18). John then comments that this was Jesus' indication of the way Peter would die. The key word in the text is "another." There is warrant for contending that this other is the Holy Spirit that Peter had already received, but he would not have had much time to understand the implications of having received it. Jesus spells some of these out. To be led by the Spirit is to be led to one's fullness. It is to be led by Someone other than oneself where one would not go were one to be without this Spirit. It is a kind of death, but it is also more deeply life: "He who loses his life shall find it."

## NOTES

[1]Pope John Paul II, *Sollicitudo Rei Socialis, Origins* 18 (March 3, 1988), p. 655.

[2]Ibid., pp. 653-54.

[3]Ibid., p. 655.

[4]Ibid., p. 654.

[5]Ibid.

[6]Jozef Tischner, *The Spirit of Solidarity* (New York: Harper & Row, 1984), p. 4.

[7]Ibid., p. 2.

[8]Ibid., p. 3.

[9]*Sollicitudo, loc. cit.* p. 655.

[10]Pope John Paul II, *Dominum et Vivificantem, Origins* 16 (June 12, 1986), p. 96.

[11]*Sollicitudo Rei Socialis, loc. cit.,* p. 658.

[12]*Dominum et Vivificantem, loc. cit.,* p. 93.

[13]Ibid., p. 94.

[14]Gerhard Kittel, ed., *Theological Dictionary,* vol. 3, s.v. "koinos," by Hauch.

[15]Ibid., p. 792.

[16]Birger Gerhardsson, *The Ethos of the Bible* (Philadelphia: Fortress Press, 1981), p. 29.

[17]Ibid., p. 30.

[18]Ibid., p. 31.

[19]Raymond Brown, *The Gospel According to John (I-XII)* (Garden City: Doubleday & Co., 1966), p. 323.

[20]Ibid., p. 326.

[21]"Pastoral Constitution on the Church in the Modern World," in *Vatican Council II: The Conciliar and Post-Conciliar Documents,* ed. A. Flannery (Northport: Costello Publishing Co., 1975), par. #38.

[22]Ibid., par. #39.

[23]*Sollicitudo, loc. cit.,* p. 658.

[24]Ibid.

# Index of Persons